Adoption is Redemption

THE JOURNEY OF FINDING WHO WE ARE CREATED TO BE IN THE MIDST OF GRIEF, LOSS, AND LET DOWN

Sara Negash

TRILOGY CHRISTIAN PUBLISHERS

TUSTIN, CA

Trilogy Christian Publishers
A Wholly Owned Subsidary of Trinity Broadcasting Network
2442 Michelle Drive
Tustin, CA 92780

Adoption is Redemption: The Journey of Finding Who We Are Created to Be in the Midst of Grief, Loss, and Let Down

Rights Department, 2442 Michelle Drive, Tustin, CA 92780.

Trilogy Christian Publishing/TBN and colophon are trademarks of Trinity Broadcasting Network.

Cover design by: Jeff Summers

10 9 8 7 6 5 4 3 2 1

Library of Congress Cataloging-in-Publication Data is available.

ISBN: 978-1-63769-662-0

E-ISBN: 978-1-63769-663-7

Contents

Disclaimer

This is a nonfiction book. The stories written in this book are true based on the author's memory of events. Some of the names of some people have been changed to keep their privacy. The names of the locations listed in the book were also changed to keep the people's privacy. The real names of some people whom to thank were kept. They have impacted the author's life in different ways with their own permission to use their names. The people that have given the author their permission to use their names were notified, and the author has received their permission to use their story and names in her book.

Dedication

This book is dedicated to every person all over the world that has been adopted or has been in foster care. You each hold a special story; it is my prayer that this book will help you overcome obstacles, trials you have gone through as you connect with my story. May this book help you heal and be whole. You are the reason I wrote this book in hopes for you to gain wisdom and healing from my story to help you in your journey. It is my prayer that you discover your identity and fulfill the purpose that God has for you! You are loved by someone that understands your story.

This book is dedicated to all parents that have adopted children or have fostered children. Thank you for being a resemblance to God's love for his children through adoption. Thank you for being the hands and feet of Jesus and taking care of God's children! God uses people like you to impact and change the world, one child at a time!

This book is dedicated to all of my brothers and sisters in Christ who have entered into the kingdom of heaven. This, too, is your story of how God redeemed you by adopting you as His sons and daughters through His one and only Son, Jesus

Christ. You are citizens of heaven! May this book take you in a deeper intimate relationship with Christ. Adoption is the heart of God. May this book inspire you to share the Gospel to those that are lost, who are orphaned in Spirit, who have yet to find the One that came down to redeem them.

Acknowledgements

There are many people that have been a part of this book for coming into reality that I would love to thank. First of all, thank you to my family that adopted me, my forever family whom I call mine. Each of you knows who you are. I don't know where I would be or who I would become if you didn't step into my life in such a big transition in my life. God has used you to save me from many heartaches and trials that I had gone through, for which I am forever grateful. You each have a special place in my heart. By making me feel like you are truly my family, you have helped me heal in many ways than you know. Thank you for adopting me and for being God's hands and feet in my life. I love you all!

Trilogy Publishing, thank you for accepting my book to be published and believing in my book to spread the Gospel and bring people to the kingdom of God! May God continue to bless your ministry!

Thank you to all of my Ethiopian family for being an incredibly loving family who sacrificed so much for my sisters and me. I love you all! May God bless you!

Sandy, Deanne, and Emma Stephens, thank you from the bottom of my heart for believing in me to fulfill the purpose that God had for me. Thank you for all your encouragement and prayers throughout the years for me to write this book and finish it. One of the reasons I am where I am today is because of all of you! Thank you from the bottom of my heart. May the Lord bless you!

Thank you to my church Pastors and leaders at Medhane Alem-Evangelical Church who have prayed for me to write this book and who have prayed for me in my ministry at church and always encouraged me in my spiritual walk. You have sowed so much wisdom in me through many ways; here is one of the fruits of your labor! May the Lord continue to bless you, your family, and ministry!

Fray Olson, my best friend, my sister, you have impacted my life in many ways. Thank you so much for believing in my book and always encouraging me to write it. Thank you so much for editing my book whenever I needed you. You have helped me in tremendous ways! I love you, sister; I am forever grateful for our friendship and for the Lord bringing you into my life.

Tarekegn Kabeto, my brother in Christ, since the day I told you I am writing a book about adoption, you have encouraged me to keep going and finish it. Thank you for all the times you kept asking me to send you a chapter for you to read; it made me sit down and write because I needed to send it to you. Because you asked continuously, you helped me decide to sit down and finish writing the book. God was encouraging me in many ways through you. Thank you for all the advice you gave me; you are a big part of me finishing this book. Thank you for editing so many chapters in my book; you are truly God-sent.

I am grateful for you! May the Lord continue to use you as His instrument!

Mandy Perez, thank you so much for always praying for me whenever I wrote the book. There were many spiritual attacks for me not to write this book, but you always fought for me in prayer along with some other people in my life. Thank you for your continuous prayers; you have made an impact in my life through your prayers for me to sit down and write every day! I am grateful for your friendship.

Abdisa Desisa, thank you for encouraging me to do what God has told me to do in writing my book. Thank you for your prayers and encouragement and advice whenever I was feeling a little bit hopeless; you spoke life into me and brought me back to myself. You always believed God would provide the publisher and that the book will get published in God's timing. That is exactly what happened! It kept my faith in believing that God would finish what He started in me. You are a blessing in my life in many ways; I am grateful for you!

Aynalem Adem and Metikiya Addre, thank you for always praying for me and encouraging me to write this book. Whenever I get tired of writing or want to give up, you both reminded me what God has said about this book and the prophecies I have received that helped me keep going. Thank you for always being there for me whenever I needed you. God bless you!

Hana Elias, thank you for your prayers and advice in writing my book and for all the life advice you have given me. You always believed that in order for me to go to the next chapter in my life, you reminded me and advised me that I needed to be obedient to what God wanted me to do at that moment which was to finish writing my book. In order for the next assignment to come into our lives, we have to be obedient to the assignment that God gives us right now. Thank you for your prayers, my sister.

Ethiopia Alemneh, you are an angel. I always believed that God would help me find the right publisher through someone I knew, as there are so many publishers out there. I believed this for years. As I was praying for the Lord to help me find the publisher, God sent you to show me the way. Thank you for recommending Trilogy Publishing. The timing was perfect! God uses you in so many people's lives, connecting them to their destiny. Thank you for all that you have done for me! You are an amazing woman of God.

Zeki Getachew, thank you for your prayers for my book. I will never forget the day that God spoke to me through you. When I came to church that day, I had lost hope for my book. I was praying and believing for God to speak to me about this book. He told me to write, and if he wanted me to finish writing the book, I needed confirmation. I prayed He would speak to me through you that day. You didn't know me. But you were led by the Holy Spirit and came and prayed for me. God revealed to you my purpose in life. God told you that I was an author and told me to finish the book that I started. You told me the Lord wants to use me through writing books. You are a man of God who hears God's voice. I never told you anything, but that Lord revealed it to you! That word you gave me impacted my life and helped me finish this book! Thank you for your prayers and encouragement throughout the process of me finishing the book!

May the Lord continue to use you in mighty ways to build His kingdom!

Thank you so much to Leamlak, Bruk Birhanu, Betrese, Eskidar Cochran, Carrie Cochran, Carrie Strawn, and Zerihun for sharing your testimonies of what physical and spiritual adoption means to you! Your desire to share the Gospel and for orphans to be adopted is incredible! I believe your stories will impact so many people!

Thank you, David Guterson, Pastor Josh McQueen, and Maureen Flatley, for writing the foreword about my book! I appreciate all of you taking the time to read my book and the beautiful words you have written. May God bless all of you abundantly!

Foreword

by Maureen Flatley

One of the most profound aspects of my work in adoption policy is being entrusted with the stories of people who have experienced this complex, often painful process. Sara Negash's story is one of those narratives. Not an easy read, in fact, often arduous, Sara's journey is illustrative of everything that is both good and bad about adoption. But armed with her deep and abiding faith, she has navigated the process and all of its challenges with a positive outlook to create a powerful message for others.

Whether you are a social worker, adoption professional, adoptee, foster parent, an adoptive parent, there are invaluable lessons to be learned from this young woman's experiences. Painstakingly, Sara deconstructs her experiences framing simple, common-sense recommendations to ensure better results for other kids.

No child should have to endure the pain and loss that Sara experienced over the years of her life. No child should be thrust into an adoptive home that brings more misery and trauma after they have already suffered. But at every turn, Sara was determined to build a life, and she has done that with grit and bravery. Her conviction to conquer her pain, her loss, and her fear is a breathtaking journey that we should take to heart. It may not be everyone's story. But it's her story and one that reminds us that faith wins.

Maureen Flatley is a Boston-based government relations consultant specializing in government reform and oversight of adoption and child welfare. Before moving to Massachusetts in 2002, her firm was based in Washington, D.C., for nearly thirty years. She has provided expert advice and consultation to the White House, members of Congress, foreign heads of state and state legislators on a range of adoption and child welfare issues. She also provides services to nonprofits serving children as well as attorneys and their clients, including children and families victimized in the child welfare and adoption systems both here and abroad. Ms. Flatley serves on the board of fostering families.

Foreword

by David Guterson

I first heard from Sara Negash in October of 2020. A mutual friend had put us in touch. Sara had some questions about composing a book proposal—something she could send to potential publishers. You would think that because I'm an author, I'd know how to do this, but actually, I don't. (I published my first book in 1989, and things were very different then.) At a loss, I found what I thought was a good article on the subject online and shared that with Sara.

It was the best I could do.

In early November, Sara sent me the text of a letter she wanted to send to potential literary agents. She wondered what I thought of it and asked me for help as she worked to get it right. Reading it, I realized that I'd met Sara before. I had attended a fundraising event where I met Sara.

I did what I could to help Sara with her letter. Shortly thereafter, she sent me a comprehensive summary of the book you are about to read. It included a table of contents from which I gleaned the outlines of Sara's story. Born in Addis Ababa, the capital of Ethiopia, Sara lost her parents at a young age and came to live in an orphanage. After some time there, she was adopted by an American family in Washington State, where she met with difficulties. With time, however, she found a loving home and family, and as a young adult, returned to Ethiopia to volunteer at the orphanage where she had once lived.

Recently I had the privilege of reading Sara's book in its entirety and was impressed by it deeply. It was clear she had written with great determination, and with inspiration, and with a clear sense of mission. Sara was not about to be defeated by the marathon task of writing a book, and her passion for goodness, truth, and love had given her the strength, I could see, to persevere. Reading, I learned about the people, events, and forces in her life that had shaped her into such a person. I came to admire and respect her as I turned the pages—her strength, her conviction, her gratitude, her faith, her resilience, her honesty, and perhaps most of all, her determination to be of service to others and to make the world a better place through word and action. It's hard for me to imagine anyone reading this book and not feeling the same way. I was uplifted by it and moved, and hope you will be, too.

—David Guterson
Author of 11 books
Bestselling Author of *Snow Falling on Cedars*

Foreword

by Josh McQueen

Everyone has a story. Each story is different. Every story matters. Some of us struggle to put our stories into words. Some of us don't feel that our stories are worth telling. Some of us are ashamed of our stories and fear what others will think of us if we tell our stories.

Sara Negash has given us a gift—the gift of her story. Letting us into the joy, pain, fear, faith, love, sorrow, tragedy, resilience, and triumph that is her life, the reader will find with each chapter that the gift unfolds into a multitude of gifts.

Those who are familiar with Africa only through movies and TV generally have preconceived ideas about life in Africa. Most of these ideas are negative, with predictable descriptors coming to mind of widespread poverty, lack of education, poor sanitation, and so forth. While economic poverty presents a number of challenges to many nations in Africa, the unseen resources and wealth found in communities across the continent are unparalleled.

Sara's story offers a window into the life and culture of Ethiopian children and families. She highlights not only the tragedy and pain experienced in many impoverished communities but also the treasures that sustain these communities—treasures that most inhabitants of developed countries will never know at such depths—namely, unceasing faith in God as the provider and the vibrant, genuine community shared between family, friends, and neighbors in a village. In a nation where a decreasing number of Americans are too busy to spend an hour a week at church or to know the names of their next-door neighbors, testimonies like Sara's are important reminders that another way of life is possible.

Some of the gifts are difficult to receive, but they are gifts, nonetheless. Sara shares hard, honest truths about the journey of adoption. While many tend to see a perfect, photo-shopped picture of adoption with soft edges, the reality is that adoption always involves pain and loss. Sara does not shy away from that part of her story. Even in the best circumstances surrounding an adoption, there is a past to acknowledge and honor, grief that can continue to be felt for years, and loss that is carried for a lifetime. When adoptive parents are unqualified, ill-equipped, or unaccountable in the midst of adoption's challenges, the consequences can be dire.

At the same time, she's able to hold that reality in tension with the glorious truth that adoption is also "greater than the universe" (as I have heard one Bible teacher put it). Few pictures compare to that of an orphaned child coming home to their forever family. Sara forcefully connects the realities of physical adoption and spiritual adoption, using her journey as an invitation to all who would be adopted as God's children. In Sara's story, adopted sons and daughters will find a friend with whom they can identify. Adoptive parents will see more clearly the trauma that many adopted children have endured. Pastors and church leaders will find a tangible witness to the metaphor of salvation that adoption is throughout the New Testament. The Body of Christ will be built up and inspired by the relentless faith, hope, and love present in these pages.

For this gift you have given us, Sara Negash, we thank you. Amesegenalo, Egziabher yibarkish.

—Josh McQueen
Adoptive Father and Pastor

Preface

The Epiphany for this book, "Adoption is Redemption," started when I was serving at River City Church one Sunday. During worship, we sang a song called "Who you are" by Kristian Stanfill. As we were singing the song, everyone in the church was worshiping and raised their hand in surrender during the song except when these lyrics came up.

"You carry the orphans in your loving arms; this is who you are. I know this is who you are. I believe this is who you are." Everyone's hand went down, and mine went up! I have seen the Lord care for me as a seven-year-old orphan in Ethiopia after losing my parents to cancer. I have seen the goodness of the Lord and how he cares for the orphans in the world while living at an orphanage in Ethiopia. For that, I raised my hand in surrender and gratitude. But as I raised my hand, I was ashamed and embarrassed to be the only one orphaned and adopted in the room. I felt like everyone in the room was looking at me. That is when the Holy Spirit spoke to my spirit and told me, "You are not the only one." I knew deep in my heart it was the Holy Spirit that whispered it to me. He repeated the same thing: you are not the only one adopted. I knew everyone in the room and their stories and knew that I was the only one adopted. The

Holy Spirit then gave me a revelation that knocked me down to my knees. The revelation I received that day changed my whole world and perspective on adoption and how it came to be. Did you know that every person that lived on this earth after Adam and Eve were once an orphan? You, too, were once an orphan, or maybe you still are. Discover God's redemption story for you by reading through this book. The Lord told me to write a book about adoption and share with the world the revelation that I received that day! In shock of the revelation I was receiving, I was on my knees uncontrollably crying, experiencing and feeling a small amount of the unconditional love God has for you for his creation.

Prophets are God's messengers in this world who hear God's voice. The Lord confirmed and encouraged me to write this book through his prophets that came from all over the world, who didn't know me or my story. God spoke to them to tell me to write the book that God told me to write. Yes, it was that specific! He spoke to me through different prophets throughout the years to continue to write this book. Each one of them came and told me that I needed to write the book that God told me to write and finish it." My friends and families were the instruments God used to encourage me to finish writing this book.

There were many trials and tribulations that I experienced when writing this book which made me want to quit on the assignment the Lord gave me many times. I wrote half of the book four times and started all over again due to losing the whole document on a computer and faced many other challenges. Every time I wanted to quit, the Lord would send one of His messengers to encourage me to finish what God has started.

This is what I know to be true is God wants this book out in the world for people to understand His story of redemption for all mankind.

There are many people orphaned physically or not who have gone through many trials and tribulations in their life and still have not been healed or set free. I wanted to write this book for each person who has lost a parent or has gone through many trials in their life due to different circumstances and is needing to be saved both physically and spiritually! As you are reading this book, contemplate on your life from each chapter and let God heal you of any wounds, hurts, and unforgiveness that you have gone through in your life. In Christ, we are made whole both spiritually and physically. I was broken, hurt, wounded, orphan, and in need of Savior, whether I knew I needed to be saved or not. You might have faced this in your life before, or maybe you are going through it now. As God came to rescue me, healed me, and made me whole, it's my prayer that you will be healed and set free as you are reading this book. It's my prayer you get to know your Savior on a deeper level through this book and that you will have the kind of faith in God that moves mountains!

Dr. Myles Munroe once said, "The graveyard is the richest place on the surface of the earth because there you will see books that were not published, ideas that were not harnessed, songs that were not sung, inventions that were not invented. In the graveyard, there is buried the greatest treasure of untapped potential. There is a treasure within you that must come out."

This is me robbing the graveyard and fulfilling one of the purposes that God has sent me to do. Read on and discover where you came from, who you belong to, and gain wisdom from this book, then go out and fulfill the purpose that God has for you and rob the graveyard and give to this world the gift that God has placed inside of you! God is faithful to finish what He started in you!

Beginning of Life

"There are two important days in our lives; the day we are born and the day we discover the purpose for our existence."

—William Barclay

Each one of us was specifically born at the time we are supposed to come to the earth for a specific purpose to do something valuable and needed for our world. I know with all of my heart that God, the Creator of the universe, created every being on this earth. I believe He created you! In Genesis 1:1, verse 26-31 (KJV) in the Bible, it says:

> In the beginning God created the heaven and the earth." And God said, Let us make man in our image, after our likeness: and let them have dominion over the fish of the sea, and over the fowl of the air, and over the cattle, and over all the earth, and over every creeping thing that creepeth upon the earth. So God created man in his own image, in the image of God created he him; male and female created he them. And God blessed them, and God said unto them, be fruitful, and multiply, and replenish the earth, and subdue it: and have dominion over the fish of the sea, and over the fowl of the

air, and over every living thing that moveth upon the earth. And God said, Behold, I have given you every herb bearing seed, which is upon the face of all the earth, and every tree, in which is the fruit of a tree yielding seed; to you it shall be for meat. And to every beast of the earth, and to every fowl of the air, and to everything that creepeth upon the earth, wherein there is life, I have given every green herb for meat: and it was so. And God saw everything that he had made, and behold, it was very good. And the evening and the morning were the sixth day.

That is how we were created. God created us! He created the first man and woman, Adam and Eve, and said to be fruitful and multiply and subdue the earth. God gave us our earthly parents to love and care for us while we are on this earth. He gave them to us so that they can call us their own children and take care of us. Birthdays are so important because it celebrates the day we are sent to this world. I was born on June 19, 1992, in Addis Ababa, Ethiopia. My Mother's name is Senait, and my father's name is Negash. I was the third child; I have two beautiful sisters. Since they had two daughters, they really had a desire to have a boy next. When our neighbors found out that my mom was pregnant, they said, "Surely you are going to have a boy this time." While she was pregnant, I kicked my mom a lot, and because of that, they thought and expected no girl could kick like this; it must be a boy! There was no ultrasound back then in Ethiopia, so they had no way of knowing what they were going to have. It all became a surprise at birth. To their surprise or disappointment, I came out as a little girl. Everyone was happy to have me as a girl when they saw me; my parents were ecstatic to have me.

I was the first out of my whole family tree, including my ancestors both on my mom's and dad's side, to be born in a hospital. It is a very big deal and something that changed my family history. All my cousins that were born after me were born in hospitals as well. Not everybody is fortunate enough to be born in hospitals like me. If you were born in a hospital, see yourself as a blessed and lucky person. The way women give birth is quite different from where I come from. At that time, a lot of people were born at home naturally. When my mom gave birth to my sisters, they were living in geter (rural countryside), in Awash Ethiopia, so there weren't hospitals there at the time. The nearest hospital was a four-hour drive. If they want to give birth at a hospital, it comes with lots of costs like travel expenses, hospital bills, and meals while they are gone. This would be easy for you and me, who live in a civilized world, to cover the expenses and go but not for them. Geter is very poor. They live on what they grow in their farms or the small businesses they have. People struggle to feed their families daily and have a roof over their head, let alone going on a luxury trip to give birth at a hospital. A lot of people in Africa that live in a rural parts give birth in their huts or in their villages or in their one small bedroom house with a neighbor helping the pregnant woman. They give birth with no pain medicine, no doctors or nurses, or technology to let them know when the baby will be coming out. They only know to push as hard as they can when they are giving birth until the baby comes out, while a couple, usually untrained professional people, help them. They are very strong women. There is no ultrasound to let them know what they are going to have so they could wait with excitement and get things ready for the newborn. There is no baby registration or baby showers, something a lot of us are blessed to have in different parts of the world. It all becomes a surprise at birth. If there were any complications while giving birth in geter, the mom or the baby dies before getting to hospital since it is so far away. There are complications and disadvantages of giving birth in a rural part of Africa. Women who give birth naturally are truly remarkable. But one of the greatest blessings is they are surrounded by people that love them. Women are helped through pregnancy by their mothers and other female family members, friends, and neighbors. The mother lays in bed for forty days to three months after giving birth and rests while taking care of her newborn. The husband, family, and friends oversee making sure that there is sufficient food and comfort for the mother during this time and take care of her every single day.

There are different religions in Ethiopia, and it is usually according to the religion the family believes in, the newborn's name is given. Everyone's stories are different. I have heard of many stories of children being presented to a witch by the parents. Some parents, if they are not able to have babies, go to a place where witchcraft is practiced and ask the witch to give them a child. By God's grace, if they end up having children, they think the witch helped them get pregnant to have a baby, so they take their child to present it to the witch in a witchcraft ceremony. If you have been given to a witch as a baby, or have gone there as an adult, or if you know of anyone that has gone to a witchcraft place, you or the person need to be set free! Parents usually go back to the witch to give thanks to the gods for giving them children, and in return, they present the child back to them when they get born. Here is the reason why you need to be delivered.

Witchcraft is the work of the devil and not from God. Witchcraft is an abomination to God. Witchcraft is practiced in a lot of African countries and other countries as well all over the world.

Some people are not taught that going to a witchcraft place was worshiping the devil and working with the devil instead of the real God. They think it goes along with worshiping the real God. All people know is going to that place gives them quick answers and quick solutions to their problems. But it is a solution that never lasts just because the quick fix isn't from the real God. The problem always comes back. People that practice this, their spiritual eyes are closed. No wonder the Word of God says, "my people are lost (destroyed) because of the lack of knowledge" (Hosea 4:6, KJV). Knowledge is wealth. Knowledge is protection. For your knowledge, people go to a witchcraft place for many reasons, to ask the witch to give them children if they haven't been able to have children yet, they go to ask the witch to make them rich and successful, or if they are sick, they ask the witch if they could heal them or if they should go to a hospital. Another reason people go to a witch is to do harm to people as well, even to their own relatives, because of jealousy or hatred towards those people. Some go knowing that it is the place that worships the devil. It is usually to take away that person's chance or opportunity that came for them and to reverse it for themselves instead. Another reason they go to a witchcraft place is to make whoever they want not to be successful anymore no matter what they do, so that person never has a breakthrough in their lives. Or other times, they try to put a bad sickness spell on them so that person could live all their lives being sick and miserable and not being able to enjoy or live life to the fullest. Witchcraft is real, and it does happen. All of this is made in the spirit and can only be broken off in the spirit, too, through the name of Jesus Christ.

The Bible says in Matthew 16:19 (KJV):

And I will give unto thee the keys of the kingdom of heaven: and whatsoever thou shalt bind on earth shall be bound in heaven: and whatsoever thou shalt loose on earth shall be loosed in heaven.

Whatever is tied on earth through witchcraft is also tied in the spirit and can only be broken off by praying against it to break off in the name of Jesus. The name of Jesus has power! It is only the name of Jesus that has the power to break off anything in the spirit realm. It is the only name on earth and in heaven that releases something when we pray using the name of Jesus. He is our Savior. When it is released and loosed in heaven, it will also be loosed on earth. So whoever was tied to witchcraft in the spirit will be released in the spirit realm. They will then be set free of whatever they have been tied over. It will immediately let go of them and leave them completely. There are many people that have been set free reading the Bible or have seen people that have been set free and know this to be true. There is evil in the world, but there is also a miracle-working God that will break off all the work of the enemy when we believe.

If you have been given to a witchcraft place when you were young that you know of or have gone there when you were older, if you have any connections with them, you need to be set free. In order to be set free, if you haven't yet, you need to accept Jesus Christ as your Lord and Savior into your heart. The second thing to do after accepting Christ into your heart is to get baptized as Jesus commands us. You will then become a child of God. God will wash and cleanse you and make you a new person in him. *"Therefore if any man be in Christ, he is a new creature: old things are passed away; behold, all things are become new"* (2 Corinthians 5:17, KJV).

You will now be known in the spiritual realm as a child of God. You were bought by a price when Christ shed His blood on the cross for all our sins. Jesus will make you a new person in Him and give you a new identity.

You can say a prayer to be set free spiritually after accepting Christ into your heart. You can have your church pastor or leader pray for you, and you can also pray by yourself by reciting this prayer in faith.

"Lord Jesus, I thank you that you are the Lord of my life and the king of my heart. I rebuke and break off every work of the enemy in my life in Jesus' name. I break off every witchcraft that has been done in my name (say your name) in the powerful name of Jesus. I thank you that every spell is broken in Jesus' name. I thank you that I am set free. Wash and cleanse me by your blood Jesus that was shed on the cross for me. I thank you,

Jesus. My old identity is gone, and I receive and believe I am a new creation in you. I say this in Jesus' name. Amen."

My aunt Mesi was a Christian, God-fearing woman. She was the one that picked out the name Sara to call me. She remembered the name Sara from the Bible, who was Abraham's wife. She is the reason so many of my family members became Christians today. So many of my family's souls have been won for the kingdom of God because of her resilience and consistency to always pray for us, including me. She is a part of the reason for me to write this book, knowing the only one and true God and for you to be able to read it. She is one prayer warrior!

I write this book myself as a new creation in Christ and to share with you what the Lord has taught me and to share with you the revelation I have received in hopes to help you understand your Heavenly Father and for the Lord to reveal many things to you through this book and bring you closer to Him.

When I was four years old, my mom got sick. She died soon afterward and was buried in her country Awash, Ethiopia. My sisters and I lost our mom at a young age, and my dad became a widower.

My Childhood Without My Mother

Every continent in every country has its own cultural way of raising children. We all were raised differently from the different languages we spoke growing up, the houses we grew up in, our surroundings, and the discipline we got when we did something wrong. In Ethiopia and a lot of places in Africa, people live in huts and or in small one-room houses at that time. My family and I lived in a small one-room house where we cooked, ate, hung out, and slept. The walls were mud walls covered with newspaper all over the house. We would take off the newspaper and glue on some new ones once a month to make it look nice. The floor was mud floor. I remember my sisters using cow poop to cover the mud and make the whole house look nice. That is what we did in our culture at that time.

When I think about it now, it is crazy to me to think we did that in our house and that I stepped on it. At the time, it was normal to me, and it is what we did, but as a young adult living the blessed life I live now, I have way different views than I had before. What does your childhood home look like? Does it compare to a house I grew up in? There are so many people that live in the streets with no shelter to cover them from the rain, the hot sun, and the cold nights. My family and I were blessed to live in a house where we were protected from everything. A few of the things that we had in the house were a bed and a wooden chest we used for three things. We used it to store our clothes in, used it as a seat during the day and as a bed at night along with a couple of chairs put along the side of it to protect us from falling. My two sisters would put some sheets on it and sleep uncomfortably there. There were people that lived better lives than us, that had a sofa, TV, fridge, etc.

We didn't complain much because we knew our dad was doing his best to provide for us. We also had a kitchen drawer for all kitchen appliances and a propane stove to cook our food. In Ethiopia, our main dish is *injera* (Ethiopia's traditional flat bread) with different kinds of vegetable or meat stew. People also eat spaghetti, macaroni, or rice if they could afford it. Since we didn't have much, my family always ate the same meal of *injera bewet* (stew) either with lentil stew or *shiro* for breakfast, lunch, and dinner. As a young child, I didn't like injera with wet for breakfast; my favorite breakfast was always *dabo be shyi* (fresh bread with tea). If I didn't have that, I always gave the biggest tantrums crying for *yesuq dabo* (store bread). My family knew it, so they always put money aside specifically for my breakfast. There was no dishwasher in Ethiopia at that time that I knew of. We washed dirty dishes by hand, warming up hot water on the stove, and dried the dishes with a towel. We didn't have a sink to wash our dishes. We washed them in big buckets, one for soapy water and the other with clean water. We didn't have washing machines or dryers for our clothes, so my sisters always washed them by hand and let them hang to dry in the hot sun. My young sisters, bless their hearts, always did everyone's laundry every Saturday. We had the smallest house in the neighborhood.

My neighbor's house looked nicer and was bigger and better, I thought. After a couple of years, they started remodeling and were able to buy new furniture. They had nice comfy couches, a DVD player, a TV, and so many other cool things. My whole childhood in Ethiopia, we never had any of those things. It was one of the desires of my heart to have those things growing up, but my family had no money. It always bothered me, why did we have to be poor? Why can't we have a TV in our house, or couches, or at least a radio or a DVD player so we can listen to music? Our house was empty, quiet, and no fun. Whenever we wanted to listen to music, we had to go to a friend's house just so that we would hear music and dance. Have you ever felt like that and asked yourself that at one time in your life? I wished we had it all but never thought it would come true, and it never did while I was there. I wanted to have a TV at my house and watch all the cool kid shows. All my friends would get together at our friend's house that had a TV and watch some shows together. I wanted it to be at my house. I never had any toys. Never played with dolls or cars or anything. My sisters made me a homemade doll, and that was my only pretend toy.

In Ethiopia, it is the norm for all the neighborhood children to get together and play outside. All of us kids were always running around everywhere cheering, laughing, crying, and playing together in the dirt, and being very noisy. There would be kids circled together playing hand games, others playing games with their feet, and others playing soccer or marbles. The adults and teenagers sit down and talk right outside of their houses or braid each other's hair. It is common to see a row of neighbors braiding each other's hair at one time. In Ethiopia, that is what you do at the time, playing or visiting with people instead of watching TV all day long or playing video games. The kids get down and dirty and play all day every day during summers in Africa and during school season. After school, they are usually out playing until late in the evening.

The only time all of us kids got together to watch TV was on Saturday and Sunday mornings to watch a popular kids' TV show called Ababa Tesfaye. Usually, there are at least twenty or more kids in a small house watching Ababa Tesfaye on a tiny TV. We loved being together and doing everything together. We always had something to do, whether it's playing in the mud or pretending to cook with mud and water, or playing soccer, or marbles or other fun games we came up with. It was always physical and active. I absolutely loved playing outside with my friends. That is one of my fondest and best memories I have of Ethiopia. When I think of my childhood and playing outside, I think of joy, happiness, and so much love. I love how Ethiopia is such a strong, very social country. We were all in each other's lives. When I would go to my friend's house to play, after playing, we always ate dinner together at their home. We don't call them to go to their house; we just show up at their house because we see each other as family instead of just friends. Their house was my house, and my house was theirs. We had a great bond, a great connection with all our neighbors. It is hard to describe how we were, but we were all super close, and if you came to Ethiopia to visit someday, you would see how we are and understand what I can't describe, and you will end up loving it too.

My dad didn't like it when we spent too much time playing outside. He was always asking us to stay home and do homework and study. He didn't mind when we played all day long during the weekend, but on weekdays it was always education time. He cared about our future, and what we were going to be making of ourselves, so he was always strict about doing our homework and studying. If we were not obedient, we would get the belt. Not everybody used that method, but some people did. Every parent has their own way of disciplining their children, and my dad's was always the belt. I could never stay mad at my dad for discipling me, though; I loved him too much. He believed education was the key to living the life we desired and wanted, so he wanted to engrave that within us.

In Africa, having respect for your elders is highly recommended. It is the rule to listen and obey them and do as they say. If they are working doing dishes or sweeping the floor or doing anything, you go and take it over for them and do it yourself no matter what age you are. No one will stand around while the elders are working; they go and pick up whatever they are doing and do it for them. It is one of the ways we show respect to our elders. That is one of the greatest lessons I have learned in my country and have carried it my whole life, which has helped me become a respectful person. Africa is one of the best continents that has great manners in respecting elders and people in general. I am grateful for my dad and the lessons he taught me as a young child and the way he disciplined me. I disliked it at the time, but he taught me many lessons in life in such a short time. I am a responsible person to this day and have so much respect for people because of what my dad taught me. When people look at me, I look different and act differently. I am unique in the way I carry myself because of my father. I am forever grateful for him.

The kind of man my dad was and the way he carried himself, no one will ever guess that he spanked us. But when father duty calls and he needs to teach us something, then there is nothing that would stop him. I don't know how your family taught you discipline, if it was abusive or if it was in a good way or in a bad way, just know it made you who you are today. If it was bad, you know how not to discipline. If it was good, then your parents taught you something valuable, didn't they? Do not hold a grudge or be mad about it for years. Forgiveness needs to kick in so that you can move on with your life and do the things that you are called to do and are meant to do. Talk about your childhood with someone you trust and let whatever hurt you come out, so you are not hurting from the inside anymore. It is better to forgive than to hold it in and let it ruin your life. Forgiveness is for you.

My dad was a security guard with three kids to raise. My sister Hiwet, the oldest who was eight years old, became the mom of the house. She had to after my mom passed away. She learned how to cook for my sis and me and fed us breakfast, lunch, and dinner every day. She learned how to clean, wash our clothes by hand, take care of my sis and me, helped us with homework, took us to school, washed and braided our hair. Everything that a mother does, my sister must do at that young age while going to school at the same time. But despite all the load of work she had to do, she was still a great student. There are lots of young children my sister's age and younger that take care of their siblings and have become a parent to their younger siblings at those young of age themselves in Ethiopia.

When their parents pass away, they absolutely have no choice but to grow up fast, mature, and take on responsibilities. That is what my sister and so many other kids in Ethiopia and all over Africa had to do. When I was in Ethiopia, I saw so many little kids taking care of their siblings. Some of the reasons were because their parents had passed away and there is no one else to take care of them but their own siblings. They are living in the streets begging for food and money at a very young age. Most of them are malnourished, some dying of HIV, some walk miles and miles away, going door to door for someone to open their homes to them and feed them or give them money for food.

Can you imagine a world like that? What if one of them was you? Can you imagine yourself being in that kind of situation? How would you have handled it? How can you be so strong for your own siblings and give them hope when you yourself are pretty much as young as they are and you yourself need food, love, and support? There is a world like that out there. There is so much we don't know about, or we forget after hearing about it. Don't forget and don't be oblivious about it. Two of my Ethiopian friends, before coming to the U.S., used to be those kids who begged for food, slept in the trees in the cold with nothing to cover them, homeless, nobody to care for them or watch over them. They got picked on by older kids in the streets and had a life that no one would ever guess looking at their life now. It's amazing how God works! They went from living that lifestyle and being in survival mode to coming to America, the land of opportunity where dreams come true, and having a family that loves and cares for them. It breaks my heart to know that there are kids out there still in the same spot as my friends were. My dad and my sisters are my heroes. I don't know how they did what they did, but I am forever grateful to them for taking such good care of me. Hiwet remembers my mom and how loving my mom was to her and how she treated her. She knew I didn't remember her, so what she did was she would show me how my mom was through her love and how much she cared for me and what she did for me. She didn't want me to forget my mom, so she was the example my mom was for her. She washed my dirty muddy feet every night that I got dirty from playing all day outside. She washed my crazy, unmanageable hair, braided it, and took care of it. She always hugged me and loved me up every single day. I remember her rubbing my back and petting my head at night to get me to fall asleep at the age of eight. Sometimes I wouldn't fall asleep unless my sis would tuck me in and rub my hair. That and everything else she learned by watching my mom do the things she did for her and my other sister Lydia and me. Even when I was being a brat and wouldn't listen to her and would hit her, she still kept her calm and still loved me. I have no idea how she did it, but I know God definitely gave her the strength to go through what she went through raising my sister and me.

There were times when it was hard. It was difficult to care for me and love me the way she did. But she kept going. She took on the responsibility, and so did my six-year-old sister and my loving dad.

School in Ethiopia

"A child without education is like a bird without wings."
Tibetan proverb

If you have no education, you have no life in Africa. Your life is at risk of surviving and becoming someone in life. How can birds fly and do what they are created to do if they don't have wings to fly? They can't. They have to have their wings in order to fly and soar high and be the birds that fly beautifully around in the sky. That is why a child without education is like a bird without wings. A child needs to have education to become and be the person he or she is meant to be and created to be. One of the biggest problems in Ethiopia and all over Africa is the inability of children to be able to go to school. There are so many kids of all ages who are so eager to learn and go to school all over Ethiopia and the whole entire continent of Africa but don't have the resources or the money.

There are over 20,000 children who live in the streets just in Ethiopia. That is an enormous number of children just in Ethiopia. Imagine how many more children live in the street with no one to care for them in every country in Africa and all over the world. I believe education is one of the keys to being successful. There are so many children working on farms and helping their parents make a living instead of going to school. My dad was one of them. He was a shepherd and didn't ever get the chance to go to school. Every day is a struggle of survival for so many families, especially children. I heard this story of these two little boys ages nine and eleven from Ethiopia who became friends living in the street. When I heard their story, it broke my heart to pieces. Their names are Bruk and Tamirat. Bruk's mom was really sick with AIDs and couldn't take care of him or feed him. She told him to go to the city and find a job to support himself because she knew she was dying of AIDs soon. Can you imagine being a mom and sending your eleven-year-old son who doesn't know anything about living to go to the city and start taking care of himself? She knew she couldn't do anything for him but knew what was best for him was to go to the city and make something of himself alone where he doesn't know anyone. Tamirat's dad got sick with malaria; he told his son to go to the city and find work because he couldn't take care of him with how sick he was. There was no way to work and provide for his son and himself.

Bruk and Tamirat begged at restaurants in the city to see if they had extra food and dug through garbage to find food to feed their hungry stomachs. Food was always scarce for them. They had to worry about how they are going to be feeding themselves next and where they're going to find shelter instead of being normal nine and eleven-year-old children. They want to go to school, but it was one of the last things on their mind and one of the last things to worry about because there was absolutely no way for them to afford to go to school if they couldn't even feed themselves. They fought for survival every day. When they were asked what their future would look like, they shrugged their shoulders, not knowing what would happen or if they were going to be alive then because they were fighting every day to survive. Bruk said he hoped he could get a job picking up garbage in the city so he could have the money to feed himself every day. That is just so sad that is all he thought he could do in this world was to pick up garbage, not that there is any problem with that, but he had no hope in him for a brighter future. The pay in Africa for picking up garbage is nothing like America. In America, someone can make a living working as a garbage man, but not in Ethiopia. In Africa, it pays very little. There are countless stories like Bruk and Tamirat's story in the streets of Ethiopia and all over Africa. Can you imagine being one of those kids? Where would you be if you weren't able to go to school and didn't graduate high school? Can you imagine being one of those kids? Can you imagine and see yourself running around in the streets to find food and dig through garbage? When the children are in that kind of situation, there is so much emotional damage of not belonging and deserving of love. They feel alone in this world with nobody to care for them, love them and take care of them. They don't feel like they have a purpose in life like there is any reason for them to live. We need to do something to be helping these beautiful children and bring them life and hope.

I was blessed to have lived in the city where I could go to school. The school I went to cost a lot of money. My dad was determined and worked hard so that he can pay for my sisters and me to go to that school. Even when it got expensive for him as a single father, he still made it somehow. Education was important to him. All he wanted us to do was to learn and be influencers in our country. I remember every night when he would come home from work; he would ask me and my sisters how we were doing in school and if I had any homework. If I did, I was told to do it asap. He was very hard on us when it comes to school. He believed in education more than anything other than God. He believed in us. He wanted to raise kids who were going to change and impact the world in some way. He believed and wanted us, his kids, to add to the world in a positive way rather than settling for less in our lives or in any job. I am grateful for my determined father.

Another school called *sibiste* opened thirty minutes away from my house. The whole neighborhood was super excited about it because it was going to be free to go to school over there. Going to school for free, what? We needed that, and the government finally opened it up for us. My sisters and my whole neighborhood friends transferred to that school because it was free. The school was huge and took in thousands of children. It helped parents save a lot of money and other children that were not able to go to school because finances were able to go to school for free. Everyone I knew transferred, including my sisters, except me. My dad refused to let me go to that school because he was worried about me. That year a lot of people, including children, were dying in car accidents. Drivers were going too fast and could not stop on time and have run over people. There were a lot of gruesome deaths, and because of how young I was, my dad couldn't live with the thought of that accidentally happening to me, so he chose to pay for my school fees to stay at my school. My sisters were able to go to that school after they begged him to let them because they were older and could take care of themselves.

The neighborhood friends and my sisters were able to walk to and from school together, which made my dad feel at peace to let them go to that school. I begged my dad for months, but he refused. I didn't know what it was, but there was something telling me in my heart I needed to go to that school. Not only because I wanted to but because I needed to, I didn't know for what reason. I just knew that something was going to happen soon in about a year or two, and I needed to go to that school. I didn't tell my dad about that because I was scared of what he would say to me. Now, as I am writing my story, I know why I felt like I needed to go to that school. I didn't know what the future was going to hold, but I felt in my heart as a seven-year-old I needed to go to that school because of what was coming. I will be sharing that part of my story in a little while in this book, but it totally makes sense now. I love how God put instincts in us, especially in me, throughout my childhood. My dad wouldn't change his mind for the life of him. I bribed him and told him that he would save so much money if I went to that school. I told him he could save more money for his dream house if he let me go to that school. He would laugh when I would try to bribe him in different ways but wouldn't listen to me. After a while, he changed his mind. I was jumping up and down with joy when he finally told me yes. There were eighty students in my classroom at Sibiste. Every classroom in that school was packed with 80-100 students and more. The classroom wasn't really big, but since it was the only free school in our area, lots of students attended the school. Students would walk two hours to and from school every day from home. That is some dedication. There were so many students that had a desire and had a whatever it took kind of attitude and mindset to go to school and learn no matter the situation. There were students in my classroom who were in the second grade that were taking care of their mom or dad because they were sick with HIV or taking care of their siblings at those young of age and still walking an hour or two to go to school and walking back to do homework and take care of the house and clean, work for people to help their parents. I was stunned to hear of many stories like that. These kids had the strength of a lion. They were warriors and fighters for their families and themselves to have a better life a better future for their families.

Do you have that kind of determination to go to school and succeed in life? If we were late to class, or if students were talking too much, or if we didn't do our homework, we were disciplined. Our discipline was being spanked by a belt on our bottoms or getting hit on our hands by a ruler or stick. They would also make us kneel for a long time on a hard cemented floor. I was a pretty good student. I was quiet, tried to be on time for class, and did my homework, especially because I was afraid of my dad. I made friends easily. I was also disciplined a few times at school, but not like some of my classmates. I am grateful for the opportunity I had to go to school there. My dad expected me to get good grades, and if I didn't, I also got the spanking at home. He wanted me to be a straight-A student. School wasn't easy for me, but I worked hard to get good grades. My dad taught me how to have a hard work ethic and to keep digging deep and pushing into my potential at a very young age, which I carry to this day. Not a lot of people my age had that opportunity or had a loving, determined father like I did. Ethiopia is a whole another cultural shock to some of you. This is why it is a blessing to be living where you do.

Be grateful that you have the opportunity that many people, many children around the world, would die to have to be able to go to school to educate themselves and be who they desire to be and have a great future like the one you have in your hands. Be grateful that you graduated and were able to go to school for twelve years and can say, "I graduated." Be grateful if you were able to go to college. As I shared, there are so many children, the future leaders, who need to go to school and can't afford it all over the world. I want to encourage you today that you can do something to change that. You can become the change you want to see in the world by sponsoring a child to go to school today. It is as little as twenty to thirty dollars a month to sponsor a child to go to school. You can help a child have a better future by caring for the children of the world. If you would like to sponsor a child from Ethiopia, check out Sele Enat Charitable Organization, Kidane Mehret Children's home in Ethiopia, and World Vision. If you would like to sponsor a child from Uganda, check out Bridge of Hope Africa Ministries. These are organizations I trust and help. But choose any nonprofit the Holy Spirit leads you to. May the Lord bless you abundantly for helping his children.

Contact Information:
Kidane Mehret Children's home
www.fcj-kmch.org
"Seleenat Charitable Organization"
Facebook page: Sele Enat Mahiber

Contact Information:
"Bridge of Hope Africa Ministries"
Website: www.boham.org

Facebook page: Bridge of Hope Africa Ministries

"And the King shall answer and say unto them, Verily I say unto you, in as much as ye have done it unto one of the least of these my brethren, ye have done it unto me" (Matthew 25:40, KJV).

Children at Seleenat Orphanage

God of Provision

Therefore I say unto you, take no thought for your life, what ye shall eat, or what ye shall drink; nor yet for your body, what ye shall put on. Is not life more than meat, and the body more than raiment? Behold the fowls of the air: for they sow not, neither do they reap, nor gather into barns; yet your heavenly Father feedeth them. Are ye not much better than they? Which of you by taking thought can add one cubit unto his stature?

Matthew 6:25-27 (KJV)

If God cares for the birds and feeds them daily, He cares about you and me and can provide for us daily as well. If you're ever in a hard situation, pray to God to provide for you and make your request known to your heavenly Father. My family and I would cook in that small one-room house. We were poor, but my dad worked hard to provide for us. He had food in the house so that we would never go hungry. There were times when life was difficult for him. When the money was tight during the years, I knew by how much attention he would give me on the days he felt stressed. He always gave me full attention, played with me, and joked around. I can see circumstances having the power to fade our connection. Anytime I saw him in this state, I always said a prayer in my heart for God to help my father.

I prayed that the Lord would provide for whatever he needs, whether it's rent, food, or school fees for us. Our meals every day consisted of *injera* and *wet* (Ethiopian traditional flat bread and stew) for breakfast, lunch, and dinner. It is considered lucky to be able to eat spaghetti, macaroni, or rice. It is not often that people eat those kinds of meals because of the lack of money during that time. In my family, sometimes, when my dad had extra money is when we had the luxury of eating those kinds of meals. Let me tell you, those times were the times I waited anxiously to eat really good food with eyes wide open with excitement. The excitement would make me hungry! Rice and salsa were my favorite food growing up. One of my favorite memories of my dad was when my dad would make salsa for us. It is one of our family's traditions for my dad to make salsa every Saturday. My dad wasn't the cook at home; it was my sister. It was special to us because it was the only time that my dad got a meal ready at home, and was delicious.

There were times I remember when we didn't have any food in the house, only scraps of something. During those times, my dad would skip meals and wouldn't eat anything. Sometimes he wouldn't be eating all day long or for two days in a row, to leave the little food we have at the house for my sisters and me. It broke my heart when I would see my dad drink just a glass of water all day. My older sister Hiwet who was nine years old at the time, would do the same thing as my dad and just eat a bite of something and leave the rest for my sister and me. That is the life we lived. A lot of times, I understood when we didn't have the means to buy food and kept silent when I would get hungry so as to not worry my sisters or my dad even more than they already were. But there were times where I gave my family a hard time because I was starving. When the hunger became uncontrollable, and my stomach started hurting, I would start crying and continue to cry for quite some time. It broke my older sisters' hearts to see their little five-year-old sister crying because she was hungry, and they couldn't do anything about it. Despite their hunger, my sisters were very strong during those times and kept their heads up, up until they saw my tears falling down my cheeks. That moment was when it really hit them, deep in the core of their hearts, of the kind of situation that we were in. The moment when they realized they couldn't feed their crying little sister and there was nothing they could do about it. I never let my dad see me crying because of how hungry I was. I always told myself I will always stay strong around my dad no matter how hungry I get, and did a good job of hiding it from him. If I was really hungry on the nights he was home, I would make the excuse of being tired and go to sleep early so that my stomach wouldn't hurt and he wouldn't notice I was feeling sick. It was better to fall asleep than to stay hungry. On other days when he was home during the day, I would play and joke around with him more than usual or stay outside to play with friends for a long time so that he wouldn't notice that I was feeling down or hungry. He had a very special place in his heart for me because I was the baby in the family and absolutely adored me. I knew that if he saw me crying because I was hungry, it would shatter his heart for not being able to provide, at least for the youngest in the house. He would have felt like a failure which is completely the opposite of who he really was. Imagine if my earthly father was able to sacrifice all he got to keep me moving, then I can't imagine how our Heavenly Father cares and loves us. He loved you and me to the point where He gave His One and Only Son. My father would take off the cloth on his back to cover me, who would not look into the mirror to elevate his motive but rather he would look into his children's eyes and see his tomorrow.

My dad was an incredible father and deserved nothing but appreciation from his kids for everything that he did and became for us. Imagine if my earthly Father was able to sacrifice all he got to keep us moving; imagine how your Heavenly Father cares and loves you. He loved you to the point where He gave His One and only Son.

My dad was an extraordinary person. Even at a young age, I highly respected my father for everything he was and for taking the responsibility of a father as a high calling in his life. At an early age, my father taught us to pray for everything that we need and want and to believe and have faith in God to answer all our prayers. He taught us how to have faith in God and to believe God at His Word. My sisters and I always did what we were taught and gathered to pray for God to provide food for us. On those days when life was tough for us throughout the years, my neighbors, not hearing or knowing what's going on in our house, would bring injera (Ethiopian flat bread) and stew (wet) for us. I remember looking at them in astonishment and wonder with my jaw dropped in disbelief of what was happening at that exact moment. My sisters and I look at each other with wide eyes; mouths dropped in astonishment at what was happening. Are they really carrying all that food to bring it to us on a day we absolutely needed it and had nothing to eat? Right after we prayed and trusted the Lord to be our provider was when the miracle happened every single time. Every time they brought it, they didn't just bring enough food for one meal; they brought enough food that would last three or four days, enough to last till my father's payday. We saw miracle upon miracle upon miracle of how God provides for His children when we trust Him and wait expectantly in faith for what we prayed for to come into existence. After we prayed, we told each other now we wait and see how God is going to provide for us. God never failed us; He came through every single time.

"But rather seek ye the kingdom of God; and all these things shall be added unto you" (Luke 12:31, KJV).

God's Word is true; we have seen this specific word work in our lives. God is a provider of all things. My father never had enough money to be able to buy new clothes or shoes for us. God provided those necessary things through our neighbors. Our neighbors' clothes that they have grown out of or disliked were all given to my two sisters and me. Our neighbors felt bad for us and knew we didn't have enough clothes and that our father wasn't able to afford to buy new clothes for us. They were willing to give, and we were blessed by their generosity. I never dared to ask my dad to buy me new clothes; I understood our financial situation and kept silent as to not making things harder or more stressful on him. At every holiday in Ethiopia, it is the tradition for children to receive new clothes from their parents or guardian to wear on holiday and celebrate. A lot of children are super excited when a holiday is coming up because it is the only time that they receive new clothes. My sisters and I never owned new clothes during the holiday season; we just picked a nice outfit out of the hand-me-downs we received from different friends. I really wanted to own habesha kemis (Ethiopian traditional holiday outfit) to wear on holidays.

That was one of my dreams to celebrate the holiday in traditional clothes. I was never able to fulfill that dream while I was living at my house because of how poor we were. I remember going shopping for the first time, for clothes and shoes in Ethiopia, with my dad and my Godmother Tizita in a place called *Merkato*. I was very excited and couldn't contain my excitement. I finally got to go shopping, that has been something I had been waiting for, for many years. Merkato is a very busy shopping center in Ethiopia. I had never seen a shopping center until then. I remember looking around and being mesmerized by how many beautiful shoes and clothes there were. I saw so many things that would have been perfect for my family. I wanted to buy it all. I remember thinking if only I had the money, I would buy this for my sisters and this for Negash. I kept daydreaming of the things I would be buying for my family as we walked through the busy, chaotic Merkato Center. I loved everything that I was looking at and had a hard time deciding which shoes I wanted to get. At last, I found the shoes that I couldn't live without. They were black dress-up shoes, closed on the feet that had a little high heel on them for when I wanted to look nice for church and for when I was visiting family members. Excitedly, I shouted, "This is the one, Negash!" Tizita asked me repeatedly if they were the ones that I absolutely loved. I told her "Yes" as I cheered and smiled, jumping up and down with excitement. That day she spoiled me with more than I expected. She ended up buying two pairs of shoes for me.

One for everyday wear and the other for dressing up. She didn't stop there; she also bought me two beautiful dresses as well. I was more than thrilled and couldn't contain my excitement to myself. I was anxious to go home and share with my sisters all about my shopping trip. I finally had new shoes and clothes for the first time in my life at the age of six. Not hand-me-downs, but new shoes and clothes not worn by anyone. I was very thankful for what Tizita did for me and thanked her repeatedly with big hugs. As soon as I got home, I bragged and bragged to my sisters and close friends about my shopping time and the awesome things I got. The only time I got new things while I lived in Ethiopia was when Tizita bought me new things. My Godmother was my dad's boss and my dad's good friend. She was a beautiful person inside and out. She really loved and adored me. She is a person that would do anything she can for my family. She gifted my dad with money at times, outside of his paycheck, bought clothes and shoes for my sisters and me. We were always invited to her beautiful home to visit. Every time we went, we were treated and fed like kings and queens. She always had traditional Ethiopian food, the most expensive meals made for our visit. She was the angel that God sent to take care of us. We saw God's love and provision for us through her continuously. My sisters always told me that I am one lucky girl to have a Godmother like her that is so tenderhearted and giving. Their godmothers lived in geteri (rural part of Ethiopia) and wouldn't have much to help themselves let alone to help their Goddaughters. My sisters have never seen them since they left geteri and didn't have any relationship with them. Meron not only looked out for me but also for my sisters. In a way, she also became their Godmother. I am grateful for Tizita; I am not sure what we would've done without her. She was a big blessing in our family.

My dad never bought clothes for himself, not even once after my mom passed away. He always wore the same thing and kept his clothes in good condition. He did everything he could so that he didn't spend any money on himself but only for his children's expenses and needs.

We didn't have much in the world's eye of what the world thinks makes life happy, like having a TV, sofa, a large house, refrigerator, microwave, or video games. In order to be happy in this world, people believe the lie of needing those things in their homes to live happily. But those are addons or luxuries to make life more fun, not necessary things in order to live happily. But I am here to tell you that is definitely not true. Money can't buy happiness. There are things that money can't buy that will give you the greatest joy and fulfillment in life. The number one thing is believing in the only one and true God and his Son Jesus Christ. One of my greatest friends and Pastor Folake Kellogg once said, "To fall in love with God is the greatest romance, to seek him is the greatest adventure, to find him, the greatest human achievement."

God was our provider throughout all the years. Rely on Him for your every need. Believe and trust He will provide and wait expectantly for Him, and He will come through for you just like He has come through for my family and me countless times. He is your Provider.

My Selfless Father

"To be a good father and mother requires that the parents defer many of their own needs and desires in favor of the needs of their children. As a consequence of this sacrifice, conscientious parents develop a nobility of character and learn to put into practice the selfless truths taught by the Savior Himself."

—James E. Faust

As I mentioned earlier, we had one bed in the house. It is the tradition in Ethiopia for everyone, young and old, to wash their feet before they go to bed every night because of the dust and muddy streets. We always wore flip flops or ran around bare feet and got our feet dirty. Even if you wear tennis shoes, you always wash your feet before going to bed. Children always wash the eldest in the house's feet, whether it's parents or grandparents. That is a sign of respect, service, and love for your eldest to do that for them. My sisters and I always took turns washing my dad's feet. We would take a bowl of warm water and bar soap and wash his feet. Grateful for my selfless sister Lydia, who always washed my feet as well. Love looks like something, and it also looks like washing your family's feet. Even Jesus lowered himself and washed the disciples' feet when they had the last supper. All four of us squished and slept on that small bed every night.

We were a family that deeply loves and cares for each other. To the world, or to you that is reading this book probably looked like our family had nothing and might see us as if we were the nobody's in the world because of our poor living situation. We had the secret ingredient to life in our home that made us live life to the fullest and made us strong despite the hard times that we have had throughout the years. It was my dad's relentless love and care he showed for each one of us. His continuous love and care made the hard times look like it was nothing. When I think about the past, my mind doesn't immediately think about how poor we were and how hard life was for my family, but instead, the first thing I think about is how amazing my father was in those hard times to show us love and care and work night and day for us. All we needed was love. Love can be shared in different ways and forms. My Dad never failed to show us how much he loved us. We were his world, and he showed it to us in various ways every single day.

Not everything will stay the same forever. We just must be patient in those hard times, knowing this too shall pass.

My dad was the most selfless person I knew growing up. There was absolutely no one like him. I am not just saying that because he was my father, but if you asked anyone that knew him, they would all tell you how a selfless, loving, and compassionate person he was. He was a unique and special individual. After my mom passed away, life was difficult for him doing everything on his own. He worked crazy shifts working graveyard and day shifts back-to-back. He worked very hard so that he could provide for my sisters and me. People saw how hardworking he was and were stunned by his character. His life was never about him but always about his kids and helping other people other than himself. We were his world. You might be thinking that is exactly what he should be doing as a father. That is exactly true, but there are many parents that don't put their kids as a big priority in their life. It is surprising when you find parents that do. Every culture, every country, and every city are different, but in Ethiopia, at that time, in my surroundings and in the neighborhood, not a lot of parents put their kids high on their priority list. We were lucky to have a dad like Negash. After my mom passed away, people that knew him wanted him to get married and boldly told him to do so. He didn't like the idea of dating, nor did any thought of getting remarried crossed his mind.

They constantly bothered him about it and told him how life would be so much easier if he just got remarried. They tried setting him up on dates and did everything they could imagine trying to get him to date again and get remarried. But absolutely nothing they tried worked. My dad's heart was broken when my mom passed away. Though she was gone, he was still in love with her; he absolutely loved how great of a mother she was to us kids. To think of bringing someone else into our lives just to make it easier for himself wasn't what he had planned for the future. My dad was a very selfless man. Everything he did was for my sisters and me. He never did anything to make it easier on himself but always watched out for what was best for us kids. A lot of Ethiopian stepmoms at the time were known to mistreat their stepchildren. They didn't see or treat their stepchildren as their own biological children. Stepmothers usually treated their stepchildren like maids and made them clean the house and do unnecessary work all day while their biological children are sitting down doing nothing. I have heard of stepmoms throwing hot boiling water on their stepkids and just being cruel to them.

My dad has seen and knew of countless stories like this and didn't want to bring any new woman into our lives to treat us like how other people have been treated. A lot of stepmoms are nice at the beginning of marriage and seem like they are nice to their stepkids, but when the husband is out of the door is when their real personality comes out. A lot of them were fake, and that was the problem. One of my dad's personal strengths was being a visionary. He always thought ahead for the future for some reason. He always thought to himself, *If I get sick and die, what is going to happen to my kids? How would the stepmom treat my kids if I was gone?* He always thought of us kids first and what our world would look like if there was another mother figure in our lives without him being there. If anything happened, he wouldn't be there to protect us. Every decision he had to make in his life was always asking himself what the best thing is for us and how it could affect or help us in the long term. On top of everything he did, everything he went through, all the double shifts he did, he still came home and was a father and a mother to my sisters and me and showed us love, and was a great parent to us even when it got difficult for him. He was selfless.

Whenever someone would ask him, "Negash, when are you getting married?" He would laugh with them and just shrug his shoulders and say I will never get married again. My sisters and

I have boldly told my dad that we didn't want him to get remarried and bring someone else into our home. We have seen how stepmoms treat their stepchildren, and we weren't going to accept that kind of treatment from anyone. Our amazing mom was too good of a role model for us. At the time, none of my sisters and I never saw what we said to my dad as a wrong and selfish thing. But as I think about my past as a young adult now, I realize how selfish I was. If he wanted to get married again, it should have been his decision, and we should have supported him. But as a selfless person, my dad would never go against his children's wishes. Another strength that my dad had was following his instinct. My dad's instinct was always on point and right. His instinct told him it wasn't a good idea, so he chose not to get married. The decisions that we make every day affect our future in a good way or in a bad way. My dad always believed that it isn't about fixing the problem for the moment but thinking about how that decision can affect the outcome of our future in the years to come. Always choose wisely. Negash was a genuine person, full of love, compassion, driven to be the best father he could be for us kids. He was respected by all and had a great reputation all over the city. Everyone who knew him loved him and always spoke highly of him.

My dad started getting ahead financially to the point that he was able to start saving for the first time again since my mom's death. My mom's and dad's dream before she passed away was to build on the house we had and make it bigger. They dreamt about it for years but were unable to get started on it before she started getting sick. It became my dad's dream to fulfill their dream, even though she wasn't by his side anymore. It was a way of honoring her and doing it in her memory. Even though it had been a couple of years at the time, since the love of his life had passed away, he still had aches and pains in his heart over her passing. Even though she was gone and years passed, he was still in love with her. I remember, sometimes he would sit down at the house, holding his hands, and looking down at the floor and think about her. He would smile, get sad and smile again as he is looking up at her picture that was hanging on the wall. My dad started falling in love with her when she was yet a young lady in geteri (rural part of Ethiopia) when he was a goat herder.

What my parents had was real and true love. He never talked about my mom to me and my sister Lydia; he only talked to my oldest sister Hiwet about it. He didn't talk to us about it because he didn't want us to be sad and miss her even more. If they were talking about my mom, when we walked into the house, they immediately changed the subject and acted like nothing happened. I always knew and realized that the conversation prior to my arrival was about my mom by the way they acted, my dad continuously looking at my mom's picture on the wall or the little, small pic he has of her in his wallet. I so badly wanted to talk about my mom too. I wanted to tell them I missed her so much too. I wanted to know more about her and how she treated and loved me, but I was always scared to bring up something that already broke his heart. I didn't want him to be sad. I knew if he knew his little princess was sad too and was missing her mom daily, it would've broken his heart more, so I kept it to myself throughout the years to not make my father unhappy. Anything to add to his happiness instead of subtracting it for everything he was doing for our family.

My Dad had the most loving and caring heart of anybody I have ever met in Ethiopia. I might be biased because he was my father, but he had something very special and unique about him that people notice right away when they see him. You can just tell. Sometimes you can look at a person and think, *wow, there is something special about this person,* just by first contact and not know what it is, but you just know that they are created to do something special in the world. My dad was exactly that person. He was full of love and compassion. He shared love with anybody he met, whether it's smiling and saying hello to everyone he saw, giving people things he knows they need or helping them in one way or another. He wasn't possessive about his stuff; he gave things away all the time to people that need them. He gave away his nice coats and jackets to beggars on the streets. When he continuously came home without the jacket he had on, we would ask him what happened. He always told us he gave it away to someone that needed it more.

During the rainy season in Ethiopia, it pours down rain; he would leave with an umbrella and end up giving it away to someone else. He buys things and gives them away to whoever his heart ached for. His heart never let him pass by a beggar without giving money to them. If he didn't have any, he would pass by giving them at least coins. My dad not only had a heart to help the poor but acted upon it in many various ways. Once or twice a month, my ten-year-old sister Hiwet and my dad fed the beggars around my neighborhood and the beggars around Yosef Orthodox church. My sister cooked delicious Ethiopian food for them. It usually took her all day cooking with my eight-year-old sis Lydia helping her here and there. There were lots of beggars and homeless people around where we lived, and outside the church, my dad had a special heart for the poor. We all, as a family, go around to pass out food and water to them. Some of the beggars had a container where we put the food in, and the ones that didn't, they used plastic bags to put it in. My dad always gave extra food to them to last them for later for when they would get hungry.

Jesus has said, *"And the King shall answer and say unto them, Verily I say unto you, In as much as ye have done it unto one of the least of these my brethren, ye have done it unto me"* (Matthew 25:40, KJV).

My dad lived his life that way. It was a blessing for me to be a part of that and learn to give and care for the poor at a young age of five. My sisters and I have learned many valuable lessons from my dad, and one of the main lessons was to have a heart to care for the poor (Proverbs 22:6). He had a compassionate and giving heart to those in need. When we die, we don't die with the things that we own, but the acts of compassion that we have done for people, the love that we shared, the compassion that we have had with people, and the lives that we have changed goes with us and lives on as the people we have been a small part of changing their life live to do the things that we have done for them and pay it forward to others. It becomes a legacy. My dad left a legacy of love, compassion, and selflessness to this world. People always said there is no one like Negash. I totally agree; as his daughter, I have seen firsthand the kind of person he was every day towards people and owns that title.

My dad kept saving the extra money he was receiving to the dream house savings for a few years. He was excited to finally have that dream come to life. He worked double shifts left and right, trying to save up enough money so he could start on it as soon as possible. He saved up a lot and was going to start building the house in a couple of months, but something tragic and life-threatening happened to me that stopped the house-building dream.

Life-Threatening Situation

One fall night, after a great day in kindergarten and a fun day playing with my friends in the neighborhood, something unexpected happened. I was in the biggest storm of my life when I was five and a half years old and almost lost my life in one tragic night. It came unexpectedly to my family and me, and to everybody that knew me. My dad was doing a double shift, trying to do everything he could to provide for us kids and save money to accomplish his dream and my mom's dream of building a house. That night he was working a graveyard shift. I was next door at my neighbor's house with my sisters and friends having fun. My eldest sister, the chef and the mom in our house at the age of nine years old, was cooking a very delicious lentil stew. (Ethiopian stew) for dinner that night. She would come to my neighbor's house where my other sister and I were to hang out for a little bit and leave to check on the stew every five minutes. We were listening to my favorite Ethiopian singer at the time and dancing and singing with our neighbors.

Suddenly, I got tired, bored, and super hungry and decided to go home. I asked my sister when the stew would be done.

She told me it was not done yet and it would be done in a few minutes. Starving, I kept telling her it's already done and that she needed to let me eat already. That night, my sister was very determined to make a delicious stew for our family. She was cooking it for what seemed like five hours but was three hours. She kept telling me to just wait. She was a perfectionist even as a young child. As I mentioned earlier, we lived in one small room house where we slept, cooked, and ate. The stove was placed close to the bed, not intentionally but because there was no other space to put it. I decided to jump on my bed while she was cooking the food to keep myself busy from my hunger. Then this thought came into my mind to learn and practice how to do somersaults and do it at school the next day in front of all my classmates and to show off. At school, everybody knew how to do it except for me.

I imagined all the kids around me at school and watching me and then clapping their hands and cheering as I would show off my skills. Then I decided to do it. My sister saw what I was doing and told me to stop. She warned me and said I am going to fall into the stew and get burned. I ignored her. She repeatedly told me to stop, and I told her," You worry too much, I won't get hurt," she said, "Sara, be careful, you're going to get burned, you need to stop now." I became ignorant and just kept doing what I was doing. She would check on the stew and then leave for my neighbor's house then come back to the house to double-check on me and the stew. She kept running back and forth, making sure the house wasn't on fire and that I was okay. She kept telling me to stop every time she came back to the house. Part of me wanted to listen to her and stop and knew

43

deep down that I should stop and that I might get hurt. The other part of me was saying, "You don't need to listen to her. You're okay; you won't get hurt. How can you land into the stew when you're on the bed? That kept playing in my mind. There was a deep, still, small voice that kept telling me, "Sara, stop. You need to stop now." After a few times, I decided to listen and stop, but then I thought of a different way to do the same thing, thinking that would do the trick and it would be okay. I started doing somersaults in a different direction of the bed, so I thought I wouldn't get hurt. I was partly upset with myself for not listening to my sister. I wanted to listen and stop, but when there are two voices in your head, which one do you listen to? I was only five and a half years old; I didn't know what the voices were, but now I know it was the Holy Spirit that gave me instincts and was telling me to stop while the enemy kept telling me to keep going and kept pushing me, I decided I would do it one more time, and then I would be done. We think in our lives that one more time of making the wrong choice won't hurt us. We say, "I have done that before, and nothing happened to me. It's okay because I am used to doing this or that whatever it is," whether it's that you are addicted to something or some substance or making the right decisions.

We tell ourselves it won't hurt us, that it is just one more time, then I am done. But that one more time we do something can be the last time we choose to live. God can try to save us from many bad things by whispering in our hearts through the Holy Spirit that we need to stop or not do that thing. He can try over, repeatedly, to try to save us from tragedy that is going to happen in our lives. We don't know the outcome because we can't see the future, but He does. Is there a time in your life where you decided to listen to that still small voice? A time where you listened to your gut feeling of making decisions in your life, and it saved you from something or someone?

A time where God said no, and you said yes to something? What happened? What were the results? Were you right when you decided to go and do things your own way? Or did you learn a lesson from thinking you thought you knew it all? God gave us free will to choose for ourselves. Even though He loves us so much and died for our sins to open the gates of heaven for us, He still gave us free will to choose what we wish. Our decisions have consequences when we choose not to follow the right. The one-time choice can be a life or death decision in our lives in some situations, and that's exactly what happened to me. I chose not to listen to my sister even though I knew she was right, and I knew deep down that I needed to stop jumping on the bed. I thought to myself if I stopped, she would win, which means I listened to her. I had this pride issue going on that I wasn't going to listen to my own sister. Pride can kill us, literally. Learn to break your pride at a young age, and if you're older and reading this and that pride needs to break off of you. I advise you right now to break the wall of pride and ask Jesus to help you. Say, Jesus, help me break my pride. Take my pride away from me in Jesus' name. Your pride can be your biggest enemy in life that will make you stop growing as a person and break off a lot of opportunities that could be coming your way. Have the desire to be teachable from anyone younger or older than you. You become more in life when you are teachable. My little pride and not wanting to listen to my instinct and to my sister led me to almost losing my life. I thought to myself, I have never seen anybody get burned because they were jumping on their bed. So I didn't think it would happen to me, so I kept going. A big lesson here is just because you haven't seen somebody get hurt doing something that you shouldn't be doing doesn't mean that it doesn't happen at all; it doesn't mean that it won't happen to you. Think it through and learn to choose the right.

As Hiwet was running back home to check up on me like she was doing every five minutes at the same time, my leg twisted in a different angle and somehow flipped over differently and knocked the lid off the hot burning pot of stew. When I hit the wall with my leg all twisted, I knew immediately that something bad was going to happen because I couldn't control the way I was falling. My leg knocked the lid off the hot, burning three hours delicious smelling cooked stew. Then the unthinkable happened. The thing that I thought would never happen happened. Ahhh! I started screaming at the top of my lungs! Hiwet was in shock. She started screaming with me. The whole pot of stew was all over me, and the pot and lid knocked off and splattered all over the house. My sister walked into this crazy horrifying scene. I kept screaming really loud. We both kept crying; I lay down, burning, literally saying, "Hiwet, help me. "Hiwet, Hiwet!" I screamed her name to help me. My sister, at the time, was ten years old and didn't know what to do. She just stood there in shock, watching me. Some of the stew fell on the gas stove and turned out the flames! Thank you, Jesus, for that. It could have been worse. My whole body was soaked up with the stew that fell on me. I felt like I was on fire. Like my whole body was on fire! I couldn't move at all. I felt paralyzed in my own body. Have you ever felt that way? If you have, you under-stand what I was going through. I have never felt like I couldn't move any part of my body. It's the craziest thing to experience. I kept screaming, "It burns (*tekateliku*) Hiwet!" As I was scream-ing and crying, I remember my eyes kept gazing at wherever Hiwet would walk. She kept walking back and forth, back and forth, trying to figure out what to do. It is a miracle that the flames were off. As my eyes gazed around, I saw the lid, and the pot was scattered. My sister, instead of leaning down and help-ing me or telling me everything was going to be okay, was pick-ing the stuff from the ground and cleaning. Not knowing what to do, she thought until the neighbors came for the rescue, she would start cleaning up and clearing up everything that was around me. I remember thinking, *What is she doing picking up stuff? Why isn't she on the ground helping me and taking the clothes off of me?*

My clothes were sticking to my skin; I felt it because of the stew; I was dying for someone to take it off of me. I don't know if you've ever been burned before but imagine a whole big pot of stew falling all over your body, you're just lying there, not know-ing if you're going to live or die, crying, screaming if there ever help would arrive to rescue you? I wanted something cold on my body to cool down the burn. We screamed for what seemed like an eternity. Literally! We hear a commotion outside, people trying to find out where the scream was coming from, but no-body came to check the house.

After fifteen minutes of screaming, finally, my neighbor walks into our house and told everybody that she'd found us. I found out later that my sisters and my scream were so loud the whole neighborhood around the block was out of their house startled. The scream felt like it was close, but it was so loud it seemed it could be from far away. I guess there was a lot of commotion because there were a lot of people outside trying to figure out where the horrifying scream was coming from. They started counting off family members, trying to figure out who was missing. They checked every house except ours. Our house was a very quiet house; nothing bad ever came out of there. They knew my dad was at work and my other sister was with them, so they thought they had everybody in the family. They forgot about Hiwet and me. We kept screaming that they finally decided again that everybody needs to go check each house in the neighborhood; thank God they did. Finally, my friend came into our house. She saw us and ran out to go get help and let them know they found the house. Love her reaction. She didn't stand there looking at me paralyzed because of what she saw, but she ran out in fear and to let my neighbors know. What would you do if you were in that kind of situation? How would you react? All of a sudden, my house was filled up with tons of people. Our tiny one-room house can only hold so many people, but somehow, everybody was squashed in there like a pumpkin trying to figure out how to help me. I kept hearing them argue on what to put on my body. Some say we should put cold water on her, while some were saying we should put lteti (mix for injera kind of like a pancake mix). I am thinking, *I don't care what you put on me, just put something cold on my burning body.* It was burning so bad and hurting that I couldn't wait any longer.

I was going in and out of consciousness! Everything was blurry to me, but I saw my neighbors frantically scared, not knowing what to do. So many people cramped in that one little room house of ours arguing about what they should do for me and what's best for me without hurting me. I kept whispering to take the clothes off me. Finally, they took the clothes off of me slowly. As they were doing that, I remember my skin pulling off with it. It was a horrifying scene. It hurt to take it off because my clothes were stuck to my skin, pulling off with it, so the skin was coming off with it. Still, they didn't put anything cold on me. My body was still burning. I couldn't really speak, but I cried. They continued arguing about what is best to put on my body to put water or *injera liti*. Finally, they decided instead of cold water to put lete on me. Oh my gosh! When they put the mix on me, it was indescribable how the cold lete felt on my skin that was on fire. Oh! It felt so amazingly good! It was so refreshing. Have you ever accidentally burnt yourself on your hand or something? When we feel the fire, even just the heat, we take our hands off right away because of the tad burn that we feel. Imagine your whole body on fire! Imagine your body feeling paralyzed, and you weren't able to move. Imagine waiting for somebody to put cold water on you. How would you have felt? They put the lete over my clothes first then started to slowly take the clothes off me. My neighbors weren't really educated, so that's why they put the lete on my body instead of cold water. It would have been better for them to put cold water on me. Not a lot of adults went to school or anything at that time. A lot of them came from geteri (rural side of the country). People that live in the geteri don't usually go to school. In a lot of places, there either aren't schools there, or they can't afford to go to school, so they work on the farms.

As they were putting the lete on me, I turned my head around and saw both of my two sisters sobbing. My heart sank as I looked around the room; my neighbors were also hugging each other, holding on to each other, crying. There was no dry eye in that room full of people. There were at least fifteen people squished in the house. They were crying like I was going to die or something. I stopped crying when they put the lete on me. They covered me up with my dad's favorite gabi (Ethiopian traditional blanket). There was comfort in wearing my Dad's gabi. My mind was running as I watched my neighbors and sisters freaking out, worrying and trying to figure out how to get me to the hospital. Nobody had a car in my neighborhood. I kept wondering if I was going to live or die that night.

Going to the Emergency Room

In Ethiopia, it's not common for people to own cars. Here in America, we live in a world where teenagers start driving at the age of sixteen and have the luxury of having their own cars. It's the norm here, but not in Africa and definitely not in my country. If you had a car in Ethiopia, you would be considered rich. The people that have cars in Ethiopia are either only taxi drivers, people that work for big companies, or rich people. They have the company's car they use, and some rich people own theirs as well. Our transportation is a lot of walking, taking the taxi and bus with lots of people as crowded as can be. It is hard finding transportation at night. A lot of taxis and buses stop running early in the evening. It was around 10 p.m. at night when I got burned, so there was no taxi we could find to take me to the hospital. In the whole few blocks of my neighborhood, nobody had cars except one. Thank you, Jesus.

One of my friend's dads worked for a company that transports goods. He occasionally, when he gets ready to go out of the city and go to different parts of Ethiopia, he would have the car for the night or few days before he leaves. He usually is out of town, but that day when I was on the verge of losing my life, the day when I absolutely needed transportation asap, he was home. Not only was he home, but he had his truck with him. I thank God for him and for his truck. That day, that night, that moment when we needed transportation the most. I know that was an orchestrated God plan so that he could take me to the hospital. Have you ever had that kind of close encounter and seen God's goodness in your life? They wrapped me up with gabi to keep me warm and put me in the truck. I remember sitting in the car thinking, *What's happening?* Everybody was running around like crazy, people screaming, trying to get things done. People are yelling; she doesn't have that much time. Take her to the hospital. I didn't even know what to think. I was shivering not only because I was cold, but I didn't know what was going to happen to me. I didn't really speak. All I wanted was my daddy to hold me to let me know everything was going to be okay. I was missing my mom.

Why does she have to die so early? Where was she when I needed her the most? Why did God take her away from me at a young age? Why? Why? What is happening to me, and why is this happening to me? Is today the last day of my life? Am I dying tonight? Everybody around me is making it sound like it was. All of these questions kept popping into my head. As my mind was running, they finally started driving. The truck only fit four people, so it was me, the driver, and two neighbors. They took me to the nearest hospital. One of my neighbors carried me out and started running in the hospital. They saw me and said sorry we couldn't take her. We don't have the doctors or medications to help her. They told us to go to a different hospital. They ran to the car and started driving. I was going in and out of consciousness. I remember there was a lot of commotion in the car. I heard them say to drive fast. Should we call for Negash? Negash needs to meet us somewhere. Oh, and there was one person with a cellphone. Cell Phones weren't big at that time in Ethiopia. There were house phones some people had, but not a lot of people had cell phones. We rushed to the next hospital. They, too, looked at me and saw my burns and said, "Sorry, we can't take her for the same reason the first hospital denied me. My neighbor started begging them to please take me in because I guess I started looking bad and could leave this world anytime soon. They told us to go to a different hospital called Yekatit 12. It was an hour and a half away from my house. When we arrived at Yekatit 12, they took me in finally, which was a miracle. Everything happened super-fast from then on. I remember being put in a wheelchair and the doctors and nurses trying to hurry to take me to the emergency room. As we were on our way to the emergency room, my dad was walking in; we met each other in the hallway. The look on my dad's face was indescribable. As I was sitting in the wheelchair, he was standing in front of me, and we both looked into each other's eyes. It was a moment that I would never forget. I have never seen my dad so sad; his eyes were shot red from crying so much on his way to the hospital. He tried to be strong, but he couldn't because it was his little princess. I can't imagine how he was feeling. He lost his wife and mother of his three children, and now he couldn't bear the thought of losing his youngest child. My dad knelt down and held my hand and said, "You are going to be okay. Be strong; I am here for you." That was everything I needed to hear. I waited to hear that from the moment I fell into the stew to two and half hours later when I finally saw my father in the emergency room. I was crying after he told me that. They told him he needs to go outside so they can start the surgery right away. I wouldn't let go of him. I started crying uncontrollably when they separated us. They put me on the hospital bed. From then on, there was a lot of chaos with nurses and doctors surrounding me. After a moment, I was out of consciousness. I remember all this because God gave me a great memory so I can write this book as a testimony of my story.

They did surgeries on me. They did a skin graft. I was in a coma for twenty-two days. I don't know what happened for those days; I was out. Can you imagine being in a coma for that long? Do you know of anybody that was in a coma? This part of my story was told to me by my aunts and sisters because I wasn't awake. My dad quit his job. He told them that he couldn't come back until I was out of hospital, or they can fire him if they choose to. His boss and co-workers understood. They told him to go on leave if he wanted for as long as he needed. One of his main bosses was my Godmother which worked in his favor. I believe that was an alignment from the Lord. The kind of man that my dad is, they knew he would never leave his children in the hospital and just come back to work. He is the type of person that would stay with his children to take care of them. He would literally give his life for my sisters and me. My dad was a devoted father. While I was in a coma, because of how badly I was burned, everybody literally everybody thought I was going to die. They were grieving like I was already dead. The nurses and the doctors told him that I wasn't going to live through it.

That he should let me go. Literally, everyone told my dad that I was going to die. Everybody thought Sara is going to die; it is just a matter of time except my father. My hero refused to accept that and believed I would live through it!

It Takes Faith to See It Through

Everybody kept feeding off of each other and kept telling my father that there is no hope. No hope for me. That I was going to die anyways, it is just a matter of time. They told him to make it easier on himself and for everybody around him and just let me go. She's not waking up; she's already dead anyways. How long has it been Negash? If she was supposed to live through this, she would have woken up already. Let her go, Negash. It's okay. Let her go! You did everything you can to save her. It's time that you should and need to say your goodbyes and let the doctors unplug the machines. That is what my dad heard every day from many people, literally every single day that I was in a coma. That went on for twenty-two days. I can't even imagine how my dad was feeling hearing all this daily. I don't know how he did it. How he lived through it. How he kept being sane. Can you imagine how easy it would have been to just let me go and listen to what so many people were telling him to do? Even the doctors and nurses told him that I wasn't going to make it. There was a sermon I once heard Pastor John Gray preach and said, "When your family is in need, you go to talk to Jesus.

When the doctors and nurses don't know what else to do other than what they know, you have got to go to Dr. Jesus! That is because Jesus makes wine out of water! You have to give Jesus the situation so He can make a miracle out of it."

My dad was in the biggest trials of his life. His daughter that he loved so much was on the verge of dying. He was in the biggest storm of his life. If you remember the story of Jesus on the boat with his disciples. Suddenly there was a storm they found themselves in. When Jesus was on the boat with his disciples, he said, "Let's go to the other side of the lake." I don't even know if my dad knows this story in the Bible, but that was what my dad was going through with me. Even Though the water was filling up the boat to the point that the boat can't stand in there anymore. That represents doubts, worries, and everything my dad was hearing from everyone filling up his mind. My Heavenly Father gave him peace in his heart that I was going to live through this. When Jesus was sleeping on the boat, that represented my story the peace and quiet that my heavenly Father gave to my earthly father. Because without peace, you will go crazy, especially in a life-threatening situation like I was and like the storm my father was in. My sisters and aunts told me my dad prayed every morning and night. If he wasn't talking to people that came to the hospital to visit, he was talking to God. There were times when he was worried sick about me dying. There were times where doubts crept into his mind, and the enemy tried to twist his mind and make him try to listen to the people around him. He is only human.

Faith is believing in something you can't see. Faith is believing it will happen when there is no way of it happening and seeing the bright side of the outcome even when it doesn't make sense. Faith is truly trusting God that he will come through. Faith is relying on God. Faith is knowing and letting God know it's not in my powers anymore. I can't do it on my own, it's saying I need you, Jesus, and I give this all to you. Do what you will with it. Faith is truly believing in God and His plans. Faith is truly believing that God will show up and that He will make a way where there is absolutely no way to provide for his kids at home with food and money to pay bills. Faith is saying that you will take care of my other two daughters God. Faith is saying that you will not only take care of my two daughters at home while I am away but also comfort them and that you will give them the peace that they need, that their sister is going to be okay, and their father too. Faith is teaching your kids not to ever give up on something when you include God, the Creator of the universe, in the equation. Faith is saying, "I won't quit on believing in this, God." Faith is saying, "I won't quit on my daughter." Faith is saying, "I know you will give me the peace and strength that I need to go through this trauma in my life right now." Faith is saying, "Not only will you give me peace and strength, but you will give me fresh new strength and new peace in my heart every single day however long I need it."

Faith is believing until God shows up with the miracle you are expecting. Faith is believing that God is already there and that he is surrounding you with love and comforting you through people's hugs and sweet notes, and remarks. Faith is knowing that God will answer everyone's prayers. Faith is trusting fully and letting go, and letting God. Faith is saying; I love you, God, I trust you, and believe that you know what is best for my daughter and me. Faith is saying, "I know whatever it is God, I trust your will, and I will wait expectantly with faith." Faith believes that I will live through this traumatic trauma. Faith is believing that God will use this crazy event in our life to change people's lives now and forever. Faith is believing that a miracle is coming our way anytime. Faith is believing when it gets hard and even when bad doctor's reports come in saying my God is bigger than this situation. Faith is telling your problem how big your God is. Faith is keeping strong. Faith is knowing with all your heart, mind, and soul that God will bring back your dying daughter to life! And that is the kind of faith my dad had! I am in shock and amazed every time I think that I will live through this. He had the biggest faith than anybody I know in my life. I am so grateful and so proud of my dad and the faith he had. Praise God for giving him amazing faith. I am so proud to call him my father. If it wasn't for God saving me, I wouldn't be alive today. Oh, my Heavenly Father, how can I thank you enough! If it wasn't for my dad's faith, I wouldn't be alive today. In the Bible, in Mark 5, there is a story of a helpless father and his dying daughter and their experience with Jesus. When Jarius saw and heard that Jesus was healing the sick, the blind, and doing miracles, he knew exactly who to go to get help for his dying daughter. He fought through the crowd, ran to Jesus, and said, "*...pleading fervently with him. 'My little daughter is dying,' he said. 'Please come and lay your hands on her; heal her so she can live'*" (*Mark 5:23, NLT*). He asked him to cure his daughter that was on the verge of dying. He told Jesus, if only you could touch her, she will live and come back to life. As Jarious was speaking to Jesus, his friend showed up and told him not to bother Jesus that it was already too late that his daughter was dead. Even after hearing that, Jesus tells Jarious, "Do not be afraid, just believe" (Mark 5:36, NLT). Jarious led Jesus to his house to show him his daughter. When Jesus walked in, he saw the man's daughter lying on the bed, unresponsive. There were a lot of people mourning and crying because they thought the girl was dead. Jesus told Jarious to have the other people leave the house, then Jesus touched her and said:

"Holding her hand, he said to her, 'Talitha koum,' which means 'Little girl, get up!'" (Mark 5:41, NLT). She woke up! Looked around and stood still. When the parents saw the miracle that just took place, they could not believe it; they were stunned because moments before, she was just lying down, not breathing. Jarious thanked Jesus. Jesus told him that his faith had saved his daughter. Wow! That story is exactly what happened to me. My dad prayed, prayed, and had big faith that I will live through it, just like Jarious that ran from his house to Jesus. He kept fighting and walking into every crack in between people to get in front of Jesus to ask him one question and to bring Jesus to his house to heal and bring back his dying daughter. My dad had to fight through so many people's opinions and advice to believe God will wake me up. When you have that kind of faith, God will answer your prayers. God will answer you and come to your rescue. He will because he loves you.

While I was in a coma for twenty-two days, to people just like the little girl in the Bible, I was already dead to them. My physical body said she's dying or already dead. The reports reported the same thing. But I was only asleep. When it was time for me to wake up, I believe Jesus touched me and said, "It's time to wake up, daughter!"

Out of nowhere, I started opening my eyes very slowly. As I opened them, I found myself on the hospital bed hooked up to an Iv! There were so many wires and wraps tied to my arms. I was attached to a lot of things; I was flowing through me. I remember waking up so scared. I gasped for air when I saw my right leg hanging up and resting on something. It was the freakiest thing ever to wake up to. It felt like my whole body was attached to so many things and machines and monitors. I was lying down, helpless because I couldn't move or talk. I was thinking to myself, what happened to me? Why am I in the hospital attached to these machines? Am I dying? What happened to my leg? It was the scariest thing to wake up to for a five and half-year-old. I started to freak out; then, my eyes started gazing around the room instead of looking at my helpless body. I was in a big painted yellow room. While lying in bed, I looked out the big window in front of me and saw big buildings and houses as I laid on my bed. The sun was out, so I figured it was afternoon. There was nobody in the room except me. Where is everybody? Where is my dad Negash? I probably was awake for five minutes when a nurse came in to check on me. As soon as she saw my eyes, she smiled big and excitedly said, "Selam, (Hi) Sara."

I looked at her and couldn't say anything. She told me she would be right back and ran out. I thought, *Where is she going? Don't leave me by myself.* In came the doctor. They started checking on me. I didn't know what they were doing, but all I wanted at the moment was to see my dad or a familiar face. I kept gazing around the room, confused, and then I heard footsteps coming towards the room. I turned my head slowly to the door to see who was coming in, and guess who walked in the door? My Dad! He stopped at the door, stunned to see my eyes open. I remember clearly when my daddy walked in; his face was shining with a huge bright smile. I have never seen him so happy like this. I was so happy and so excited to see my daddy's face. But my face wasn't making the excited looks that I was feeling inside. I felt trapped in my body. I looked at him and felt relieved. My dad and I had another moment that I will never forget, the first time I woke up after twenty-two days of being in a coma. He ran to my bed and started talking to me, and kissed my forehead. I don't remember what he said, but I started crying because I was so happy to see him and because I was so scared of what was happening to me. He kept encouraging me and holding on to my hand. With my confused look, he realized that I was wondering what happened to me. He told me I got burned, stew fell on me, and that everything is okay now.

"You're alive, and God saved you," he told me. Out of all the words he spoke, the words that stayed with me were when he said I am going to be okay. It was terrifying to wake up to something like that. I can't imagine how my dad was feeling to see his daughter alive, and the joy and happiness and all the mixed emotions he was feeling at the moment. His daughter that was supposed to die opened her eyes. Faith is seeing it through! I remember seeing him cry, but it was happy tears this time. The doctors and nurses were in shock to see me alive and awake.

Waking Up From Coma

There were so many people that were in that big hospital room that kept coming in and out to see if it was true that I finally woke up. They couldn't believe their eyes. The news spread fast that I woke up from coma. People kept coming to see me and look at the breathing miracle. I guess the whole hospital staff and family members that were there knew about me and my condition and how I was in a coma for so long. There were rumors about me probably dying and my dad fighting to save me. So when they heard I woke up, they all wanted to see with their own eyes if it was really true. My neighbors and sisters, as soon as they heard about the news, got on the taxi and drove two hours to see me. I still couldn't talk but nod my head and look at people. I remember every person I saw coming in that door to see me. They literally stood at their track at the door, paused and couldn't believe what they were seeing, smiled really big then walked in the room. They were all shocked to see me alive and would start tearing up right away. People I didn't even know but knew my family members or friends, friends of friends came to visit me and would look at me and start crying because they were so happy to see me.

When I saw my sisters walking into the room, I lost it and so did they! I was so happy to see my sisters that I loved so much; we were all crying tears of joy. As soon as I saw my sister Hiwet, all the memories kept rushing back on how I got burned. Hiwet and I have a history that changed our lives forever. We have a bond that can't be described. When you go through a big traumatic trial like that with someone, that bond and love are there forever. My room was full of people with tears for days as different people came in to see me. This time though, they weren't crying because I was dying; they were crying because God came through, and their sister and friend that was supposed to be dead was alive right in front of their eyes. They saw God's work; their faith wasn't strong. They saw God in a real, presentable way, for some for the first time in their life. God is so good. They all gathered and prayed and started thanking God for my life and for saving me. They knew with all their heart that it wasn't the doctors; it was totally God. My dad couldn't keep it together; he was full of tears of joy. The only way he could express his joy was through his tears and kept thanking God for saving his daughter. I can't imagine how my dad was feeling the emotion that was going through him. How he endured everything, everybody was saying to him, to let me go and then seeing the fruit of his faith. He saw a big miracle in the biggest storm of his life. He saw God coming through. He saw what faith does when you just believe. He saw his Heavenly Father answer the biggest prayer in his life to save his daughter. He saw God working from heaven down to earth.

My dad's faith started from the moment he walked into the hospital on the night I got burned to the moment he quit his job. My dad didn't know how long I was going to be in the hospital or if I was going to live or not. My dad had huge faith that I was going to live through this for some reason, no matter what it took. Everybody kept telling him repeatedly that he should let me go and that he was just wasting all his money on me. The people he looked up to, like his siblings, my doctors, and nurses kept telling him every day; she isn't going to live through this; just let her go. I was at one of the best hospitals in the city, and that was what the doctors had to say. It doesn't matter what the reports or what people or the doctors say; God is the Creator of life. My God is bigger than the reports. God is the author and finisher of our faith and life, so when God says, "Come back to me, daughter," is when I am supposed to go to heaven, not when the doctors think I am supposed to go. God sees what the human mind can't see. They didn't want me dead by any means; I guess they were trying to be realistic with my dad because of what they saw with their human eyes.

But God wanted them and my dad to see it through supernatural eyes the way he would see it. He totally did give my dad that vision and faith of seeing it through his eyes instead of what he was hearing. You know what I have come to realize? Yes, I should be dead the way I was burned. But we have a God that can heal the sick, raise the dead and do the impossible and work miracles before your eyes. My dad could have given up and said, "Well, maybe there will be no miracle," he could have stopped praying because the prayer was taking too long to be answered. He could have said she isn't going to live through this and lose his faith, but instead, no matter how hard it was, he embraced the process, the process to my healing. But I am so grateful to my dad's big unshakeable faith in God. That's the reason why I am alive today right now while you're reading this book. My dad knew the only way I was going to live was through God's miracle and his healing power. I am so grateful to be alive today writing this story of how faith in God can change your world.

How one person's life can be changed because of your faith. I am so grateful that God healed me, and it is because of him and only him that I am alive today. Jesus is my healer. I am so grateful that my dad didn't give up on me. I am so grateful for his faith in God and for knowing sooner or later, God will make the impossible possible and let me live and recover from it. Life is precious. We take life for granted sometimes, maybe a lot of the time. Life can be taken away at any moment; we must live life to the fullest. God saved me from coma for a reason and a purpose to accomplish his purpose in my life. God has a plan to use my story for his glory, just like he will use what you went through for his glory. God is using my dad's faith to show people and dads with dying sick daughters and sons out there to have unshakeable faith in God.

God is using my dad's story to birth miracles out of people's storms if you choose to let them impact you. I knew when I was jumping on the bed, and there was a small still voice telling me to stop so that I could get burned. It shows even when we don't listen to God and mess up. He loves us so much that he takes our mistakes and what could and should have killed us because of the bad choices we make and turns them into miracles. When that happens, you can only think and know it was only God. I don't believe in coincidences; I believe in divine appointments. I believe you are reading this because God wants to show you something through my story to use my story to help you to continue to have faith in God in what you believe Him for. Maybe you are one of the few that have lived through a big challenging storm in your life and need to know you are saved and alive for a reason and a purpose? I don't know how this story connects to you, but only you do, but I hope you can see it through my story that you have a kind, gracious Heavenly Father that truly loves you and wanted to remind you that God is surrounding what is surrounding you and that He has you and your situation in his loving arms. He will do a miracle in your life and solve the problem in your life. Just be patient and wait and believe in His timing and keep having unshakeable faith because the God of the universe is on your side. Just keep remembering the Bible verse that says, *"What shall we then say to these things? If God be for us, who can be against us?"* (Romans 8:31, KJV) See it through; God is going to use your story for his glory. You're going to be making Jesus famous through your story and life because of what He has done for you and how He can or has changed your life.

My dad is my hero and a great role model and example for me and for so many dads out there. You never give up on God, your kids, or anything that's worth fighting for. You keep fighting, and if it's God's will, it will happen.

This is a lesson that I will carry for the rest of my life. My dad taught me the biggest lesson you can teach your children is to have big unshakable faith. I am always reminded when I think small and ask God to do small things. I am reminded of how big my God is, and this thought always comes to my mind, have big faith like your dad. God will come through. The miracle isn't going to come in our timing, the way we want it, or when we want it, but it's going to come in God's timing, and God's timing is perfect. He wants to teach us lessons through the process of birthing the miracle. My dad learned patience, perseverance and learned to rely only on God. Just believe and patiently wait because your miracle might be around the corner. It takes faith to have faith. Thank you for making a miracle out of me, Jesus. I am forever grateful.

Learning to Persevere

It was a third-degree burn! They did surgeries on me. They did a skin graft from my right leg that was hanging up when I first woke up from my coma. My arms were wrapped up still. I kept being fed through the veins with Iv nutrition for a while. I was awake from my coma but still sick. Waking up from my coma was a miracle but also a process of so many things to come and endure. Just like the story I shared in the earlier chapter about the girl that woke up from her sleep when Jesus touched her, I was awoken. The next thing that Jesus told her parents was to let her rest and give her water. My body needed to rest just like that and keep healing and keep getting taken care of by the doctors. I still had to lay in bed for a month and a half after I woke up. During that time, I was on IV the whole time. All I did was wake up for a little bit but go back to sleep, then wake up again as the doctors and nurses were taking care of me because I still wasn't healed all the way for me to go home. They were changing the wrap from my scars daily. I would scream and cry every day as they changed the wrap because it hurt a lot. It was the most painful thing that I have ever experienced. I couldn't talk, so it was hard to communicate and share with them how I felt. I felt paralyzed in my own body, not being able to move as

I wanted because the scars were fresh and were hurting me. I feared what was going to happen to me or if I was ever going to be able to walk and talk again and be a normal five-year-old. I had to be strong and go through all the pain. I was getting two shots a day. I cried every time I got shots; I hated it. I slept a lot for another month.

The only thing that gave me peace that helped me so much when I couldn't say a word was having my daddy at my bedside whenever I woke up. He was always there right there with me. My dad was a special person and one of a kind. When I started noticing what was going on around me and feeling better, I wondered where he was sleeping. Every time I woke up, he was awake; he barely slept. The room I was put in didn't have another bed in there, so my dad would usually fall asleep sitting on the chair. Sometimes he would sleep beside my bed on the cement floor with a thin sheet on the floor and a little blanket over him. I was horrified when I saw that because day in and day out, he slept on the cement cold floor uncomfortably for two months. I hated seeing my dad sleep on the floor. I loved having him there, but I was worried about how he is doing in his health. I was afraid that he would get sick from sleeping on the hard cold cement floor for so long. I asked my dad a few times to sleep on the bed with me or for us to trade places for a night, so he doesn't sleep on the cement floor, but he refused every time because he wanted me to sleep comfortably and heal. We agreed on one thing if he wouldn't sleep on my tiny bed with me, he had to get a mattress to sleep on from then on. I don't know if someone bought it for him or if he bought it himself, but there was a mattress brought in for him. I was happy he was finally sleeping on something more comfortable. That was a huge relief for me to see him sleep on a mattress so he doesn't get sick. He wasn't sleeping well for a while or eating well. He was there day in and day out, being there for me whenever my scars hurt me, for when I cried or felt lonely. My dad and I had an amazing bond that I will never forget during the hospital months. I am grateful for the precious time I had with him. When I was finally able to talk, he would give me these bright smiles encouraging me to keep talking. He was happy to hear my voice finally again. He would say elelelele (it's like a hallelujah chant in Amharic), then he would look up and thank God. He prayed with me and thanked God for the new strength I was gaining. Even after I woke up, there were some big decisions that my dad had to make for my health. Even though I was awake, there was still a slight chance that I was still not going to make it. He kept trusting God through my healing process. It felt like when one thing was solved, there was another problem coming one after the other. He still had two other kids he needed to take care of, but my aunts and neighbors took care of them while he was in the hospital. He wanted to spend quality time with them, too, but he couldn't. If he had my mom by his side, life would have been much easier, but she had already passed away; it was hard being a single father and going through what he went through. I remember seeing my dad cry a few times, which was good for me to see. I always saw him being strong for our family and never showed his emotions until we were in the hospital. Crying is not a sign of weakness but a sign of releasing worry and things that you have been holding on to in you for too long that hurt. It is a way of healing your hurt heart.

I also felt free to cry around him and show my emotions when I saw him crying, which never happened before at the hospital. Even though my dad was perfect for me, I missed my mom a lot during my hospital days. I wondered why God took her away so early in my life and had a hard time accepting it.

I had lots of visitors coming to visit all the time, young and old. My favorite was when my sisters and friends came over. My room was always full of flowers, cards, and people. I was bored when there were no visitors because my room was empty with no TV, so they entertained me while I was lying in bed. I didn't have a phone to entertain me. I looked at the plain white walls all day. One thing I was grateful for having my dad as a company.

My Christian Aunt Mesi came over to visit my dad and me every day while I was in the hospital. She brought homemade food for my dad and spent quality time with us. She asked my dad to trade her places for a few days so he can go home and get a good night's rest. While she stayed with me but he refused her offer every time. He wouldn't leave my sight. My aunts and uncles were always praying for my recovery. My aunt Mesi and my other aunts and uncles that were believers especially would have their church and their pastors pray for me in every prayer group. Prayer is powerful; I am alive today and writing you this book because of many people's prayers being answered. Grateful for Mesi; she's a prayer warrior; she is an incredible woman whom I love so dearly. She has continuously prayed for me throughout my life and even to write this book.

I longed for the day I would go outside to play. I wanted to be a normal five-year-old; I wanted to run around with my friends like I was doing just a few months ago. It is crazy that life can be fun and easy and change in a drastic of a second. After a little while, I was getting tired of being in the hospital. I wanted to walk around outside and smell the fresh air. After a while, when they saw I was feeling better, they put me in a different room with lots of patients. The hospital had a lot of patients and not enough room, so they put ten patients in one big room with different sicknesses of different ages. I was ecstatic to be changing rooms to not be alone and isolated from everyone anymore. I said goodbye to boredom and said hello to entertainment. That room was always full of patients and visitors; there was no quiet time other than when we were sleeping. It was great for both my dad and me as he was able to socialize with other parents, and I was able to make friends and play with other children. By that time, I was able to walk around with an Iv pole with me for weeks, which was a miracle. I started feeling better every day and was able to start eating regular food, glory to God. I became close friends with an eight-year-old who was fighting for his life just like me. After becoming best friends with him, I found out he had cancer which broke my heart. Just a couple of days before I found out, there was another child from our room who had cancer and had passed away. We had the best time of our lives with my friend. Whenever he felt sick, I would sit by his bed and entertain him and be there for him. I loved that he wasn't scared of my scars; that took so much worry off of me. When my scars looked the scariest all over my arms and leg still wrapped, he liked me for who I was. We were inseparable. He took me in and didn't judge me. Our friendship was short-lived because he also passed away soon after that, which devastated me. I was heartbroken and missing my friend.

But God gave me strength every day and stood by me while I was in the hospital.

God was surrounding what was surrounding me. He had stretched out his arms and was over my hospital bed. He was with the doctors when they were doing procedures on me. He was guiding them every step of the way to make sure that everything they did was for my good. God gave my dad wisdom when he had to make tough decisions. God never left our side. The Lord was our comforter, our healer, our guide, and provider through all this trauma.

The hospital bills were very expensive for me to get the right treatments and surgeries I needed in order to be alive. It was very expensive to stay for three months in the hospital, but God provided for everything.

"But my God shall supply all your needs according to his riches in glory by Christ Jesus" (Philippians 4:19, KJV).

God supplied my every need and blessed me. My dad used the money he was saving for the dream home he was going to build for my hospital bills. The money still wasn't enough to pay for all the expenses. My aunts, uncles, family members, neighbors and friends of friends, and my dad's coworkers all donated money to pay for my hospital bills. They did a fundraiser and got a lot of money to be able to pay for all my expenses. The Lord blessed me through each person and used them to supply for my every need. May the Lord bless you all abundantly.

If it wasn't for God providing and for each person donating the money, I wouldn't be alive today. There are so many people that die because they can't afford the hospital bills they receive; I was definitely lucky that I had people that loved me to support me financially. I thank God for all of you!

On my hospital journey, I learned to have patience; I learned to fight for my life. I learned to persevere, and I learned to work through what I have. I learned to accept my body with my new scars, which was hard to get used to. I learned to love people that are in life-threatening situations just like I was and brought out a desire and compassion for people that are in critical health conditions.

My doctors told me that I was going to be able to go home soon. I was excited to go home, but I was also nervous because my home was at the hospital for three whole months. During my hospital stay, I was a very happy person, always smiling and full of joy, which came not from me but from the Lord Himself. People were always surprised by my attitude and how well I was taking what was going on with me, but I know it was only through God's help that I was able to go through everything with a positive attitude. I will never forget when the doctor uttered the words I have been longing to hear for so long, "You're going home tomorrow!" I couldn't sleep that night; I was tossing and turning with excitement, waiting for it to be morning already so I could go home.

I Am Coming Home

"I am coming home. I am coming home to tell the world I am coming home. Let the rain wash away all the pain of yesterday. I know my kingdom awaits and they have forgiven my mistakes. I am coming home; I am coming home."

—Jasmine Bussiere

I woke up early in the morning on the day I was going home. I was full of different kinds of emotions. I didn't know which one of my emotions was outweighing the other. I remember being happy, jumping on my bed, chanting, "We are going home today." I was laughing, excited, and nervous all at the same time. I couldn't believe everything that happened to me, being in the hospital for three months almost losing my life, and now I was going home? After so many trials, tribulations, and fighting for my life, I was finally going home alive and well,

That in itself was a miracle!

I feared what people were going to say about my scars and how bad they looked. Both of my arms were covered with scars. My scars were so fresh at the time that everywhere I was burnt, it was all white! The miracle in it was that my face and neck were completely untouched. I am a dark-skinned girl with white scars all over my arms. I thought it looked very gruesome and ugly at that time because it was fresh, so I was worried about the response I will be getting from people that knew me. I didn't know how they were going to accept me when I came home. I was worried about the gossip that was going to go around; even if it was good gossip about my news of coming home, I was still nervous. I kept how I felt and all the emotions I was feeling inside without telling anyone. I so badly wanted to tell my dad, but I didn't know what to say or how to bring it up. I kept thinking to myself, *He is probably going to think I am going crazy for feeling the way I did.* It was strange why I would feel all those emotions. I was just going to my own home, my house, my own sisters, my own neighbors I knew and loved. I was going home to everything that was familiar but yet I was still nervous, excited, and scared of what people might think and how the transition is going to be.

The nurses told me that my dad went to the store and would be returning soon. As I was waiting for him to come back, I started looking out the big window from my hospital room. I was very mesmerized by everything I was seeing and took it in. As you can imagine, it was refreshing to see what I was going back into. It was a very busy city; there were so many cars driving by. I saw people talking as they were walking, hugging, and shaking hands. I remember looking at houses and big buildings and just thinking, *Wow, it looks so beautiful outside, and in just a little bit, I get to walk out and feel it and experience it again and smell the fresh air.* It was crazy to me to think it was finally my turn to go home. I have seen so many families and friends from the hospital going home after months of being at the hospital one by one. I always wondered when it would finally be my turn to go home. It felt like that day would never come. It was so unbelievable to me to think that day was finally here.

Finally, for the last time, guess who walked into the hospital room with a beautiful big smile on his face. My daddy! I was so excited to see him! I ran up and hugged him. He couldn't believe either that it was finally time to go home. He can finally take me home after experiencing so many trials and watching me suffer. If he could, he would have taken me home right away, but my health wasn't at its best. Finally, he can take his daughter that he absolutely loves and cares about so much, home to where she belongs, back to our house. He had agony seeing me suffer for so long. He had patience and faith that I will come back to him, that I will live through this trial because of the one and only God that was going to save me. He surprised me with new clothes and shoes for my welcoming home.

We had lots of bags and stuff that we were carrying when we got off the taxi. I was helping my dad as he was holding on to my other hand while we walked. I was very quiet during the long two-hour taxi ride. I would talk to him a little bit, but I was busy taking in everything. I was taking in the smell of the fresh air, people interacting, the busyness of the city, and thinking about what people were going to say when they saw me. Since I was young, I never liked attention and being the center of it, so that made me nervous too. We got out of the taxi and started walking home. It was quite a distance of at least a mile from where the taxi dropped us off to my neighborhood to get to my house.

As soon as one of the neighbors spotted my dad and me walking, they ran to greet us. There were a few of them running to us at full speed to help us. They took off all the bags and a suitcase from us and carried our load down for us. As we got closer and closer to my neighborhood, I started getting nervous. My dad noticed that, I think, because he grabbed my hand. We walked together, holding hands as he brought me back home. There were people playing outside, people selling onions and potatoes, etc., in the streets as my dad and I passed every store and every house. People came out of their houses and stopped what they were doing, and stood there clapping, smiling, welcoming me home. As we kept on walking, more people kept coming out of their houses, and if they were sitting down outside, they stood up and showed respect, all of them clapping, smiling, and shouting, welcome home, Sara! It was a scene that I wasn't expecting. They stood there in disbelief and amazement, in awe to see a living miracle in front of them. They saw me with my father, who stood like a rock in his faith and belief in fighting for his daughter's life. It was very emotional. I held my dad's hand tighter. I was crying with happiness and full of emotions to see everybody welcoming me like they were. My dad started crying happy tears when we saw everybody's reaction. As we got to our house, there was a big crowd of people that surrounded us. I saw all my friends, neighbors, aunts, uncles, my sisters, so many people gathered around us that kept clapping louder and harder, shouting, praising God. Praising my dad for what he did. They were so full of joy with so many emotions. Their prayers were answered! I came home safe and sound. After a few minutes of crying and taking it all in, everybody wanted hugs! They kept coming at me one by one to hug, kiss, and congratulate me. They all told me how proud they were of me and thanked God for me. It was an emotional moment. I was filled with so much joy. It was so amazing to see everyone show so much affection and love towards me. We had a feast afterward!

My neighbors and sisters cooked for my welcome home party! There were lots of different types of Ethiopian food. They killed a goat for my welcoming home party. That is a big deal for my culture, especially for my family to have a goat killed. In Ethiopia, we kill goats, lambs, chickens, or cows to celebrate holidays or special events and make lots of different types of stew to feast. My family was blessed to have chicken for holidays but nothing else, so when I heard about the goat being killed to welcome me home, I was surprised. Everyone that contributed showed me they loved me. They made lots of different kinds of meat stew. They went all out. It was a party, and everybody ate and had a great time! It was a celebration, a welcome home party for the little girl that almost lost her life. But because of God, I was saved and back home safely.

Thank you, Jesus! God is amazing! Just like My family and neighbors were missing me, God misses you! He is pursuing you. I am reminded of the Parable of Prodigal son story Jesus told as I think about my story of coming home (see Luke 15). The Prodigal son had everything in his father's house, but he decided to get his share of the inheritance and left his father's house to live his life as he pleased. He realized after facing many trials, he decided to go back home to his father. Just like the prodigal's son decided to head home to his father and started going that way, His father met him from far away as soon as he saw him from a distance. As soon as you decide right now to come back to your Heavenly Father, He will meet you at your place as you are reading this! He sees you! He sees the struggles you've been through; He sees how much you have been fighting; He sees the people that have done you wrong. He has forgiven you for what you have done, for leaving Him, or for pursuing other things. Just like my dad had agonies seeing me suffer and almost die, your Heavenly Father feels that for you. He is hurt to see you suffer without him. He wants you to come back to Him. He will run and meet you where you're at in life as soon as you decide to come back to Him. He will take the baggage off of you. He will take the burden off of you and run to your rescue when He sees you coming to Him. He will know and run to your rescue! He will not judge you, but He will accept you and meet you where you are at! He will love you; He will clothe you with the best garments!

Your Father in heaven is filled with love and compassion for you! It says, *"And he arose, and came to his father. But when he was yet a great way off, his father saw him, and had compassion, and ran, and fell on his neck, and kissed him"* (Luke 15:20, KJV).

He is going to embrace you with his love, and you will feel his presence which is indescribable; there is nothing like it. It is one of a kind! Wouldn't you want to feel that? He wants to clothe you with his protection and love and shower blessing over you! Heaven will be having a feast and celebrating your welcome home party! They will be singing and dancing for your safe return home! Because maybe you felt like you were dead because of all the trials in your life that kept coming at you; now, as you accept Christ, you are alive! We are alive through Him. He brings dead things to life! You are found through Him! He loves you! He wants to come into your heart and dwell in it and be in you as you are in him! He is full of love and joy! You will find happiness when you accept him in your life! Life will start making sense, and your purpose in life will come to life! But first, you got to let Him and give Him permission to let Him in your life! He is not going to come into your heart if you don't open the door. He is a polite God and waits for you to let Him in. He is knocking at the door of your heart.

Are you going to let Him in? Do you want to feel loved, do you feel alone in your life, do you feel helpless, do you need healing, do you need somebody to save you, do you need somebody to come to your rescue, do you need somebody to fight for you, do you need Him to come to heal your hurt heart and your wounds of life? What do you need Him to do for you? He is the answer to everything you need! He is the best firefighter because He comes to your rescue, the best lawyer because He fights for your life, He is the best surgeon because He has a healing power that heals you and saves you. He is the best therapist because He heals your troubled and wounded heart and soul. He is the best financial adviser because He provides for you. He is the best Father because He has greater love for you than even your earthly father. He is the best lover because He fills up the part of you that needs to be loved with His love and doesn't hurt you. Jesus is the best brother because of how much He loves you. He died for you. He is a loving God, a loving Father that loves you more than you can ever understand. You don't have to do anything to earn his love. All He asks you to do is to believe in Him!

He says, "Believe in me, and I will be whatever you need me to be listed above and more!"

Are you ready to accept Him as your Lord and Savior? Before you knew about Him, before you were even conceived, He knew you. He already took the first step in faith and died for us because He knew that we all needed Him to redeem us for the sins that we were going to commit. But He died on the cross to take away the sins of the world to make a place in heaven for you because no unclean thing can be in heaven. The greatest love story ever told is when Jesus died on the cross for you and me! He loves you! He chose you first! He chose you before you even knew Him. Now it's your time to choose Him! You have a choice to decide to let Him into your heart and be your Lord and Savior! All you must do is believe and take a leap of faith, just like He took a leap of faith for you. Say this prayer to accept Him into your heart. Say this out loud wherever you are reading this. He will hear you!

Pray this with faith: Lord Jesus, I believe that you came down from heaven because of your love for me to die on the cross! I believe that you died on the cross for my sins. Forgive me for all my sins for all the wrongs I have done. I believe you rose again from the dead on the third day. I believe you are my Lord and Savior! I accept you into my heart right now! Lord Jesus, come! Come into my heart! Change me from the inside out. Come in my heart, Lord Jesus! Say this in your loving name, Jesus, amen.

One of the Few

I was so excited to be home finally! I was excited to sleep on my bed again. I was happy to see my friends and live life again like the five-year-old that I was. I played with my friends outside now too. I would go to the hospital once a week to get shots so I could feel better. We would take a taxi or a bus to get there. I started feeling better and gaining my strength back. It was so good to feel like the old me again. Now I would like to transfer our thoughts on God.

After we accept Christ into our hearts and lives, what do we do? What is the next step? How do we keep feeling better? We must keep going to the source that made us feel better the first time. For me, it was a process of healing, so I had to go to the doctor every week to get my shots and do my checkups to keep going to help me feel better and fully recover. Jesus teaches us a lesson in anything and everything. If you have accepted him before but have fallen away again, you have the chance the privilege to accept him again. You can always go back to the last page and say the prayer right now; it's never too late to accept Christ as long as you are alive. It is better to accept him now and act on it like it is an emergency!

Jesus came to your rescue; I encourage you to accept the rescuer. After accepting Christ, we must keep being connected to the source, which is Him. We need to start attending church regularly! You can pray about which church to go to and see what is right for you and ask God to lead and guide you to a church that is going to keep you connected to Him. God rested on the seventh day after creation. That day is a day of rest for us, but it is also a day of worship, a day of us showing our gratitude, a day to worship our Savior. It is a day where we keep getting connected to the source. In order to do that, we can get connected to the body of believers that are believing the same thing and pursuing God!

The doctors helped me in my process of healing. God gave me great doctors to take care of me, and He guided their every step, their decisions, their advice, and their hands when they did surgeries on me. They also had a group of nurses that took care of me and knew what they were doing. They also were loving and nice to me and cared for me not only as a patient but as a person that they knew and cared about. Even though I was in the midst of the storm, God was calming the waves and put protection over me with people that cared for me. I was surrounded by doctors, nurses, family, and friends that truly wanted the best for me.

Just like what I have mentioned, God brings people into our lives to help us grow in him. When we go to church, the pastor shepherds us and takes care of us, and feeds us God's Words. Just like my doctors took care of me because they knew what they were doing, and God was leading them by the hand and showed them what I needed at the time. God also gave us pastors to do that for our souls. God shares with them what we need to hear, what they should preach on. They hear Words from God in order to share them with us. They have to spend time with God for them to know what to preach every week. We go to church to be fed. We need to keep being fed each week with God's Words.

When I started going to one of the non-denominational Christian churches called Awaken that God led me to, the pastors always knew what was happening in my life during that time. I was so surprised and thought, *How does he know what I am going through?* It was always so accurate. The thing is, he doesn't know what I am going through. I don't go to him and tell him. But because he spends time with God, the whole week, praying about and putting a sermon together, that when he gets up on stage and shares about what God has been putting on his or her heart, he or she speaks right to the heart. They speak into our lives and what we are going through because it is God speaking through them. Nobody knows what we really need, but God fills up that thing that we need, and he uses people to show us and guide us. He knows every step of that thing that we need.

First, I had my doctors take care of me. God gave us pastors to Shepard and take care of us! Jesus said, feed my sheep! Pastors are feeding his sheep by being pastors and feeding our souls! Doctors are feeding his sheep by taking care of our physical health! I had nurses too, man and woman taking care of me and following what the doctor had ordered. God gave us leaders in the Church to help us grow in who we are in him! They are people that truly care for you, who you are as a person! It fills them up to do God's work and do what they are called to do in the church. There are life groups going on, whether it's youth group, college-age group, marriage group, women's group, men's group, you name it there is one. And if there isn't one that you need, maybe you need to step up and get it started because if you need it, it's a big chance that other people need it too! God gave us leaders. The only thing that we need to do is we need to keep plugging in the sources. The sources that are around us. God gave us families to care for us and love us! If you don't have a family that you are close to, the people at your church are your family! Know that you are brothers and sisters in Christ. God layers and circles people around us to grow and take care of us and to become closer to him in our spiritual walk with him just like he put layers and circles of doctors, nurses, family, and friends around me to take care of me in my physical walk to recover. I started realizing that I wasn't the only one with scars. Thank you, Jesus, for that! I knew there were other people all over the world that got burnt like me too, but I didn't see one with my eyes; therefore, it made me superconscious. I felt like I was the only one. I had scars on both of my arms. It was super white and very gruesome, I thought at the time. I was embarrassed by it.

Every time people looked at me, they looked at my scars first. They would look at it and wonder what happened. Some would feel bad for me; some would see my strength in how I overcame it; some were curious about how I got burnt and wanted to know my whole life story about it. People were curious, but I was very ashamed of my scars as a young little girl until I grew up. I didn't want anybody to know how I got burnt or what happened to me. I felt like I didn't fit in. I thought people wouldn't like me because I have scars. I felt like everybody always talked about me behind my back. I cringed in my own body for years! I didn't accept myself for who I was. I started wearing long sleeve shirts that covered my whole arm. I was ashamed of the way I was. I was afraid to let people see what I have underneath my sleeves. I wore long sleeve shirts whether it was hot or cold outside. I think you are getting the picture of how I felt about myself. I felt like I couldn't make lots of friends if they saw who I really was underneath my long sleeve shirt; I thought people would feel grossed out when they see my scars. I thought they would feel like I am a completely different person because of my scars. I was afraid to hear other people's opinions of me. I thought scars aren't beautiful but ugly. They are not pleasing to look at. I would cry and say, why do I have to have scars! Why? Why me? Why did I get burnt? Why was I in the hospital for so long? Why can't I be an ordinary little girl like everybody else? Why? Why? Why? These questions and so much more flooded my mind.

I think what I just shared with you of how I felt about my scars kind of relates to us on how new Christians and us Christians feel about being one of the few followers of Christ in this crazy world! Some of us feel like we are the only ones that believe in God in this world. The way I felt like I was the only one with my scars, maybe you are the only one in your family that believes in God! So you feel overcast? You feel outnumbered, maybe? Maybe you are the only one in your friends' group that is a believer. Do you sometimes feel like you don't fit in the group because you are a believer? Do you feel like people won't like you if they found out you were Christian? Do you feel judged? Do you feel judged when they do see you for who you are? You being you, and it shows you are different and unique because you know who you are and what you believe in? Have you covered up who you are in Christ and your beliefs about God because of what people made you feel like? I think we all have felt that in our lives in one way or another, whether it's with a sickness or disease we have or in our Christian walk with Christ. I think we ask ourselves sometimes why we believe in God when there are a majority of people that don't. We feel different, and we know we are different! We cover it up with things that come up in our lives or go along with the crowd doing things that they do, whether it is partying and\ drinking and not attending church or whatever it is in your life. We become followers instead of the leaders we are created to be. We need to learn to embrace what we have and fully take ownership of it and be proud that we are believers! I learned to embrace what I have.

I remembered God made a miracle, waking me up from my coma and breathed life into me, and made what felt like my dead body rise to life again! I forgot about the miracle because I was too worried about what people thought of my scars. I was so caught up in that and worrying if people would like me because of that; I didn't remember that God Himself changed my life! I am a living miracle of his healing power and prayers being answered! That is so amazing! It is so incredible! How can I forget His goodness? How can I not accept myself for who I am with my scars when I know he saved me from so much! We think and worry too much about what people think and want so badly to be accepted by them. I have great news for you! Jesus already accepted you for you! You don't need anybody's approval. Don't take it to heart if people judge you because of your faith because the only judgment that matters is the one at the end of your life. Think of that time when you felt God's presence. Think of the time when you accepted God as your Lord and Savior for the first time. Do you remember how happy and emotional you were feeling? Do you remember being saved and what that felt like? Think of the joy you felt and the blessings He brought you because you chose to follow Him. Embrace yourself in who you are in God. I decided that I didn't care about what people thought about me and my scars. I knew there were people who were going to like me for who I am and those that might turn the other way because of my scars. Those who turn away because of my scars don't belong in my life. They don't deserve to have me as a friend. I am not going to change. My scars will take time to heal completely. As I share with you my story, I hope you are connecting your story to mine to have a new perspective on life.

When we accept God into our hearts, He will change our life right now. We can't forget His goodness and mercy and the fact that He shows up when we need Him the most. He answered, He is faithful, and He comes when we call on Him. Our faith and belief in God define who we are in Christ. Those who are followers of Christ have a unique form of DNA that defines who they are in Christ.

I met a lady one day during work, and her name was Lisa. Like a lot of people do, she asked about my scars and how I got burnt. I was wearing a short-sleeve shirt that day, so it was easy to see my scars. I was asked by different people, whether it was at work or someplace else, about my scars. But every time, I would not feel ashamed, but instead, I would explain to them the story and how it happened. I included how it was God that saved me from a terrible outcome, and I am here because of His grace. I spoke of God's mercy and His goodness and how He still saves every day. Give God the glory for your story. It is because of Him that you are alive and able to share your story. The curiosity of those people regarding my scars allowed me to share God's work and He who answers every prayer, who heals the sick, and who makes miracles happen all the time. For those who were believers, it strengthened their faith in God, and for others, it allowed them to start including God in their life. Now going back to the lady I mentioned, Lisa.

She asked how it happened and how long ago it took place. I told her with confidence my story and that I have accepted myself for who I am. I was smiling, sharing my story and how blessed I am to be alive. After sharing my story, what came next surprised me. She opened up to me and shared how she also has scars from being burnt a few years back. They were third-degree burns, as are mine. Lisa shared about her life of living with her scars. We immediately had a connection. I had never met someone that had the same story of having third-degree burns for like fourteen years. We couldn't stop talking; we had so much to say and had a lot in common. We became sisters. She hugged me tight and got my cell number before she left so that we could keep in touch. She was deeply moved by my out-look on my scars. She wanted positive energy too, and to have each other encourage one another.

Our DNA is our connection in us Christians. When you ac-cept Jesus into your life, you start living as a godly woman or man. People are attracted to you because of the unique aspect of you. Maybe you are a smiley and helpful person, or in the way you carry yourself, you are different, and people can sense it too. There is something that makes you stand out. There is a glow in you that people can't fully grasp, so they ask questions to understand what it could be. They look at you and think that you are an overcomer. It looks like you have gone through a lot, but you fought through it. They notice something they don't have within themselves and are bold about asking you questions. Others will take time to get to know you and find out over time who you are and what makes you who you are. They find out your DNA. The DNA that separates you from other people is God. The blood of Jesus separates you. The blood of Jesus has fought death and has given life to those who believe. His blood has made you a new creation and alive in spirit. The reason you are powerful, big, and loving now is because of God's work in you. There are going to be those that you have a conversation with that are going to love your outlook on life and your perspective. Who you are and what you want out of life is a match, and you become brothers and sisters in Christ. Isn't that amazing? You might be one of the few followers of Christ and feel like one of a handful who believes and follow Christ. But you are shining bright like a diamond because of your DNA in how the Lord has made you.

"Let your light so shine before men, that they may see your good works, and glorify your Father which is in heaven" (Matthew 5:16, KJV).

My Father

"A father is respected because he gives his children leadership, appreciated because he gives his children care, valued because he gives his children time, loved because he gives his children the one thing they treasure the most—himself."

Unknown

This quote describes my dad perfectly. My dad was the most selfless, loving, caring, amazing person I know! Since the first time he found out he was going to be a dad, he was devoted to being a father! He took being a leader in the home, and one of the greatest blessings that God gave him was to be a father to us and his three children. Every morning he had a reason to wake up, which was for his kids. He woke up every morning with a reason and purpose. A purpose of being the greatest father he can be to his girls. He woke up every morning with strength to work hard, live, to love, and provide for us kids. There were times when life was hard for him. It was rough to be a father and mother to three little girls. He prayed day and night. He had his pocket Bible that he kept with him so he can be reading God's Word every day. God says when you're weak, I will make you strong! When you mourn, I will comfort you.

His grace is sufficient for us! My father taught me at a very young age to lean on God when life gets rough. Not only when life gets rough but to have God's presence with us at all times, every day and every morning. He taught me by example. I watched him do it every day. I watched him read his Bible every day. I watched him pray every morning. I watched him just out of nowhere in the middle of the day, praying wherever he was at. I watched him have strength when he should have not had strength and was a strong person and father. I was always in awe of my dad. It was amazing watching him live life in the way he did. You can look at him and know that he was a great person because of the way he lived his life and in the way he talked, acted, and treated people and his daughters! He went to church every Sunday. Not a lot of people in my neighborhood went to church on Sundays. They went when they felt like it or if it was a holiday or something.

But my dad went no matter what every week to hear the Word of God and worship Him. Since I was young, I noticed things. I noticed things around me and how people acted and how they were. I noticed my dad even more because he was just so unique and so special than any other person around the whole neighborhood. That amazed me as a seven-year-old. I started going to church with him, and I wanted to be like my dad, worshiping God at church. We had precious moments like that, and I am so grateful for those moments. When we saw people we knew on our way to church, he always stopped and acknowledged them and talked to them and introduced me proudly, and held on to me as he was talking to his friends. People just loved my father. My dad and I had a special relationship! A relationship that is indescribable. As I shared about when I was at the hospital for three months, my dad was right there with me day and night. He never left my side. The father and daughter relationship we had got stronger and stronger. There was nobody I loved, like my dad growing up. He was everything to me. I wanted to do whatever he wanted to do. I wanted to be with my father at all times. I loved being around my dad and sitting by him, and talking to him. It always felt like something was missing when he was working and not home. I couldn't wait to be around him when he would finally come home.

My story of my father and me reminds me of our Heavenly Father and us, his kids. God gave us earthly parents to love and care for us but ultimately though He is our Father in heaven! He is the father of all creation. When you have a son or daughter, you love your children so much that you would do anything for them. Your children mean the world to you. Any loving and great parent would say that about their children. You see, just like our earthly parents, God our Heavenly Father has a magnificent love for us, His children. A love that is so big that us as humans can't comprehend. Your parents have a connection with you, or you as a parent have a connection with your children because they came out of you so instantly; you already have that love and connection with your children because of it! God, our Heavenly Father, created us! In Genesis, it says, let us make man in our own image, and in the image of Himself He created man and woman. Since God created us, He instantly has a love for us because of that connection because He created you first but used your parents to get you here. God has an infant love for us. Infinite means unending. Isn't that amazing that no matter what you do, God still loves you? God pursues you every day, every minute, every hour, and every year. He gave you life, and as long as you live, He will always love you and pursue you. We serve a mighty, loving Father. Time spells love.

God loves it when His children spend time with Him. Just like any good father loves spending quality time with their own children and talking about deep things that matter. Our Heavenly Father longs for that. He waits and says maybe today my son or daughter will come back to me. Maybe today they will decide to spend time with me to talk to me about things that matter in their life. Just like my dad was right there with me the whole three months of my hospitalization, God is right there with you during the hard times in your life. You might not notice it sometimes, and maybe you already have and have felt His presence in your heart. He is there to help you and hold on to your hand wherever you go, every day, whether you're happy or sad. God loves His children! Your Heavenly Father is available to you every day. Have you stopped to hold on to his hand and talk to him? Have you stopped to feel his presence? When you know and feel God's presence, you would never want to leave it. It is a feeling that you can't get anywhere or feel anywhere but in your Heavenly Father's arms. Spend time with him because he cares about you more than anybody in this world and loves you more than anybody in this world! If you haven't had a great father and if your father on the earth has left you or betrayed you. Just know and remember that you have a Heavenly Father who is infinitely in love with you! Who wants to hold you in His arms. Who wants to wipe away those tears and comfort you? He is the best father! The best Father who can fill that part of your heart that is hurt and cover it with His heart with His love. His love is bigger and better. Pursue Him and ask Him to pour out his love on you. I love being around my dad. But I love spending time with my Heavenly Father. Just remember you have a Father that will never abandon you, that will always invite you, and carry you in his loving arms! It says, "Seek me with all your heart, and you will find me!" (Jeremiah 29:13) Seek Him, and I promise you, you will find Him!

I became who I am and my attributes as a person because of my earthly dad. I was raised by a man of God, a man of faith, and a father who would do anything for his daughters. A father who taught me many life lessons by saying and doing and by living it out himself! My dad was a Christ follower, and his actions were too! If you're a young man or a father reading this, I hope and pray it encourages you to have that relationship with your Heavenly Father! Let Him show you and teach you what a loving Father He is for you. So he can be that loving Father you need in your life. Accept Him and ask Him to teach you and show you and pursue Him and let your actions speak more than your words about following your Heavenly Father. As you are doing that, you will be a great father to your son or daughter if you become a parent. Fathers are so important. So important to God and us. He created a man first to be a father to His children on earth. You are important to God. He wants to be a father to you so you can be a great father to your children.

There is absolutely nothing like a father's love. There's absolutely nothing like our Heavenly Father's love, either. Everybody young and old needs it. Find it and let God show you what it feels like to be loved by a father and likewise go and be a father to somebody out there that is in need of a father and a father's love! Another reason why I love my dad is because He gave me Himself. He gave me all of him and gave me his attention. Our Heavenly Father gives us Himself 24/7. We don't need to fight for attention; He gives us full attention when we pursue Him and talk to Him day and night way more than our earthly parents. I am grateful that I had the time to spend time with my father. My dad was doing great, and his health was great until I was seven years old. He started getting very sick, and what came next completely changed my life!

Appreciating Time

To everything there is a season, and a time to every purpose under the heaven: A time to be born, and a time to die; a time to plant, and a time to pluck up that which is planted; A time to kill, and a time to heal; a time to break down, and a time to build up; A time to weep, and a time to laugh; a time to mourn, and a time to dance; A time to cast away stones, and a time to gather stones together; a time to embrace, and a time to refrain from embracing. A time to get, and a time to lose; a time to keep, and a time to cast away; A time to rend, and a time to sew; a time to keep silence, and a time to speak; A time to love, and a time to hate; a time of war, and a time of peace.

Ecclesiastes 3:1

"The most common thing that God gives any human is time. What you are and what you become depends on how you use your time. There is a time for everything, and it is called life. Time is life and Life is time!"
—Dr. Myles Munroe

Everything and every season in our lives is measured by time. Time can't be stopped, but time can be controlled. Time is valuable for everything. Time with your family and loved ones is valuable and worthwhile. It is very crucial; God gave us time to live in this world. God is eternal, but He gave us time to live in this world with our mortal bodies to complete our assignment and fulfill the purpose He has for us. He gave us time to spend with our families and loved ones. Maybe he gave you children to raise and a time to raise them and help them become the children that he has created them to be. We need to take time seriously and not waste it. Time is a gift from God. That scripture shares about every part of our life that we go through. There is a time for every feeling we have, everything we go through, everything that we lose, and for everything, there is time.

I understand this verse more now because I have experienced things and have felt a lot of those things that were described. I have gone through a lot of the times and seasons that it says, and I am sure you have too. Some of these seasons are not expected, nor are they things that we would want to go through in our lives. But they come no matter what; you just have to brace yourselves and know that there is a time for everything and that a brighter side of that time is coming, as the scripture says. I was too young to embrace or even understand this hardship, a part of my life I am going to be sharing with you right now. This is the hardest chapter of my life to write about! I avoided it for a while because I didn't want to go back in my memory to see everything. But it is something dear to my heart, something that has hurt me even for many years, even as a young adult. But I know that God has healed my heart. I know my God is a healer. He is a healer in everything, even a wounded heart. He is the best heart surgeon. I have always wanted to close up and not share with people this part of my story, but God has sown up the wounds in my heart. I hope through my story you are going to let God heal you from any hurt that you have gone through. He is the healer, and He will heal you. There is no more pain, no more sorrow when you let God into that part of you that's hurting and let him heal you. Are you ready to be healed? But first, you got to let it out so that he can heal you from it. This is a time for you to get healed from any hurt wounds. Whether it is losing somebody you love, or somebody that has hurt you, or any hard trial that you have been in that has wounded your heart. Let somebody in your life that you trust and talk about those things and tell God about it too. Let him and ask him to come into your heart and heal it in the name of Jesus! As it is written, Jesus said:

"You can ask for anything in my name, and I will do it, so that the Son can bring glory to the Father. Yes, ask me for anything in my name, and I will do it!" (John 14:13-14, NLT)

Something unexpected, something unseen, something unwanted, something happened that changed my family forever. My dad, my hero, best friend, the only parent that my two sisters and I had left, got sick and got diagnosed with cancer. At that time, I was seven, Lydia was nine years old, and Hiwet was eleven years old. We were all young girls. Here was a strong, healthy person who took care of his body and his health and yet was diagnosed with cancer. My dad went to the hospital, and they gave him some medicine, but at the time in Ethiopia, there was nothing to treat cancer. Our country was so poor that there was no way to cure cancer or have equipment needed for that kind of sickness at that time. Nor did they have doctors that knew a lot of info about it. My dad got worse and started to get weak. He was the only person working to provide for his three girls. He was a selfless father, as I described earlier, so he kept working hard at his job day and night. It got to the point he couldn't work anymore. He was lying in bed day and night. He lost a lot of weight. He wasn't skinny before, but as the days and months went by, he started getting more sick. It was hard for him to eat food. It got to the point that my sisters and I were making his food and feeding him for breakfast, lunch, and dinner, or whenever he would actually eat.

We had to pick up his head and put a pillow behind him so he could sit up to eat and not choke on his food. He was helpless and couldn't move his body or walk around. My aunt would come down and take care of him for us as well. She stayed many nights, many days, and months taking care of my dad and sacrificed being with her family. I am so grateful for her. I don't know what my sister and I would have done by ourselves. She surely was a huge blessing that the Lord sent for us. We didn't know what he wanted or needed; we were not even in our teenage years yet. We were children. He had doctors' visits once per week. It was hard for him to leave the house because of how weak he was getting. We rented a taxi to take him to the hospital. He was carried to the room or put in a wheelchair. At home, he just lay in bed. Before he got worse, he would eat and walk around the house and then lay back in bed. It broke my heart seeing my dad so sick like that, so helpless. I wanted my dad to be healthy again. I wanted to hear his voice and talk to him and climb on his lap and be his little princess again. I missed my dad and the way he was before he got sick. We were all waiting for a miracle! So many people prayed for him till nothing was coming. He would do better for a few days; then, he would get really sick again. I will never forget one time when my sister Lydia and I were taking care of him for the day. My aunt had gone home to visit her family for a little while, and my sister was out shopping for groceries. She told us we needed to watch my dad and stay at home with him. Somebody always had to stay with him. We spent time with my dad while he was lying down helplessly. It was hard for him to speak, but whenever he needed water or food, he would sound it out. Before he could finish the word, we would say okay and get it for him. I remember sitting him up and feeding him and making sure he had fluid in his body. We loved taking care of him but hated seeing him like that. All of me just wanted to break down and cry as I was feeding him. This time instead of him taking care of me, I was taking care of him. It is just crazy that time and things can change so fast. I needed to be strong for my dad, and I couldn't let him see me crying because that would just break his heart to see his little girl crying for him. He needed to know I was going to be okay. I missed talking to my best friend. My dad knew me so well and could tell just by looking at me. He would motion to me to come to lay down on the bed with him. For a moment, it would feel like everything was normal, like he wasn't sick anymore. He would just look at me with this sad look, just heartbroken for me as I lay under his arms. It was hard for him to move any part of his body because he was so weak, but he would slowly get his arm out of the blankets no matter how much it hurt to get it out and hold on to my hand as he motioned to me to come to sit by him and hold on to his hands. He would hold on to my hands for a long time as I sat on the bed next to him. He couldn't really speak, although sometimes he would. His hands and whole body were weak and almost immovable, but he would try so hard to hold on to my hands for a while. I could see he missed me, and that was the only way he could show me love or any kind of affection! Can you imagine your own dad being that sick as a young daughter or son? Maybe you have experienced this, and if you have, you know what I mean and the struggle I had to go through. Out of nowhere, not having anybody comfort me and love me in that way was very hard, and he knew it too; that's why he would try his best.

There were times where I just wanted to break down and cry in front of him and just lose it. There were so many times when I was praying for him to feel better for God to take away this cancer. My neighbors, friends, and family took care of us kids a lot of the time and brought food for us and helped us financially, and just being there as friends. I was so grateful for them, but there was nothing that could bring my happy chipper-loving dad back. I didn't like staying at home and watching him sick like that. I would spend time with my friends or just sit outside a lot taking everything in and talking to God.

One time as my sister Lydia and I were taking care of him by ourselves, my dad asked us to do something for him that was a hard decision for us to make. My sister Hiwet before she left the house to go get some food as an eleven-year-old, told us to take care of Negash. Don't leave the house, don't let him out of your sight. Don't let him go outside if he asks. Just make sure to keep an eye on him all day since he was feeling better those days! She didn't want him to be worse. We agreed. It was just a beautiful day spending and sharing special moments with my father and my sister that I will never forget. He asked us what we wanted to be when we grew up and took time to speak life into us as soon as he got the chance to be able to speak. He also kept telling us we have to take care of each other and love each other. My sister and I used to fight a lot. It was usually me causing the problem. She was the sweet loving one. I don't know why I was the way I was when I was young but definitely wasn't nice to them. God has transformed my life and heart because I don't even know of or remember the girl that used to fight. My sister told me aschegarinesh! (You're a problem maker!) I stopped fighting with her when my dad was sick, though, because I didn't want to add stress on him or her.

He was talking like he was leaving soon, like he was going to die soon. I would always interrupt him and say, "Negash, stop!" You are not going to die. I need you. We need you to stop talking like that. We love you, and we aren't ready for you to leave us. You are not leaving us, period. Stop! He would nod his head and would stop, but deep down, he knew with the look he gave me and in the way he talked about it that his time was coming for him to leave this earth soon. He would just shrug his shoulder. My dad always had that feeling even way before he got sick. When my neighbors would tell him to get married (there were other reasons why he didn't want to get married), but deep down, he would ask, "What is going to happen to my daughters when I leave, when I die and God calls me?" I remember him bringing that subject of his time to die during other conversations; I always got so mad and would stop him from saying it. I knew he was missing my beautiful mother and his bride a lot. He believed in God and had so much faith and a strong relationship with God, and he believed in the afterlife. So he would say, when I go and get to see your mom, what are you going to do, Sara. He was getting us ready for what was to come because he felt it in his heart it was coming soon. He didn't want to die. He loved us and loved life, but something in his heart was always telling him to get his girls ready for what is to come.

He didn't understand why or anything, but he followed his instincts. Great lesson by my dad here is to always follow your instinct even if it doesn't make sense and you haven't seen the reason why to believe what is coming. Just believe and do what you feel in your heart to do. He believed and did what was on his heart to do, which was to speak life into us. He mentored us and was a great leader and father to us. He wanted to leave a legacy of his children doing amazing things by how he taught us and treated us. He was always dropping down wisdom on us and talking to us about life and how to be better in our lives and pursue our dreams and goals. He always told us you have to get yourself ready for the unexpected. He mentored us a lot about life even though we were only seven, nine, and eleven years of age. We were mature from the start because of what my dad's teaching. People would always ask us how old we are. They see how mature we are, how respectful we are, how helpful we are and how hard-working we are, and loving we were because we stood out. You get your identity from your parents in how they raised you.

My dad gave us his identity and who he was by his teachings. Dads take notes! Start teaching your kids manners and who you want them to be from their early childhood! People would always be surprised when we would tell them our age. We proudly say we are Negash's daughters. My dad raised Champions from the start. We stood out the most from all of our kids our age; we people knew it and saw it and were amazed by it. He felt in his heart that he needed to tell us and teach life lessons and raise up champion. He just knew that he wasn't going to live a long life, and he used it all up to pour life into us. I want you all to be taking care of yourselves, he would say! He was a thinker and such a great and smart guy! There were times when I didn't want to apply what he was teaching because I didn't want him to die soon after he taught us these things. I was always scared and terrified of my dad dying, especially when he would keep bringing up and saying if anything ever happens to me and I am not there anymore. You know how to live and take care of yourselves. He looked at the future for us and wanted to teach us so much before it is too late. You never know when bad things come, so be prepared; that is a life lesson right there. He taught me to love, to be knowledgeable, and use wisdom throughout the years.

As my sisters and I were taking care of him and sitting beside him, he asked us if he could please go on a walk. He wanted to see the outside, the beautiful sunshine, and feel the breeze. He wasn't able to be outside for a few months because he was bedridden. It wasn't good for him to go outside with how cold and windy it was. My sister had strictly told us not to let him go outside. We immediately told him he couldn't. We told him if he leaves the house, he is going to get more sick. He begged us to just let him see outside. My dad was stuck in a one-bedroom house laying in a bed with no TV or anything else to do other than laying down all day. He wanted to see things that we take for granted looking at every day. He wanted to look at the beautiful blue sky, the beautiful green trees, hear and see kids playing outside in the neighborhood. He wanted to finally walk and use his legs. He wanted to feel alive again. He kept asking and asking us to let him go. I looked into his eyes, and his eyes filled with sadness. I didn't know what to do. It broke my heart. Half of me wanted to let him go and let him experience his walk. I remember being stuck in a hospital for three months staring at plain white walls and not being able to go outside when I really wanted to. And now I am telling my own dad that he couldn't have that! Another half of me was saying, no, you can't let him because he is going to get more sick. It is going to be my fault if I let him and he gets sicker. Which one do I do? Even though my sister was older, I was the outspoken one, so the decision kind of laid down on me. I told my dad, please stay in bed because we love you and don't want you to get more sick. He said Sara, out of all people, you remember what it feels like to be stuck in a room and not be outside. Even though I didn't want to believe it or know it, I knew my dad's time was coming and that he was going to pass away soon. I just felt it but didn't want to accept it. With how sick he was, he wasn't going to live for very long, not even a few months; there was no cancer treatment he was getting, nothing to help him. He was slowly suffering, and his cells and body were dying. How can I not let him go on a walk and let him have his one wish in the world, which was to go on a walk and let him feel alive again one more time? I felt so bad for him; my heart ached for him. I begged my sister to let him go and let him have his one wish in the world. I told her if you were in the same situation, wouldn't you want to go on a walk and feel alive and see everything and everyone one more time? She agreed.

My dad's face lit up with happiness when we told him he could go. We bundled him up with warm clothes and put a gabi (blanket) over him. We told him not to go too far and to take it slow. He agreed. He was listening to us. This time, even though he was the parent, and we were so young, he took our advice. He knew he raised wise kids with a great mindset that he would trust us and listen to our ideas and concerns. It was so nice and so sweet to see my dad walking around the neighborhood all bundled up with a cane to help him walk. He was full of smiles as he passed each house and stopped to say hi to the neighbors and his friends at each house and carry on a conversation. Everybody was so happy to see him and to see him talking and being more alive. This was the Negash they knew and loved that they missed so much. He was so full of joy. It made my heart smile to see him that happy. I teared up a bit just experiencing that with him! I walked with him, making sure he was going to be okay as he was smelling the fresh air and looking at everything like it was the first time he saw any of it! It was such a special moment that I will never forget. He thanked my sister and me for letting him experience life again. He felt alive for the first time in a long time and hugged us. Oh, it was so precious! We then tucked him back in bed. Hiwet got home and heard about his walk. She was upset at first, but she knew he needed it, so she let it go. My dad slept well that night and was happy; you could see it. I was glad we let him go and experience the little things we take for granted.

Soon after his walk, he got really sick again. He got so sick to the point that people knew any day he was going to pass away. I totally wasn't ready for what was coming, and neither were my sisters. Everybody whispered about how sick he was and that he had a few days left. He kept holding on every day. When they felt maybe today he's going to go, he kept holding on for another week, then another week after that, even though he was so sick. They knew he was holding on to his last breath for a reason, and it wasn't until he decided and felt it was okay for him to go that he would go. People were amazed at how long he was holding on. My dad was a strong warrior! He was a fighter. He wasn't going to go until he knew his daughters were okay and can handle it, especially his youngest daughter, who was me. My aunt asked me to make coffee, and that is when the tragic thing came!

My Hero's Last Days

As that scripture states, there is a time to be born and a time to die. God sent us to earth for a period of time and wants us back to him after we complete our assignment and purpose! Nobody can escape death. It is a way of life just like it says there is a time to be born and a time to die! Some people go too soon though from our lives. I don't think we are ever ready to let people that we love and cherish go. Even when we believe in God and the afterlife, we are still never ready to let people go. That is one of the hardest things to go through is letting go.

In the middle of October, on a beautiful sunny day, my little one-room house was filled with people. My aunts and uncles from geteri (countryside) came to see my dad. They were his brother and sisters. My aunt that had been taking care of my dad for so long was there as well. My dad was lying down on the bed and listening to conversations. He seemed like he was doing good that day. We were all getting so excited that he's finally started feeling better. He looked like he was getting better that day. His countenance was changed. He was just himself but laying down on the bed. It felt like he was just resting. Everybody was having a great time laughing and joking around and spending time together and talking to my dad! I was in the house spending time with all of them. My other two sisters were doing dishes outside and spending time with the neighbors. Everybody was happy; it was all a great morning. My aunt asked me if I could make coffee for them. I jumped for joy with excitement and said yes. I would love to make some coffee for you all. My dream was finally coming true to make coffee, the Ethiopian way. It was such a big deal for me to actually make coffee and to be asked to do it. Ethiopia is known for having the best coffee in the world.

Coffee originated from Ethiopia, as some of you may know. You drink coffee at social gatherings. We have a coffee ceremony. It's beautiful and cultural. Only older people get to make coffee usually, not young ones, especially not me. Since I got burned, my sisters wouldn't let me make coffee or be around the propane stove at all. They were worried that I would get burnt again, so they wouldn't ever let me make coffee. Every time I asked, they refused for a long time. Making coffee the Ethiopian way also represents that you are grown up and taking responsibility and becoming an adult. It shows that you are growing and maturing, and you have that trust and leadership with it, especially when you are making it for a full room of people that are way older than you. That is a huge step into going from childhood to adulthood. That is what is represented in my culture and house. My eldest sister was always the one that made coffee. Even Lydia didn't make coffee as much. For my aunt to ask me to make coffee instead of them was a big deal. She said, "Sara, do you know how to make coffee? Make coffee for us!" I waited for somebody to say Hiwet or Lydia can do it. Sara is too young, but nobody said anything. They all said we want to have Sara's coffee; we want to see what it tastes like. I couldn't help but be excited. Finally, that day came when I can show people that I am grown up and responsible and what an honor it was to be making it for a full room of people. My dad, when he heard my aunt, looked at me and smiled. I was like, yes, I got my dad's blessing too. My house was one room like a studio apartment, but we had a sheet dividing the room in half for house things that we put in the other room.

I started getting the *cini* and *gebena* (traditional cups and jug for making coffee) from the cupboard and turned around to put them into the other side of the room; as I turned around, I just had a feeling to turn around and look at my dad. My dad and I had special eye contact three times that I will never forget. They were precious moments with my dad. The first time, I turned around and looked at my dad; he was looking at me with this proud look on his face, and smiled at me, and looked deep into my eyes. I stopped and smiled back at him and put the cini (cups) and gebena down, and came back in to get more stuff. After I got a couple of things in my hand, I felt it in my heart again to turn around and look at my dad again. I turned around again, and this time he was looking at me with this sad, emotional, but proud look. I stopped and looked at him and stood up straight, and smiled at him. He kept looking deep into my eyes, and I did too. It is hard to describe, but a look that said it all. He knew he was going to leave soon that he was going to die, but he needed to know that his daughter was going to be okay first. He needed to see me do something that showed him that I was grown up, that I could take care of myself, that I can take responsibility, that I can make coffee the Ethiopian ceremony way! It was a way of showing adulthood even at the age of seven. My eyes were tearing up as I looked deep into my daddy's eyes, and he was looking at me with so much emotion. He didn't have to say anything, but the look he gave me said it all. It said that he was sorry he was going to leave me, didn't want to leave me, but proud to see me become who I was, he was waiting and waiting and holding and holding on until he saw me do something that will give him peace in his heart that I was going to be okay for him to go. He needed to see me make coffee. It wasn't the making of coffee that was so important; it is the act of making coffee and what that represented. It was so emotional. He looked like he was going to cry.

His eyes were filled up with tears because he knew that goodbye was coming. He knew he was going to die now because his work was complete. He knew it was time for him to go. He didn't need to hold on anymore and fight because his baby, his Sara, was going to be okay. As I looked at him and wiped away my tears, he looked at me with this saddest look. The saddest look I have ever seen and would never forget! I looked at my dad and didn't understand at the moment why he was looking at me like that. He had never looked at me like that with so much emotion, and I knew he was leaving, that he was dying with the way he looked at me and that it was kind of a goodbye. As I turned around to go to the other side of the curtain and put the stuff down, my dad was turning his head to keep looking at me. He wasn't going to miss it; I put the stuff down and came back to get more stuff for the third time. As I was walking back, I was trying to contemplate why he looked at me like that and just had such a heartfelt connection I didn't even know what happened. I was just soaking it up and putting it in my heart and trying not to cry and hold it together and be strong for him.

The third time I came back in to get more stuff, something told me in my heart again turn around and look at your dad. This time I turned around with haste and with my heart beating! My dad's eyes were still focused on me. He looked at me again and tried to smile; I smiled. As I looked down for a second and just out of nowhere, he made this loud noise and started having a seizure. It scared the crap out of me, and I dropped the things I had in my hands and watched him. He was having a seizure. My aunts and uncles jumped up and were holding him down as his body was shaking. My aunt started shouting out orders! "Hold down his arms and his legs and his head. My aunt started calling out orders to straighten him out to my aunts and uncle, straighten him out. I stood there like a statue, not knowing what to do and trying to figure out what was going on, and watched my dad have a seizure. I was freaking out. My heart was trembling. Then suddenly, the seizure stopped out of nowhere. I saw my dad, my hero, my kind, loving, sweet, selfless daddy, die in front of my eyes. That moment changed my life. Did he really die, or is he just having a seizure? I heard his sister say more; he died.

I felt like I was dreaming. You are not talking about my father. My dad, my best friend. I stood there puzzled. My aunt saw me and told me to get out. I wanted to know what was going on, so I started picking up the cini and gebena and get things out of the way. I got some stuff and slowly was walking to put them away when she told me again. What was happening to my dad? I wasn't going to leave the house. She kicked me out and locked the door. I sat outside, trying to figure out what just happened. I found my sister Hiwet and wanted to tell her what was going on, but it didn't seem real. I said Negash got really sick, he was having a seizure and told her what my aunt was saying to straighten out his legs and arms. My sister, who was only twelve years old at the time, didn't understand it and said it's okay; he probably got more sick. There is nothing to worry about. I was trying to make sense of it all. I didn't know what to think or do as I sat there with my sister for a half and a half hour for them to open the door. They were taking so long in the room. I thought maybe I did not hear about him dying and was trying to make sense of it all in my little brain. I kept asking my sister if my dad was okay. She told me to stop asking her and said he was going to be ok. She didn't understand why I was asking her. She didn't see what I saw and heard; I didn't know how to tell her.

I didn't know how to put it all in words, but I tried to tell her she told me to stop. My heart was beating really fast; I didn't know what to do with myself! Then my sister saw my aunt pick some leaves off of a tree right outside of our house. As soon as she saw her do that, she started running into the house really fast; my sister lost it! She started screaming, yelling really loud. It was a huge cry; her heart was broken. She kept saying no, no, no, Negashiyay! She was running to get into the house as she was screaming to see my dad. She knew that he passed away. In Ethiopia, you use those leaves that my aunt picked to wash dead people's bodies before they are put in a coffin. Cutting that off represents that my dad died, and that's when she lost it. I started crying with her and started screaming! No, Negashiyay! Did he really die? No! My sister was so loud when she was screaming and bawling her eyes out that all the neighbors started flooding out of their houses to see what was going on. They knew as they saw us dropping to the ground helplessly crying and screaming that our father just passed away. I was a mess, but my sister was even way more of a mess than I was because she knew what death represented. I didn't understand what dying meant, but she did. She felt like the whole world just collapsed to the ground on her. She felt buried in it with no strength to get back up.

My dad held everything together; now it was just her! She was left with two other little girls to take care of when she was only/twelve years old herself. She kept crying, "You can't leave me, Negashiyay! I need you! I need you, come back! Ahh!" She was saying; my mom is gone, now you can't go too. She held me and hugged me and cried her eyes out loudly. I cried and cried with her. I then started telling myself Negash is going to be back. I thought he was just going to be gone for a little while and come back again. I didn't know what dying meant. I kept telling myself it's okay; he will be back in order to comfort me. That is what I wanted to know and needed to tell myself to get through it. I didn't want to believe or understand what death really meant and that I will never see my daddy again. Lydia was sobbing. We were all so broken! My neighbors, aunts, uncles, and everybody that knew him came flooding to our house and our neighborhood crying their eyes out. Our place was flooded with people that were mourning for my dad.

In the African culture, when somebody dies, it is a huge deal. People get together and cry very hard. In Ethiopia, when someone passes away, mourning days are three days long. People just come to cry and sit and be with the family that lost the person. It's actually kind of scary to be around as a young girl. Can you imagine 50-100 people and more getting together and crying loudly! That's what it was for my dad's death! People from geteri and from every part of the country came to say goodbye to my dad. There were more than 600 people at his funeral. My neighbors, aunts, and uncles decided my sister Lydia and I were too young to go to a funeral. Yes, we were, but it was going to be one last time to say goodbye to our father. Thank God for my sister Hiwet because she wouldn't take no for an answer. She told them that we are going to say goodbye to our dad and will not miss it. She was the head of the house now. They dressed all of us up in black dresses and shoes. We went to the service for the funeral, and oh my gosh, can you imagine over 600 people wailing and crying so loudly! Africans know how to mourn. It scared me. All these people were crying for my dad, were crying because they miss my dad because he meant a lot to them and have impacted their life in different ways. All of these people were there to say goodbye to my dad; I cried and cried for what seemed like hours. There was mourning time for at least forty-five minutes. My two sisters, close friends, and I were in the front. I cried for so long to the point I couldn't cry any longer. I didn't understand why people were crying for so long. My dad is going to come back. He is just gone for a little while, I thought to myself. They were mourning very loudly that it was freaking me out being in the front and surrounded. People kept saying my dad's name, Negash, come back! Come back, Negashiyay! Come back for your daughters.

What are they going to do without you? Come back, Negash. They started calling out my sister's names and my name and crying! It was my first time at a funeral as a seven-year-old. There were so many real raw tears. I wanted to get out of there and cry somewhere else all on my own. I just wanted to be by myself. Our eyes were shot red.

We went to bury my dad after a while. That's when it started to hit me. It was hard to watch and see my dad's body, his coffin being pulled down to be buried in the ground. I started crying again and fell to the ground screaming, "Dad, come back! Daddy, come back. No! Negashiyay, I can't live without you! Come back! My sister Hiwet lost it and was running after the coffin to just lay on it and not let them put it to the ground. Saying goodbye is the hardest thing to do, even if it is a dead man's body. It makes it a reality that he is gone forever from this earth. People had to hold her down. Lydia doesn't like attention, but she was crying standing in a corner. We lost the one and only person that we loved and cared about so much that was everything to us in this world. We finally said goodbye, and they buried my hero. What a tragic day it was. What a horrible memory that I couldn't erase from my brain. All the people at the funeral went to our neighborhood, where we had food and drinks to celebrate my dad's life. They sat outside in the neighborhood. My sisters and I were depressed and couldn't bring ourselves to eat. People had to make us eat. A lot of people stayed and told us how much they loved our father and tried to be there for us. Nothing was going to bring him back, absolutely nothing. In Ethiopia, mourning lasts a whole week. So even after my dad's burial, there were people coming to see us for the whole week. Usually, the mourners are sitting in a bed where people would come and visit and eat breakfast, lunch, and dinner. The neighborhood ladies were busy cooking for hundreds of people for each meal. Everybody kept coming to hug and kiss us, especially me, since I was the youngest. I was tired of hugs and kisses after, especially the two days. I just wanted my dad back, nothing else. Everything changed after this time. We were left as orphans; life really changed after that week!

My Sister

There are different things that come up in our lives that change our lives drastically. There are different events that come in our lives, different trials, and different situations that change our lives from one way to the other in an instant at times. As the scriptures tell us, there are different seasons that come up in our lives. There is a time for everything, and the times started quickly after my father passed away. My sisters and I were left as orphans. I was seven years old, and my two sisters Lydia and Hiwet, were nine and twelve years old. None of us were old enough to get a job. Hiwet was worried sick about how she was going to take care of us both and how she was going to pay all the expenses that my dad took care of when she was only twelve years old. She was the head of the family and now in charge. Both of my sisters and I really looked up to her for everything, but yet she was just a child herself. There are lots of children in Ethiopia and all over Africa that is in charge of their families at that young age and younger, usually caring for five or six of their siblings. They worry, cry, and also have to be strong for their other siblings. Life is very difficult. They feel helpless. You never know who you are and what you have in you until life strikes you and that automatically changes and shifts your life in one way or another.

Can you imagine being nine or twelve years old and being the father and mother to four or five of your siblings? You're going to ask yourself, but how? I am only a child myself. How can I do this and take care of my siblings when I am like them myself? I am only a child, and the world is so big and everything in it. Me? Can you imagine doing that? There are countless stories of countless of them all over Africa. You grow up fast. I can't imagine the way my sister was feeling. I am reminded of a story in the bible about the prophet Jeremiah and how God called him to do something so big at a young age. He is doubting himself and who God created him to be, and what God wants him to do. He questions and asks himself, "Can I really do what you have called me to do, God?" Jeremiah thinks to himself; it's way too big of a plan you have for me. I am only a child or a lad. I don't have the strength to do what you have called me to do. I don't feel I have it in me. Who am I to lead so many people? People are going to look down on me and not listen to me. Who am I to do what you have called me to do. What am I supposed to do? Isn't that what we feel at different times in our lives? We feel incapable. We feel helpless. My sister was crying out to God during that time of what felt like the world was crumbling at her feet. She felt, "How could you do this to me, God? Why do you have to take away my mother and father? Why now? We need them. How could we survive without them? How can I be the leader of the family? Who am I? I don't feel like I have the strength to do what you have called me to do or the ability." God was calling her to a bigger calling in her life. She was feeling helpless but yet she knew who to go to get the help and strength that she needed to do what she needed to do. She was crying out to God for help and for Him to show her who she is and to give her the strength that she needs because she felt inexperienced and felt out of place. As Jeremiah was saying that, God spoke to him and said this, Jeremiah chapter 1:4-5, (NLT): *"I knew you before I formed you in your mother's womb. Before you were born I set you apart and appointed you as my prophet to the nations."*

What God just shared with Jeremiah should give him confidence that God knows him! It should give us confidence that He knows us before He even formed you in the womb. He knew us. He already set you apart. To give you an illustration of that. A person that came up with the idea of having a camera to take pictures, at first they had the idea, then they started patterning it. They wrote down ideas of how it was going to work and which button was going to be which. They wrote the plan then they put the plan together for people to use. If customers had questions about how it worked, all they need to do is go back to the instructions that they have received about the camera and or send it back to the company that they bought it from to get more knowledge so that it can get fixed. Just like that in our lives, when things go wrong, or we hit a stumbling block as we live our lives, we need to know to automatically go to the one that made us the One that created us. The one that thought us out and knew what was going to happen next. The One that holds the world in his hand. The One that is Alpha and Omega. He is the beginning and the end and knows what is going to happen in our future. Not only people's futures but our own future. He knows your future. We need to go to our Creator to get the help we need so that we can get back on the right track by the one that knows us more and sets us apart to become the person that he created us to be.

Hiwet was mourning and heartbroken for probably a couple more weeks after my dad passed away. As I explained the way she felt, feeling unequipped and everything. She prayed to God to give her strength and to help her, and teach her how to do everything. As I remember and think back now on how she was, I feel like she became a superwoman out of nowhere. She has the confidence that I had never seen in her before. She started to believe in herself and felt equipped and ready to take on any challenge she faced. There was a strength about her that nothing was going to break her, but she was going to break it. I remember feeling like what on earth happened to my sister. Who is this girl, and what happened to the other Hiwet I was experiencing? I loved the new strong, focused Hiwet, but was wondering what came over her. I know now it was all God that gave her the strength to be the strong superwoman that I was experiencing, nothing else. She was going to school and getting great grades and passing her classes while she was a mom and dad to her two younger sisters. She always amazed me at how she did everything and how she made time for everything. She would stay up late at night, studying and doing her homework. She always put me in bed and would pet my hair so I could fall asleep. She always cooked delicious food for us. Everything she started doing, she did with excellence. She did our laundry for us on Saturdays by hand since we didn't have a washing machine. We helped, of course, but it was all her, mostly cleaning the bedding. She made sure everything that parents do, she was doing it as well. Whatever came at her, she worked hard to make it work. She felt equipped out of nowhere. Her confidence was very high; I was always so amazed at how hard she worked and how she did it. God totally gave her the strength that she needed to keep going. He gave her new strength. He says that He will strengthen us in our weakness. I can testify that He was her strength in her weakness.

Life's Challenge

Did you wonder how in the world we paid for rent, electricity, food, and school supplies? Even though we didn't know God's plan, God had it all planned out. He uses people to carry out His plan and to be His hands and feet for His children around the world. All of our aunts and uncles had a meeting together to try to figure out what to do with my two sisters and me. Some had ideas to possibly separate us and have each one of us live with different aunts and uncles if they can afford to have another person in their home. While some agreed that was a great idea, others disagreed on separating us. They are family; it is not healthy to separate all of them, especially after losing both of their parents. They knew we needed each other.

They thought to themselves, if we have all of them stay together, then we need to do something about how they are going to be paying bills. They all agreed each of them should give 30 biri a month to us, so we can pay for rent, electricity, water bill, food and other necessities that we needed. We were so fortunate to have aunts and uncles that actually were able to give an extra 30 biri to help support our family even though they had a family of their own. In other families, if both parents die, the kids are usually sent to a different aunt or uncle's house, and the aunt or uncle takes care of them. They are usually separated from their siblings. Some could be living in the city while the other sibling lives in the geteri (countryside). That creates family division, and they wouldn't be able to see each other often. Some that live in the geteri most of the time aren't able to go to school and study because the family that is taking care of them can't afford to pay for their school, let alone even food to eat for the day. If they have a farm, they usually help out at the farm all day.

It doesn't matter your age in Africa; you start working when you are very small. Children mature and grow up fast because they have to due to circumstances. In order to survive, you have got to be strong; you have got to change and be willing to change. I am so blessed that God had a plan for my sisters and me to be together. Some of the aunts and uncles sent money to us each month so that we were able to pay for the bills we had. I just knew it was God providing for us through them. My sister Hiwet was very excited to hear that they would help us. It took so much burden off of her just knowing that there are people that are going to help her and our family. She would cry with happy tears because she knew it was God providing. She saw people being the hands and feet of Jesus. Hiwet did a great job using the money wisely. She budgeted really well. It paid the bills. We are forever thankful that God provided in the way he did for us through our families. We were very fortunate. There were also times where our aunts and uncles had a hard month or two and weren't able to pay the money they said they would help us with because some of the months, they were having a hard time financially for their families as well. We understand that they could only help when they were able too but those months were tough on us as well. When Hiwet would worry, we would worry with her. Then we will remember back on how God has been providing for us before through prayer, and then we would gather together and ask the Lord to provide for us. My aunts and uncles were faithful to their word and blessed us. At the times they weren't able to, God started growing our faith. We felt small and helpless. But I remember thinking we need to pray and God is going to provide for us. There were times where my sister felt like God was not going to come through to help us because he stretched the waiting period till the last minute we felt. But we all know that God's timing is perfect. He is never late, He is never too early, but He is always on time. There were times where He wanted to stretch our faith and show us who He is and literally witness it before our eyes of how God answers our prayers.

There was a time when Hiwet had no money on her, and we had no food in the house. We usually ate injera and wet for breakfast, lunch, and dinner. You might be thinking, Don't you all get tired of it? The answer is yes at times, but when that is the only thing you have to eat every day, you feel blessed to just feed your stomach. We were even out of the flour (teff) to make injera with. Hiwet asked the neighbors if she could borrow money from them until our aunts and uncles would give her money, but they said they didn't have money to let her borrow to buy food. Sometimes though, they would let her borrow money. She always returned it back. When they said they didn't have money, she asked if she could borrow injera from them and that she would return it when she had the money to prepare the food. She was shocked that they weren't helping her when they knew there was no food in the house. She was embarrassed to ask, and she didn't know what else to do. My aunts and uncles didn't live close, and they weren't going to bless us for a few more days. She felt helpless. She grabbed both my sisters and me and told us, "You need to start praying because there is no food in the house," and explained the situation. As we were sitting there, trying to figure something out, she said, "Unless you get on your knees right now and start praying for God to do a miracle and bring you food or money, you're going to be drinking water for the next three days for every meal." I worried because I was already so hungry. How in the world am I going to drink water the next few days when I am already starving right now. But we knew who to turn to for help.

> *Don't worry about anything; instead, pray about everything. Tell God what you need, and thank him for all he has done. Then you will experience God's peace, which exceeds anything we can understand. His peace will guard your hearts and minds as you live in Christ Jesus.*
> *Philippians 4:6-7 (NLT)*

So the three of us got on our knees and prayed and asked God to answer our prayers and provide for us. I remember that day so clearly. We had nobody to turn to but God. "After we prayed," my sister said, "now we wait for God to answer our prayers." This time she said it with so much calmness and peace in her heart. There was something that shifted after we prayed. We all had peace in our hearts and while we were waiting on God to answer our prayers somehow. That is what happens after prayer. We gave it to God, we gave God our worry and made it known to Him what we needed afterward, just like that scripture states and the peace of God which surpasses all understanding will guard your hearts, and your mind is what it states, and it is what we felt. As we were talking about something else and laughing, not even thirty minutes later, there was a knock on the door. My eldest sister's friend came over carrying something. We all looked at each other in shock and amusement. We had no words when she came and said, I brought you injera! She was carrying a big stack of injera that was already made. She just said, here, I made extra. That Injera would have lasted a week; she had a big family that eats a lot, so we knew it was not that she made extra; it was God telling her to give it to our family. She gave it to us and left. We thanked her and were left speechless. We were in awe of God and how quickly he answered our prayers. We serve a mighty God. We ate a lot and were filled. She even went home and brought wet (stew) for us. We were mesmerized by God. She gave us so much food it lasted for four days instead of three days. On top of that, someone gave my sister money, so she was able to buy the teff and other food she needed to buy. Thank you, Jesus, for providing for us. The scripture tells us God will always be there for us even when we don't have our other families to take care of us. Use that scripture, declare it over your life, and you will see many great breakthroughs in your life. Just believe that He will come through because He is able, and He will. He is capable of meeting our needs.

Another way that God came through in our lives was when we needed school supplies. We all went to public school where it was free. I switched schools a little while before my dad passed away to a school that was free. It was very hard to convince my dad to let me go to that school, but I am so grateful he let me switch finally because after he passed away, we would have not been able to afford to pay for my school on top of everything else. I would not have been able to switch schools in the middle of the school year either. God worked that out so perfectly. The times when there was no money for schoolbooks, pens, pencils, erasers, and school uniforms and shoes, we would pray, and people out of nowhere would bless us by buying this and that of what we needed for school without even asking them. I remember that happened a few times. We were so amazed at how real God was working in our lives using people we knew and we didn't know to meet our needs. I remember one time when I needed school supplies; my neighbor sold drinks outside of her house as her business. People, especially men, would come and drink tela and hang out. I always would say hi, and if somebody asked me a question, I would answer it and be always nice and polite. My dad taught me to be a person of character at a very early age in my life. I kept what I knew and how to act just like he taught me. Everybody knew my sisters and I were Negash's daughters even after he passed away. They knew by our great attitudes and who we were as a person.

People that didn't know us would see our character and would ask us who our parents were. We would proudly tell them we are Negash's daughters! Because of how mature we were for our age and beyond our age, people were always surprised. People wanted to bless us just because of the people we were and how we treated others. I am so grateful for my dad for instilling everything in me and teaching me so much before he passed away. He used his time on earth so wisely. He accomplished his purpose on earth by raising his children for sure. Everything he taught really blessed us, and because we obeyed, we got blessed for the attributes that we had at that young age. So the man that was drinking tela asked me some questions about my life. He was a nice person. I didn't tell him what I needed, but he right away saw and heard my other neighborhood friends talking about school and how their parents bought them school supplies and said I want to buy you your school supplies. It was very expensive to buy everything I needed, but he said he wanted to bless me! So he bought everything I needed and my sister's school supplies as well. My sisters and I again were dumbfounded on how real God is and how He is there to meet our needs. That took the burden off of us. This kind of miracle happened quite often, which we were grateful for. At other times, people would randomly give me 10-100 Ethiopian money for no reason. But it would always be when we needed money. I would give it to my sister to buy whatever we needed to buy. It covered some of the expenses that we needed to pay for, and if it was extra, we would treat ourselves to making spaghetti or rice instead of injera for the night. We loved those nights. My sister made the best rice in the world. Sometimes people would randomly surprise my sisters with some money too.

We had lots of hard times financially for our family, but God always came through every single time! He is faithful and always answers our prayers! People would invite us for meals and for holidays. In Ethiopia, for holidays, we always had feasts. It is the tradition that people always kill chicken, goat, cow, lamb for the feast! We have never killed a cow or a goat or anything for holidays. We never had the money to buy the animals. When my dad was alive, we would buy chicken, though, so we can have traditional chicken stew. Sometimes He wants to stretch our faith and see if we believe in him still when He doesn't answer something right away. Sometimes after the wait, He will show up in the last three seconds! But we have a God that is so faithful that will never leave us nor forsake us!

"But my God shall supply all your need according to his riches in glory by Christ Jesus" (Phillippians 4:19, KJV).

The Reason for My Smile

What is the reason for your smile? Is there something that makes you smile every day? Is it something tough that you have gone through in your life but, in the end, changed your outlook on life and made you smile? I ask you this question for a specific reason. Your smile is a signature of who you are. Your smile says a lot about you. There are different reasons why each person smiles in this world. The reason for your smile could be because God has blessed you with so much like family, friends, children, or job. I believe we smile for different reasons in different seasons in our lives. There is a season where your smile comes naturally because everything is going well in your life.

There are different seasons where your smile wants to fade away when some things aren't working out in your life. There are seasons where your smile vanishes away when you go through big trials in your life. Think of the last time you lit up a match and how fast the fire went out when you blew it out! Just like that, in the blink of an eye, something tragic can happen to us that tries to take our smiles away, and it is up to us to choose to not let what happens to change our smile or, even worse, take it away for a period of time. The tragic thing that happened in my life that tried to take my smile away was when my father, my best friend, passed away. I already explained in the last few chapters about how close my father and I were and how much he meant to me.

When my father passed away, I had a hard time with it; my heart was broken. The first few days, it didn't seem like he was gone. It felt like he was just gone for a little while and that he was coming back soon. I was very young to understand what death meant; at times, I would even question and ask myself why my sister Hiwet was crying so hard. Why was she so heartbroken? He is just gone for a few weeks or even a couple of months. He will come back, I thought and expected to happen. It didn't really click that he was never going to come back. I was seven years old, and my mind and imagination couldn't comprehend for my dad to be gone for so long. It didn't make sense for my dad to be cut off from my whole life as young as I was. That just can't happen, I thought. After a couple of weeks of my dad's passing, people stopped coming to check up on us and bring us dinner like they were doing the first two weeks. Our house was always full of people visiting or bringing lunch or dinner to hang out with us and eat with us, so it didn't really feel like my dad was gone. We were surrounded by people so much that it didn't hit me personally. I loved spending time with the people that came over. It started getting lonely when fewer and fewer people were coming to our house.

Our house became quiet. It was the plain newspaper-covered wall room with a bed and a few other items in our house and my two sisters. I started asking and questioning myself when Negash was coming back. I kept thinking that he would come back in a few weeks. Another week would pass with no sign of my dad coming back. I didn't realize what death meant. I didn't understand in my little seven-year-old mind that I was never going to see my dad again. My dad is gone forever. I then started praying and asking God to please bring my dad back. I started pleading with God more and more because I missed him. No answer and no Negash. It finally started to hit me that my dad was never coming back. I cried by myself several times a day, every day for a long time. In Ethiopia, the culture is when family members die, you always hang their picture in a frame on the wall to remember them. There were four people's pictures on our wall in our house. It was everybody that passed away in our family. It was my grandma, my dad's mom that I loved so much, my uncle, my dad's brother, there was my mom's picture, and now my dad's picture was on there too. I remember walking into my house one day and closed my door and literally cried and cried for hours looking at pictures of everybody that passed away in my family. I was sobbing like crazy because I missed all of them. I would be playing with my friends; then, suddenly, I would think about my dad and start crying. I didn't want my friends nor anybody to see me cry. I was so mad at God for taking my mom and dad away, especially my daddy. I would yell at God and say, "It was already hard enough to lose my mom, and now you have taken my dad away? My Negash! Why? Why? Why? I need my dad. I need my dad to take care of me. I need his love. I am only seven years old; Lydia is nine, and Hiwet is eleven. How can you take him away from us, God, when we are so young and when we need him? I was crying out to God every day. We need our dad, God. Don't you know?"

I was so mad and so mad at myself for the way I was talking to my God to my Heavenly Father. I did that for over a week. Then I finally came to my senses. I would repent and ask God to forgive me for speaking to Him the way I did. That was definitely not the way that my dad taught me to speak to God. I would cry and say, "God, I am so sorry. But I don't understand. I don't understand why my dad has to die? Why didn't you heal him? Don't you know that we need him? God, we have no parents. We will never have parents for the rest of our lives. How could you let that happen?" I told myself I would never smile again. I would never be happy. I will always be miserable because I have no parents. That is how a lot of you have felt if you have experienced losing someone that you love. I was so unhappy with myself. I told myself I would never be happy again. I decided I wouldn't smile anymore. I lived every day unhappy and miserable for a few reasons. A couple of the reasons were I was so upset with myself for talking to God the way I did. He is God! He created the universe, and I was talking to Him like that. He could touch me, and I could die in an instant, and I knew that. I was so disgusted with myself for treating God that way. I felt I disappointed him, which I did, and I also felt like I disappointed my dad by talking to God that way.

For weeks I was miserable and didn't want to be happy nor smile. One of the times I locked myself in the house and was crying while my sisters were gone, something came over me, and I realized something. Something made me ask myself. Why are you crying? Is crying going to bring Negash back? No! I have been sobbing and crying every day for hours, but nothing was bringing him back. I realized something; I can never bring my dad back. He is gone. I missed him so much, and I always will. Something made me realize in my heart that my dad can watch me from heaven. This thought came into my mind, if your dad was watching you from heaven would he be happy with the way you're acting? Would he want you to cry every day? Or would he want you to keep smiling? What advice would Negash give you if he was here? What would he say to you? Would he want you to keep smiling and live every day as happy as you can be? Would he want you to have joy and peace? Would he tell you to keep going in life and make him proud and become somebody that is going to impact the world? If you have lost anybody that is close to you, if you feel defeated or helpless, ask yourself those questions. What would they want me to do? Free yourself from thinking negatively otherwise. Because the people that love you would want what is best for you and move forward.

As I pondered all these questions that came into my heart. I stopped crying and realized what my dad would have me do is to be happy no matter what! I realized something, the devil would want to be sad and miserable, and he was using my dad's death and was going to use my dad's death to bring me sadness and live a life that is miserable. The enemy was using this to make me question God and my faith. He was trying to stop me from focusing on life and fulfilling the purpose that God had for me by using my dad's death. The devil wouldn't want me to reach greatness, and he would have used what isn't coming back to me, my father, as a burden and make me feel like I can't live my life or do any kind of accomplishment without my father.

When I felt defeated and sad, it was like I was feeding strength to the devil. Oh heck no, that was not going to happen. I was a daughter of my respected father, Negash, and child of the Most High God. I decided that day there was no way that I was going to let the devil win anymore. A special friend of mine once said this, "Whenever you are going through a tough trial in your life, whether it's death or not seeing a close friend for a long time, be Strong! Remember, the devil brings many things to get you off track but always knows what you are aiming at." Crying and being sad do not solve anything. It's one of the devil's ways to bring fear to our heart and body so that we may lose hope and not believe in the God who created us and knows the plans that He has for our lives. Being sad and miserable is giving the devil what he wants, and being strong and happy is what my dad and my Heavenly Father would have me do.

That day I had a conviction inside of me that from that day forward, I decided I am going to smile every day. I decided I am going to be the happiest person I know. I am going to smile through the trials! I am going to make my dad proud and do the opposite of what the enemy wanted me to do. I am going to live my life to the fullest and work hard and make something of myself and make my dad proud. He can look down from heaven and see me, even though I couldn't see him. I knew that day that God was not going to let me down, but he was going to take care of me. I knew it in my gut, so there was nothing to worry about. God reminded me that day that he was the one that created me and gave me earthly parents to take care of me, but he says, "I was his first before I was my parents' child." I am a child of the God of the universe.

He was my father, and I knew my father wouldn't abandon me, not God. So I had full confidence that he was going to take care of me and provide for me and that I just needed to trust him and believe in him. I knew when trials hit who to go to. My earthly father really instilled that in me and showed me by example that I go to my God, to my Heavenly Father. I knew that God would take care of me because of the ways that He had provided for our families, even when my father was alive. God reminded me of how I survived and lived through getting burned. If he can do miracles to wake me up from a coma after 22 days of being non-responsive, he can do anything. As I was thinking about how we were going to live our lives without our father around, this scripture comes to mind.

Matthew 6:26 (NLT) says: *"Look at the birds. They don't plant or harvest or store food in barns, for your heavenly Father feeds them. And aren't you far more valuable to him than they are?"*

Well, when you put it like that, God, yes, of course, I am more valuable. You are more valuable, and therefore, He will take care of you, believe and trust in Him. That day was so significant in my life and everything I experienced. It changed my life forever. Since that day, I was always known to be the happiest person people know. People always complimented me when I was young, and as I got older, too that they love my smile and being around me. You can ask anybody that knows me from everywhere in Ethiopia and America what kind of person Sara is. They would say she is very happy and joyful. People always complimented me on my smile and how beautiful it is. I even won the best smile from a big competition I was in after I came to America at an acting and modeling competition in Los Angeles. I forgot the reason behind my smile as the years went on because I was always so happy. It became part of me and who I am as a person. I am very humble, but I want to share with you how people saw me and know me as a person because of that one decision I made when I was seven years old that have changed my life and have impacted so many people's lives by my smile and joyous attitude and being around me. All it takes is a decision to be happy no matter what comes at you in life or what you have been through. The trials and heartaches you go through make you a stronger person. The scriptures say in Proverbs 18:21 (KJV): "Death and life are in the power of the tongue: and they that love it shall eat the fruit thereof."

I totally believe in that. I spoke about life in my situation and life to be happy and to have life instead of death, and I am eating the fruit of it, which is happiness and joy every day. This smile doesn't come from me but from God himself strengthening me. Thank you, Jesus. Speak life to your life and situations. Choose to be the happiest person you know. This world needs more smiles; more people need to have joy and live happily and not feel defeated in what we call trials of life. God calls us to rise to the occasion to rise and to speak into our lives. What comes out of our tongue is so powerful, whether it's life or death. If you're speaking negatively to yourself or about your life, you're speaking death to your life. You need to speak Life, as the scripture says. I dare you to choose today while you are reading this and decide to be happy in spite of everything wrong that is happening in your life right now or if it comes later. Choose to be happy. Inspire people to be like you. Jay Danize once said, "Your smile is your logo. Your personality is your business card, and the way you make others feel is your trademark!" My favorite quote of all time:

"Use your smile to change the world and don't let the world change your smile!"

Unknown

Only He Makes the Impossible Possible in Your Life

Have you ever dreamed of something big, something extraordinary, something impossible for your life? Have you ever dreamed of something unimaginable? Something you want and desire that is and seems impossible? My two sisters loved to dream big. They would dream of having the biggest nicest house and how they would decorate it. Hiwet says she would have a nice big TV, radio so we can listen to music whenever they wanted, and have nice sofas. They would have nice bedrooms and have a bed of their own and nice bathrooms like Americans. In Africa, especially in rural parts, the bathrooms aren't the same. The toilet is a big hole that you squat on and do your business. They would dream of having nice cars, so they didn't have to walk anymore to places. So a car would make life easier.

They walk miles whenever they go to a store or somewhere or at times take a taxi if they have money. It seemed they would dream of bigger and bigger things; every night, their dream got bigger and bigger. I usually would never join them when they were dreaming as they laugh and joke around. I thought it was impossible. They were too big of dreams for me to accept; I didn't want to dream of something big and be disappointed. Since we just had each other at the time and with both of our parents gone, there was no way those things could be accomplished. We were too young to work and still had a long way of school that we needed to finish. They loved to daydream and think of things they would do if they were able to financially. They would ask me what I would do, what my dream was, and how I would decorate our new dream house. I wanted everything they wanted and dreamed about, but I was thinking to be realistic because there was no way those things would happen at this time in our lives. One of the craziest impossible dreams they had was coming to America. I laughed at their remark when they blurted out coming to America. What in the world are they thinking? They went to the impossible! There was no way they could come to America, but they kept dreaming. I told them they didn't have any family members there that they knew there, not even a friend. They didn't have money, so there is no way they were going to America; I always told them that it was impossible. When would they ask me if I would want to go to America?

I told them no because it is impossible for me to go there. But deep down, it's not that I didn't want to go to America; if it ever were to happen, I didn't want to be separated from my sisters. But to me, it really was a waste of time and energy to dream for something so big as to come to America when it is impossible to get here! America was like heaven to them. They would hear of so many stories about America and the way Americans lived so extravagantly. They dreamed to have that kind of lifestyle. During their dreaming season, we were trying to get more help for our family from the district. It was a couple of years after my dad passed away by this time, and life was still hard for the three of us. Our district found us a Christian organization that found sponsors for kids that are in need from America! Isn't that crazy? I was getting help from people in America? When I knew there was no possible way America and I can ever touch or the people of America and I could ever connect. God wanted to start revealing who He is to me! Their mission was to find families that would sponsor kids from Ethiopia that got accepted to the organization and find families for them to sponsor them. The sponsorship covered school fees, uniforms, health care, and also clothes, and other necessities. My aunt had a friend who worked for World Vision and told her about my family and how we lost both parents, and that we needed help. I got chosen to be in it, and so did four other friends around my neighborhood that lost both parents, one of the girls was Mitikay. They all have a special place in my heart. They had an age limit, so they only chose me out of my family, and the other four were sibling groups from different families. We were also excited and blessed to be helped and be a part of the organization. We became friends right away. It came at a time in my life when I needed it the most. I was eight and a half years old, and life was getting worse financially for my family. God brought that organization right on time. I was surprised that a family that didn't know me would care enough to sponsor me from a different continent and pay for all those things I needed. They didn't need to do that, but they wanted to; I was very grateful. I felt they showed the love of God to me. When I shared the reason for my smile, I felt like God was telling me in my heart that He was going to take care of me because I was His child first. He was keeping His word and promise by using people, using this family that sponsored me in a completely different country to take care of me. Isn't God so Amazing?

I was always mesmerized by Him. It's a promise that God will keep His word and will always take care of you, his children in unexpected ways. I loved getting new clothes from the organization. The organization that I was with also had a Bible club on Saturdays. I learned to worship God and learn more about God on Saturdays with other children my age. It was a completely different religion and church than I was used to. I was going to an orthodox church which is more formal and traditional. I remember being in an atmosphere that was a lot of fun but still felt the presence of God as we worshiped and had Bible study. I don't know the person that sponsored me through World Vision but thank you from the bottom of my heart. May God bless you tenfold; thank you for investing in my life. It truly changed my life and was such a huge blessing. It took the burden off of my eldest sister. I now see the importance of sponsoring a child. You can be changing somebody's life literally and make a difference in this world by sponsoring a child for such a small amount of money a month. I urge and encourage you to look into that and sponsor a child from an organization of your choice! Sele Enat Charitable Organization is an incredible nonprofit organization that finds sponsorship for children in an orphanage in Ethiopia. It is an orphanage that has a special place in my heart with incredible leadership. They love the children there like family, and they make them feel at home. Their website is www.seleenat.org. World Vision is also a great organization.

I was going to school and loved my classmates. I was in fourth grade at the time. I was happy and living the African life. The district we were in always kept us in contact to try to find help for my family and the other two families that the siblings have come from since we were orphans. They would help us occasionally with clothes or money, food, or find an organization to help us.

One day the district called and told Hiwet that they found something that can be life-changing for us if we get chosen and that we need to meet them at their office in a couple of days to hear more about it. Hiwet was super excited, and I was scared to find out what it was. We went to the meeting, the other two families, the siblings that were being sponsored with me with World Vision, were also there. A car pulled up, and there was an American woman and an Ethiopian lady and their driver that came through the doors. I was shocked and excited to see the American woman, we never really saw Caucasian people in Ethiopia, so it was exciting. I looked at her and was still scared and shy, trying to figure out why she was here specifically to interview my siblings and me. The American woman's name was Merrily Ripley. As she videotaped us, she asked us how old we were and what we wanted to be when we grew up. The Ethiopian lady explained and translated the unimaginable coming to my life. That thing that I thought was impossible? That thing that I thought would never and could never happen was at the stake of an interview and a decision by a person. Guess what it was? The impossible, coming to America. The lady told us she owns an orphanage here in Addis Ababa, Ethiopia. The orphanage has about 96 children, from babies to thirteen years old. It is a house where they are taken care of, fed, taught while they try to find families that would adopt them to bring them to America. I could not believe my ears. I was interviewed to possibly find a family in America that would adopt me? Do you remember what I have shared earlier in this chapter about how my sisters dreamed about coming to America? It wasn't me that had a dream to come to America; it was my sisters! And lo and behold, I was the only one interviewed because my sisters were too old. I was ten years old at the time, and my sisters were twelve and fourteen. What in the world? They are the ones with the dreams of coming to America, but I was the one that thought it was impossible and the one that got interviewed. I always thought, why dream of something that will never happen? I remember even when we had the conversations, I had even doubted God when something in my heart said, what if God wants to take you to America? Is it impossible for Him? I said to myself, yes, how could it possibly happen? That is impossible. But God can move things and align things in your life the way He wishes and can bring what is impossible to be possible in your life. I didn't know what adoption was or that it existed in Ethiopia.

One thing that I haven't mentioned yet that I wanted was parents. I wanted to have parents so badly. When I saw my friends with their mom or dad, I would be happy for them, but deep inside of me, I desired what they had. I wanted to be loved, taken care of, held and hugged, and kissed by a parent.

I wanted to have a mom and a dad again. I knew my parents weren't coming back from death. But I didn't know how it could happen, but I knew if I prayed and let God know, He can send somebody to love me and become my parents. I remember praying for God to give me parents when I was eight years old, then forgot about it after a while. My neighbors and my eldest sister talked about the orphanage and how cool it would be if I got accepted to go to the orphanage. *Are they crazy? I thought to myself. There is no way that I was going to leave my sisters. It doesn't matter where I was going and getting chosen to go too, but if it is without my sisters, I didn't want anything to do with it.* They would ask me, Sara, what if you got chosen. I would yell at them and tell them to stop talking about it. I told them I wasn't going anywhere. Hiwet would tell me, if they chose me, that I was going. She would tell me I wasn't going to pass up an opportunity like that. That kind of opportunity definitely doesn't come to our neighborhood or city often. I didn't like it when they talked about it. Since Hiwet was the eldest, she needed some advice on what to decide if I got chosen. I was scared deep inside, thinking I could possibly be chosen to go into the organization. It scared me to leave my sisters; they were the only ones I had left in this world. To think about leaving them, leaving my friends, family, neighborhood, and everything I knew, to go to an orphanage where I didn't know anybody, and to go to a new continent where I didn't know anyone or the language shocked and scared me. I was not ready. I was super attached to my sisters. My sisters were my everything. They knew how upset I would get when they talked about it in front of me, so they would talk about it behind my back. They were excited for me and for the new life I would have. It was an opportunity of a lifetime. They loved me and wanted what was best for me. We waited to hear back from them for a couple of weeks.

It took one day and one phone call to change my life forever! The unexpected and impossible were coming to pass. One evening, I came home very late from school after hanging out with some friends. I thought I was in trouble with Hiwet because I didn't let her know where I was and was gone all day. Usually, she would be upset with me, but that day when I came home ready to be scolded, she greeted me with a hug and smile. As I walked into my house, my aunt, my mom's sister, and her husband were there visiting. Everyone seemed very happy, I kept waiting to be scolded, but there was nothing. I looked at them confused; Lydia kept giggling when I knew there was something they were keeping from me, I didn't know. I went to get water, and my sister couldn't hold on to whatever they were hiding from me anymore, and blurted out, "You're going, Sara. You're going, Sara." Confused and scared, I asked her where I was going. That's when they told me the news, that I got chosen to go to the orphanage.

Hiwet said, "You're going to the orphanage that finds a family to adopt you in America; you're going to America." What? My heart sank; I didn't know what to think. She asked if I was happy. I said, "No!" They all wished they would be the ones chosen to go, but I was the one they wanted. When I asked them when, I couldn't believe my ears, she told me I was going the next day in the morning. What? It was too big of news to wrap my mind around; I was going and got accepted and going tomorrow. I started crying and said, "I am not going! I am not going; you can't make me go!"

My heart became full of fear, and I started shaking. I couldn't leave my sisters. My sister hugged me and spoke life into me, along with my aunt. I couldn't sleep that night; I was tossing and turning and couldn't believe that this was the last night that I was spending with my sisters! There was no time to say goodbye to my friends at school, or to play and spend time with my friends in the neighborhood, or to say goodbye to all my aunts and uncles that I haven't yet seen. But God was going to do what I thought was even impossible for him! I thought going to America was impossible. It wasn't even my dream. I thought it was too big of a dream and was even scared to dream of something so big as to come to America! Friends that are reading this, learn from my story that anything is possible for God. Don't doubt Him in your life. He can take and turn your situation around through one phone call, through one organization and bring something to you that you thought couldn't ever happen. He can bring something that will change your life, something that you think you didn't want or need.

"In the beginning was the Word, and the Word was with God, and the Word was God" (John 1:1, KJV).

God can speak anything into existence. He can speak into your situation and make your dreams come true. Anything, absolutely anything, is possible for Him!

Love is Letting Go

"A journey of a thousand miles begins with a single step."
—Chapter 64, *Dao De Jing*, Laozi

The next day my journey of a life that I have never dreamt of and never expected was starting. I didn't know what to expect nor had any clue of what really was happening. Nothing was hitting me yet. We woke up early in the morning and got ready for the big day. My sisters were excited for me, but it didn't really hit them that it meant they needed to let me go. There was a sacrifice in it; they didn't realize that I was not going to live with them anymore in the house and that we weren't going to be a typical family anymore. We weren't going to grow up together anymore. I didn't know what to do or say; I was in shocking mode as well. Word travels fast in my seferi (neighborhood); people come in early in the morning to say goodbye to me and wish me good luck. Some of my friends and neighbors were crying as they said their goodbye. People were crying left and right; our house was filled with people. I hated goodbye. Part of me wanted to leave without saying anything to anybody.

My aunt and uncle had to leave early in the morning; they prayed for me and left. It didn't hit me that I was never going to live in that house again. It didn't hit me that I wasn't going to play in my neighborhood or be around everything I knew and everybody I loved so much. I hugged my sister Lydia goodbye; she started crying. Out of nowhere, it hit her that this was real and that I was leaving. We said our final goodbye and held on to each other while Hiwet was telling me we need to go asap, so we weren't late. My sister Hiwet was walking me to the office; we had long ways to walk, which was great because I wasn't ready to let her go. As we were walking on the dirt road, I held on to her hand tightly, thinking this is the last time I would be walking with her. As we passed some people we knew, they would ask us where we were going so early in the morning. My sister proudly and happily told them I was getting ready to go to America and told them the story. Everybody was excited for me and this opportunity when they asked me what I thought of it. I would tell them that I didn't want to go to America. Hiwet would tell them it was because I was sad to leave but that I would be thankful for it in my life later on, which she was right.

But to be honest, it is not that I didn't want to go to America; it's because I didn't want to leave my sisters. I couldn't imagine my life without my sisters. We finally got there; both sets of the siblings were there too. Ethiopia and Nati were siblings, and Mitikay and her sister; I was happy to see them and was grateful that I wasn't the only one going. Love how God worked that out. He knew we would need each other. After my sister and the other adults signed some papers for the agency to give them legal rights of the agency being our guardian, I started crying. I couldn't help it anymore. How could my sister give me away just like that? Did she not love me? Was I really a burden for her?

How can she give them rights of guardianship when she knew I would rather stay with her at the house. I would rather live in Ethiopia with my sisters, did she not understand that. That is all I wanted. Did she not realize that I loved my family so much. Did she not realize I am going to miss my friends? Does she not know that I cannot imagine my life without her? I knew she loved me, but I didn't understand at that time. If I was everything to her, why would she give me away like this? All of these questions flooded my mind as they were telling them more about the organization and their visiting rights, and what they do! Then finally, the thing I was dreading was coming. I was hoping that this was all a dream; I didn't want it to be in reality. It was time to say goodbye and go. My heart was beating fast like an earthquake shaking the ground.

I was shaking and couldn't stop my body from doing it, and felt like I was going to faint any time. All of us kids that were going to the orphanage were crying, sobbing uncontrollably. As we were saying goodbye and hugging our siblings, we didn't want to let go. All of our siblings were holding us so tight and crying. It was an emotional time. My sister told me, Sara, I love you. I love you. Be strong! Always know how much I love you, and I am going to miss you every day. God knows what's going to happen, and he will keep you safe. I am doing this because I love you. I want what is best for you. There is nothing here. You can make something of yourself in America. You can't let this opportunity pass you by. You will have a family to take care of you. You are strong. You are Negash's daughter! *Iwedishalewi ye ne konjo.* I love you, beautiful," she said all that to me in between her sobs as we both held onto each other. The Ethiopian lady that worked for the orphanage had to pull me off my sister to get me into the car. After she finally pulled me off, I ran back to my sister, then the driver came and grabbed me to put me in the car. They were doing it in love, but it was hard to leave. My friends, too, had a hard time saying goodbye to their other siblings; after quite some time, they all got into the car sobbing. I was crying just seeing them heartbroken. After we got in the car, all our family were standing in a row crying and waving goodbye to us. We cried for a while in the car then stopped, waiting to see where we were going! That day changed my life, and it was the beginning of a crazy, awesome journey!

The title of this chapter is "Love is Letting Go". I truly believe in that. When you love something or someone so much, there will be a time where you need to let go for a time. My sister, at a young age, had to make a very important life decision; for me, it was kind of like a life-or-death decision. When those times come in your life, and you need to make a decision, you need to do it out of love and sacrifice. You need to do it out of selflessness. You cannot be selfish and look for ways to make it better for you, so it doesn't hurt you. You need to give it away or give them away because of the love that you have for that person. For those who have experienced the same thing I have experienced, if you have been given away for adoption, know it is because your family loved you that they decided to give you away to a family that can give you better opportunities and provision than they could ever give you due to their circumstances of living. Know that your family didn't reject you but loved you enough to know what is best for your future. If you have held resentment over the years for your family giving you away, forgive them. It wasn't easy for them to let you go, it was the hardest decision of their life, but they were hoping for a better future for you. My sister loved me so much that she took her selfish desires and wants out and thought, what would be the best thing for Sara's life? She thought to herself, *I know I love her and want to keep her here, and it will be easy for me, but because I love her so much that I am going to let her go, so her life is better than mine. She will have a better life in America. I can't give her all the opportunities she deserves to have. I can't give her everything that her family in America could offer her here in Ethiopia.*

So she decided if I love her so much, I need to let her go. That decision changed my life forever. The word love can be a noun or a verb. I think love should be a verb, an action word. When you love something or someone, instead of telling them you love them, you need to show them in action. Like the phrase, people say, "If you love me, show me." I know that my sister loved me so much, and she showed it to me by letting me go to the orphanage, to get adopted to a family she didn't know, to let me go to a country that she has never been in, a language that she couldn't speak. But she knew that for me to have a better life, I needed to go. She did that because she loved me so much, just like your family. I am so grateful for my sister Hiwet. Thank you so much, Hiwet! I can never thank you enough for making that hard decision to let me go so that I can have a better life. Thank you for answering yes to my destiny that God had for me. Thank you for your Yes, it has forever changed my life. I am grateful for it every day. Love is sacrifice.

When I think of love and the demonstration of love, I think of two stories from the Bible: one of them is Abraham's obedience to God and his faith in God. Abraham loved God with all his heart, mind, and soul. He showed God that he loved Him by being obedient to Him when God asked him to do a very hard thing to sacrifice his son as an offering to God. In the Old Testament, in *Genesis 22:2 (NLT), "Take your son, your only son—yes, Isaac, whom you love so much—and go to the land of Moriah. Go and sacrifice him as a burnt offering on one of the mountains, which I will show you."*

When God asked him to sacrifice his one and only Son Isaac that he dearly loved so much, Abraham had to make a very hard decision that was life or death for his son. He chose to take his selfish desires of having his son and decided to be obedient to God whom he loved and worshipped and took Isaac with him to do as the Lord had commanded him. This is incredible faith. After he arrived at the place God commanded him to go, he was getting ready to kill his son; then God stopped him by sending an angel to let him know to not put his hand on his son Isaac! God was testing Abraham. Abraham's love for God, obedience, and faith for God were tested by his son that he loved so much. He passed the test! His love for God was greater! Because of it, God gave another message to Abraham by an angel, an angel called Abraham's name once again and said Genesis 22:16-19 (NLT):

> *This is what the LORD says: Because you have obeyed me and have not withheld even your son, your only son, I swear by my own name that I will certainly bless you. I will multiply your descendants beyond number, like the stars in the sky and the sand on the seashore. Your descendants*

will conquer the cities of their enemies. And through your descendants all the nations of the earth will be blessed—all because you have obeyed me.

One man's obedience and look at the blessing! God won't ask you something so big as to sacrifice your children like He asked of Abraham, but God will ask you to give something up to show Him the love that you have for Him. Each person's sacrifice is different; maybe it is drinking alcohol, smoking, or giving up your weekend of partying. Maybe He wants you to sacrifice time that you have been wasting on watching TV too much and use that time to work on one of your gifts of writing books, drawing, writing lyrics, or working and crafting on the talent that He has already given you! That is letting go of something that you like or love to do something else to better your life, to do what He has called you to do. I don't know what that thing is but pray and ask God what it is and let go of, and do what He has called you to do. Maybe it is letting your son or daughter go to college outside of state. Maybe it is letting your son or daughter go and do mission work outside of your country or continent and letting them fulfill the calling that God has in their lives and supporting them. What you let go for love will always come back to you! Will repeat that again! *What you let go for love will always come back to you.* Abraham's son that he was going to let go was returned to him. My sisters let me go, but we were going to meet someday in God's timing again.

One of the greatest love stories ever told is one nobody on earth can out pay or do. I talked earlier about how love is an action word. We say to people, "If you love me, show me." Right?

Haven't you asked somebody in your life that? Maybe it's your children. You tell them to show you that they love you by being obedient and listening to the things that you tell them to do. Just like that, if somebody told me they love me, I want them to not only tell me, but I want them to tell me they love me by showing it to me in action by doing something for me. That is how we humans think. God showed us the greatest love that He has for us by sending His One and Only Son to die on the cross for us!

John 3:16 (NLT) says, *"For this is how God loved the world: He gave his one and only Son, so that everyone who believes in him will not perish but have eternal life."*

God loved us so much that He gave His one and Only son to give us eternal life. What a big decision that He had to make to let go of His son when He knew all the pain, everything that Jesus was going to go through. He is the Alpha and the Omega, the beginning and the end; therefore, He knows all things. He showed us He loved us by sending His Son as a sacrifice for our sins. He is a Perfect God. His son was Perfect. He still sent His Perfect son to be blamed for all the things we do and to carry the sin of the world and go through so much pain and suffering so that we can have eternal life if we believe in Him! The only thing that He asks of us is to believe in Him. He chose us before we even chose Him. We choose Him by believing in Him. By believing in Him, we can have eternal life! God is love! God is love! God is love! Thank you, God, for loving me and everyone in the world so much that you would send your one and only Son to die and wash away my sins and the world! We can never thank you enough or repay you for what you did for us so that we can live with you again! I am forever grateful for what Jesus did on the cross for you and me. We can show God that we love Him, and we are forever grateful for what Jesus did on the cross for us by loving one another. It was because of love that brought Him to this world. In John 13:34-35 (NLT), Jesus gives us a new commandment, *"So now I am giving you a new commandment: Love each other. Just as I have loved you, you should love each other. Your love for one another will prove to the world that you are my disciples."*

Let us love one another. Let us show love to our families and friends and strangers and love them because we love God.

I mentioned earlier that what you let go of because of love will always come back to you. I think of Jesus going back to heaven, going back to His Father, who let go of Him because of the love for the people He created. Abraham's son was returned to him. What a joy that Abraham had when God told him his son would live, and he returned back with him! I can't imagine the joy God had when His One and Only Son returned back to Him. What a joy it is going to be in heaven when we return back to our Heavenly Father. As we learn to love and love others. Love can be difficult at times, and so we have a scripture to remind us what love is and how to love.

> *Love is patient and kind. Love is not jealous or boastful or proud, or rude. It does not demand its own way. It is not irritable, and it keeps no record of being wronged. It does not rejoice about injustice but rejoices whenever the truth wins out. Love never gives up, never loses faith, is always hopeful, and endures through every circumstance.*
>
> 1 Corinthians 13:4-7 (NLT)

Adoption Advocate International

Adoption Advocate International was founded in 1983 in Port Angeles, Washington, by Merrily Ripley. A widespread famine affected Ethiopia from 1983 to 1985. It was the worst famine to hit the country in a century which left over 100,000 children to be orphans. There were pictures and videos of children dying of starvation on TV all over the world. If you were alive during that time, you probably remember watching it on the news.

When Merrily Ripley saw the news, it broke her heart to see so many children starving and dying, and decided to do something about it. She decided I might not be able to help all the children in Ethiopia, but I can help change one child's life at a time. She traveled to Ethiopia to see what she can do about it and to learn more about the country's rules and regulations. She got together some friends from the U.S. who also had the same passion to help children and opened an orphanage in Addis Ababa, the capital of Ethiopia. The founders envisioned an adoption agency that would serve children in need of adoptive families, with special emphasis on children particularly in need of assistance because of geography, special needs, age, or the need to be placed in sibling groups. AAI was a 501 (c)(3) tax-exempt, non-profit organization licensed by the State of Washington. The agency's vision was to find a family in America that would adopt each orphan child that came to their orphanage in any of the states in the U.S. They also had a sponsorship program for children who were too old to be adopted while living with their guardian in Ethiopia.

A.A.I has helped orphan children of all ages to be adopted not only in Ethiopia but in China, Thailand, and Ghana. When they opened the orphanage in Ethiopia, they called it Layla House, which means another house. It was a transitional home for children before they came to the U.S. Merrily had envisioned the orphanage to have lots of nannies to take care of the children and made sure she had enough staff to feed and take care of the babies at Layla House. Each child that came to Layla House had a unique story. There were babies that were put in a box and put in a garbage can be abandoned by their parents that got found by AAI staff who brought them to the orphanage. There were babies that were left at the orphanage's gate that were brought in and taken care of. There were many heartbreaking stories of babies and children whom AAI had helped. They took in all kinds of children, including special needs children, and didn't discriminate. The staff in the U.S. worked hard to find families for each child that came to the orphanage so they can get adopted and come to America. They wanted to impact and change the children's lives, and that is exactly what they did. Merrily envisioned the orphanage and made sure that Layla house was a place that the children felt at home, safe, and taken care of, and fed very well. Each child was loved by the staff at AAI and by the children. She worked hard to make sure the lifestyle we were living at Layla House was like the lifestyle we would have in America, so it would be an easier transition for us and for the families that would adopt us. AAI has helped over 6,000 orphan children find families in the U.S. during the thirty-one years they were in service just in Ethiopia. They have helped thousands of children find sponsors to be able go to school while still living in Ethiopia. They have impacted and changed thousands of lives forever. AAI was in service from 1/1/1983–3/18/2014.

> "*Be the change you wish to see in the world.*"
> —Mahatma Gandhi.

Merrily became the change she wished to see in the world and started an organization that changed thousands of lives, including mine. Her vision and drive were to help children who can't help themselves. She has fulfilled her purpose in life, caring for the children of the world. Even in her old age, at eighty-four years old, she still cares and is a foster parent to children in the U.S. I hope you are inspired by her story to fulfill your purpose in life. Because of her yes, dedication, and commitment to her calling, she changed the generation. Thousands of adopted children have gone back to Ethiopia to visit and helped orphans who are in the same place they were in years ago. She not only changed the lives of the children that got adopted, but she was also a part of the impact the adopted children made in Ethiopia. If it wasn't for her saying yes to her calling, the adopted children would not be able to fulfill their calling as well to help orphan children. Thank you, Merrily, for everything. Thank you for all that you have done in Ethiopia. Merrily is leaving a legacy in this world. Thank you for saying yes to your calling and for not quitting even when it got hard. Thank you for persevering and fulfilling your purpose in life. It is because you said yes to the plan that God had for you that I am able to say yes to God's plan in my life. Because of it, my life is changed forever. Thank you for your yes! May the Lord bless you abundantly!

*Merrily and I looking through a Memory book I made for her of
Layla house children that she has impacted! Lots of adoptees and
Parents that have adopted children from A.A.I. wrote to her showing
their appreciation and gratitude for all that she has done for them
with a before and after picture of how much their children have grown
and blossomed because of her yes to fulfill her purpose! Her memory
is wonderful. Even years later after retiring, I was amazed to see she
remembered so many of the children and their story along with their
families. Her last words to me were "there are more people we need to
help"! Let's change one life at a time!*

Our Advocate

There is physical adoption and spiritual adoption. Adoption Advocate International (A.A.I.) was the advocate for orphans to find and unite orphans to their forever family. A.A.I. became the bridge to connect orphans to the families that would adopt them here on earth. Jesus is the advocate for us to connect us back to our Heavenly Father in heaven. He is the Advocate for us to be adopted sons and daughters of God. After God made the first man Adam, he told him he could eat from any tree in the garden of Eden except for the tree that had the knowledge of good and evil. He commanded him not to eat from that tree.

"But the LORD God warned him, 'You may freely eat the fruit of every tree in the garden except the tree of the knowledge of good and evil. If you eat its fruit, you are sure to die'" (Genesis 2:16-17, NLT).

The devil came as a serpent and tempted Eve to eat the fruit of the knowledge of good and evil. He lied to her that she wouldn't die if she ate it, but she would become like God, knowing both good and evil. Eve was deceived by the father of lies, who is the devil, and ate the fruit that was forbidden and also convinced Adam to eat it. After they ate, Adam and Eve were kicked out of the garden of Eden because they disobeyed God and committed a sin by partaking in the fruit. Adam and Eve, the first humans, gave birth and lived for many years. They became the mother and father of all human beings that would live after them. All humans are fallen and born in sin because Adam and Eve sinned, and we came from them. When God told Adam that when he eats from the fruit of the knowledge of good and evil, he would surely die, he was speaking of spiritual death, not physical death. We know that because they lived for many years, but they were separated from God. They were living in God's presence in the garden of Eden until they committed sin. Sin and God cannot live together because God is holy. The Bible tells us that we are born of body, soul, and spirit. It is our spirit that connects us to God.

"God is a Spirit: and they that worship him must worship him in spirit and in truth" (John 4:24, KJV).

We died spiritually because of sin. We were separated from our Creator and Heavenly Father. All human beings were orphans in spirit. We were walking around alive physically but dead spiritually. We had no relationship with God because of sin. There was nothing that could connect us back to our Creator. God forgave our sins and made way for us to connect back to him by sending His one and only Son, Jesus Christ. Jesus was conceived by the power of the Holy Spirit by a virgin called Mary. Mary is a virgin who found favor with God and was engaged to a carpenter named Joseph when an angel appeared to her and gave her a message from God that changed her world and our world as well.

> *You will conceive and give birth to a son, and you will name him Jesus. He will be very great and will be called the Son of the Most High. The Lord God will give him the throne of his ancestor David.*
>
> Luke 1:31-32 (NLT)

Mary's reply in Luke 1:34-35 (NLT):

> *Mary asked the angel: "But how can this happen? I am a virgin." The angel replied, "The Holy Spirit will come upon you, and the power of the Most High will overshadow you. So the baby to be born will be holy, and he will be called the Son of God."*

The angel Gabriel also appeared to Joseph in a dream and told him not to be afraid of Mary's pregnancy and not to leave her.

> *As he considered this, an angel of the Lord appeared to him in a dream. "Joseph, son of David," the angel said, "do not be afraid to take Mary as your wife. For the child within her was conceived by the Holy Spirit. And she will have a son, and you are to name him Jesus, for he will save his people from their sins. "All of this occurred to fulfill the Lord's message through his prophet: Look! The virgin will conceive*

a child. She will give birth to a son and they will call him
Immanuel which means God with us."

Matthew 1:21-23 (NLT)

Jesus was born in Bethlehem in a manger because there was no room for Mary and Joseph because they were traveling at that time. Jesus is God on earth, He could have been born in the world's richest palace, but He came down and humbled Himself to be born in a manager. Jesus came to fulfill the purpose that God had for Him, which was to die for all of our sins to reunite us back to our Creator and Heavenly Father.

For God so loved the world, that he gave his only begotten
Son, that whosoever believeth in him should not perish,
but have everlasting life. For God sent not his Son into the
world to condemn the world; but that the world through him
might be saved.

John 3:16-17 (KJV)

Perish means eternal death. God sent His Son Jesus so that we don't die spiritually forever; He sent His Son so our spirit can be alive again. Jesus, who is Holy and never sinned, took the sins of the world on Himself to die on the cross for us. In the Old Testament, people offered sacrifices of goats and sheep for their sins year after year in order to worship God because, without the shedding of blood, there was no forgiveness. Because of sin, we were never going to live in heaven again with our Heavenly Father. Jesus came down to be the perfect sacrifice to take away our sins.

So Christ has now become the High Priest over all the good things that have come. He has entered that greater, more perfect Tabernacle in heaven, which was not made by human hands and is not part of this created world. With his own blood, not the blood of goats and calves, he entered the Most Holy Place once for all time and secured our redemption forever. Under the old system, the blood of goats and bulls and the ashes of a heifer could cleanse people's bodies from ceremonial impurity. Just think how much more the blood of Christ will purify our consciences from sinful deeds so that we can worship the living God. For by the power of the eternal Spirit, Christ offered himself to God as a perfect sacrifice for our sins. That is why he is the one who mediates a new covenant between God and people, so that all who are called can receive the eternal inheritance God has promised them. For Christ died to set them free from the penalty of the sins they had committed under that first covenant.

Hebrews 9:11-15 (NLT)

If it wasn't for Jesus, we would have been orphans spiritually forever. If you are a believer in Christ and have accepted Jesus as your Lord and Savior, you have found eternal life! But if you haven't yet believed and accepted Jesus into your heart, know that you are still an orphan in spirit. You are still dead in spirit and need to accept Jesus as your Lord and Savior in order to have eternal life. Accept the Perfect Sacrifice, which was slain, and shed His blood on the cross for you so that you can have eternal life with the Father. Accept Jesus into your heart, who became the bridge and the advocate for you to connect you back to your Creator and Heavenly Father. Christ has paid the price in full for all your sins that you can never pay by yourself; all you have to do is believe in him to be set free of sin forever. Our promise is stated in 1 John 2:1 (NLT):

> *My dear children, I am writing this to you so that you will not sin. But if anyone does sin, we have an advocate who pleads our case before the Father. He is Jesus Christ, the one who is truly righteous.*

The Journey Begins— Layla House

As we were driving away in the car with five of us, Desta and Bruk, the bus driver, I remember thinking, this is the last time I am driving by our neighborhood forever! All of my friends were crying in the car, so I tried to talk to them and comfort them as a big sister. The car was silent; they told us we were going to the hospital and didn't tell us the reason why. Scared to ask them, I kept quiet to myself. When we got there, they poked a needle in our arms and got some blood. I hated shots but was used to it because of my journey when I got burned and spent three months in the hospital. All my other friends were super scared of needles; it took a while to get it done. No matter what, though, they were not going to leave without getting the blood test from each one of us. While I was in the hospital room, I was thinking why they were taking blood. Then it finally clicked in. They were taking blood to see if we had Aids. I then started freaking out and was wondering what if I had AIDs; what happens then? I didn't think I had it but thinking about it started worrying me. What if my friends had it? I then started praying and asking God to please let us all be HIV-free!

I didn't think we would be able to come to America if we had AIDs. I didn't want to freak out any of my friends, so I decided to keep quiet about why we were taking the shots. I didn't think they knew, and I didn't want to bring it to their attention if they didn't. After we finished, we left. We drove to a big orphanage and saw so many kids there. They were all eating lunch; I felt so scared to be there for some reason. I was hoping it was not the place they were taking us. My heart didn't feel right; I didn't feel like I was supposed to be there. I saw some of the workers there. They didn't really look inviting to meet them, so I was hoping that that wasn't the place. After they picked something up, we were on our way again to somewhere else. I remember thanking God for not having us there at that orphanage. Finally, we got to a place where there was a big blue gate! Bruk the driver honked his horn. There was a guard that peeked in and saw the big red van, then opened the big gate for us to enter. My friends and I looked at each other like we knew this was the place. This is the orphanage that we were supposed to be at. While I was in the car and looking out the window, I saw so many children. There were a lot of children playing.

The boys were playing soccer while the girls were playing jump rope and some Ethiopian games, and some were running to the car to greet Bruk and Desta and to see who was in the car. There was a lot of laughter and joy in the place and in the kids. You can just see it through their smiles and how much fun they were having, and the joy they carried. You can feel it as well. My heart was at peace with the place before I even stepped out of the car. I was scared to be there only because I didn't know anybody and didn't have any friends other than my friends that came with me. We were so outnumbered. As my four friends and I got out of the car, we were looking around, shocked that a place like this exists in Ethiopia. Desta asked a girl named Hiwot and Mihret to show us around and get us situated. As Mihret was showing Ethiopia, Nati and I were amazed at how nice the place was and everything. Another friend there took Mitikay and her sister to show them their new home. It was so big and spacious! There were boys' and girls' rooms for older kids, and there was also a separate house for kids that were younger. The big girls' room was very big. There were lots of bunk beds. It could fit at least sixteen girls in that room sleeping separately on the bed. Outside of it, there was a classroom. There was an office that the kids weren't supposed to go to. Then beside it was the eldest boys' room, which was also very big but not as big as the girls' room. There was also another separate house in the same gate where there was a kitchen, a big dining room with lots of tables and chairs. Then just outside of it was a big living room that had a TV and three big sofas, and a bookshelf with lots of books. It was very bright and inviting in there. The wall was yellow, and in the living room, the wall was painted with flowers and different kinds of designs in there. No more newspaper-covered walls like my house.

It was beautiful. The floor was nice and clean. No dirt floors in the whole place. I remember admiring how big and beautiful the whole place was. I felt like I was already in America with how nice everything was. The bathroom had a toilet like I have never seen before. I was used to having a toilet which was a big hole that you squat on and do your business, but this bathroom was like bathrooms you see on TV when we watched

American movies. It was luxurious. I didn't know how to use it, but thankfully my friend thought to show us how to use it. I was thinking to myself, where has it been all these years. Another cool thing about the bathroom was there was a bathtub in the bathroom too. As they were telling us, this is where you take a shower, and how to use the knobs to use hot water. It was a dream come true for me because I loved taking hot showers. The way we did it at home was by boiling water on a propane stove, that is, if you have gas, and getting a big bowl to sit in it and grab water with a cup and pour it over your body. It was too much work; I was thinking how Americans have it so easy. Loved the setup of the bathroom, seeing it for the first time. We then went to another building that was a house for babies and kids that are less than eight years old. The babies and toddlers had their own big beautiful room with lots of cribs. I was told somebody from America came and painted the wall in the room with trees, monkeys and did the Lion King theme in there. The girls had their own room. That was where the girls that came with me to the orphanage were staying. There was another room for the boys under eight years of age as well and a bathroom in that building. I stayed with the eldest girls in the big girls' house. There were three bathrooms in the whole orphanage; it worked out well, though, for all of us. My first day at Layla house, as I was experiencing what the children do and the way they do things there, I remember being so excited to be there and want to get used to everything. There were lots of children so I could have lots of friends. It seemed like every one of the kids was taken care of and fed very well and were very happy. I was excited to be a part of the family. I was very shy, though, so that didn't help my desire to make friends quickly, but I knew I was at a good place, and it was definitely the place that God wanted me to be at.

I met two sisters there who were very sweet and very busy. They had lots of appointments to go with one of the employees there and were going in and out of the gate. As I asked my friend, she told me they were going to appointments because they were getting paperwork done for their process to go to America in three days. What? That just blew my mind. I asked again, is this really true? Are they really going to America? This orphanage really find families to take people to America? She said Yes! Merrily and the A.A.I. staff found a family for them in America; now, the process is finishing up. I was astounded that what I have been hearing is really true; people do find families to adopt them and go to America through this orphanage. I was so excited for them and wondered and imagined when it would be my turn to go to America.

She took me to the living room, where we ate and hung out there. In the hall of that building were pictures of lots of children on an Ethiopian mesob. Mesob is an Ethiopian flat handmade decoration.

The hall was filled with pictures of Ethiopian kids with American families. I was told that after six months of living in America, the parents that adopt children from Layla House send updates of the kids with pictures and messages on how they are adapting to the new culture and family. There were so many pictures of Ethiopian kids that went to America from Layla House over the years, from the same orphanage that I just got put into. I still couldn't believe this was all true. They are an organization that keeps its promise to find families for orphans. I thought it was too good to be true. They told me they were excited to go and meet their families! The girls that were getting ready to go to America told me I was going to love Layla House; though they were excited to meet their families and go to America, they said they were really going to miss Layla House. After seeing so many of their friends go to America, they were excited that it was finally their turn. After talking to them, I knew I would fit into Layla House. It was just a matter of time. We played some games with some of the kids. It was a very loud place with so many kids running around and screaming and playing. The older boys were playing soccer for hours; I didn't see anybody standing by themselves alone. They all had friends to play with or if they got tired of playing a game. They went and joined another group that was playing something else. It was awesome to see.

At 6 p.m. in the evening, one of the kids rang the bell very loud; I was startled and was wondering what the bell was for. Then saw a flock of kids running and screaming dinner time! Dinner time! That night after everybody got food, one of the kids got up and said, "Let's pray." All the kids closed their eyes, put their arms together, and bent their heads in honor of God as they were giving thanks to Him for the food and to bless and nourish it to their bodies and to provide for those that don't have food to eat. After the prayer got done, they all clapped with a rhythm; you could tell it was what they did every day. They were giving God the glory and honor by clapping afterward to give Him thanks. They all started eating and chatting with the kids that were sitting with them at their table. We ate delicious spaghetti. I could see they fed them good when I saw a lot of the kids going again for seconds. After dinner, some of the kids played outside while other kids washed all the dishes that were used. They took turns washing all the dishes for every meal.

At 8 p.m., after everyone put their pajamas on, they came to the living room to do devotions which they did every night. That was new to me; it was awesome to see children seeking God. They prayed and sang lots of worship songs that I didn't know. It was beautiful, though. Someone shared a bible story, and then they closed it out with a prayer. What amazed me was all of them were totally focused and submitted to God as they worshiped and prayed. I was very observant, and you could tell that all the kids did their worship out of their hearts and not because they were made to. I had never seen little children that were Holy Spirit-filled and on fire for God. That night Mitikay and her sister, Ethiopia, and I slept together in a big bed in the big girl's room. As I laid down and pondered on everything that happened that day, I thanked God for everything. I prayed that God would take care of and protect my sisters. I thanked him for bringing me to Layla house and for him to please help me to transition easily. The girls in our room were nice and let us sleep in when everybody got up early and got ready for the day. I heard someone say, they are new; let them sleep. What a nice gesture!

After we got ready for the day, we went back to the hospital and came back to the orphanage. I stood by the office. Because I still was trying to figure out if they found out if we had HIV or not. They didn't tell us anything, and it was worrying me. As I think about it now, I think God knew because he let me hear this conversation. I feel like it was a divine intervention of me listening and being there at the right time. I heard the worker Desta who brought us to the orphanage, say to this other worker there who does paperwork in the office, as I eased dropped standing by the office. "I am so excited. Can you believe it? All of the five children that came yesterday are all HIV-free! They don't have any sign of any disease. They are all healthy and good. Praise God! Wow, I am so happy! This doesn't happen a lot! When I take five kids, there usually is at least one kid that has HIV, but all these kids don't! God has his hands on these kids." Yes, He does. I was beaming with joy and super excited to hear the news! I couldn't stop smiling. I waited there to hear the whole conversation as I was thanking God so much for answering my prayer and for our great health and being HIV-free! My heart would have been broken to lose any of my friends I have shared so much of my life with already and now here to take the journey together. I was my sister's keeper. I promised to myself that day that I will always take care of these four special friends of mine; I will always watch out for them and be their big sister. Nobody knew them like I did. Nobody has shared their life story and where they come from like me. I was excited that they were going to take the journey of finding a forever family and going to America together with me. As well as with the group of kids that were already there in the amazing organization. I was excited to start this new journey with all of the Layla House children. It was the beginning of something good I felt in my heart; it was the beginning of an amazing journey together.

There were ninety-six children, including babies, in 2003, at Layla House! That is a lot of children! There were a few women that did all the laundry for all the children every week. We had five house mothers that take care of the eldest kids. They took turns working morning, afternoon, and graveyard shifts. They were all very amazing, beautiful, sweet ladies who had a heart for kids. They loved their jobs, and it showed how much they truly loved us by how they cared for us. We all adored them. We had two favorite house mothers that we loved so much. They didn't see it as a job but a place they went to spend time with their family. They took care of us so we can also take care of the little ones, made sure we learned how to take care of ourselves. They played with us. They did everything that mothers do for us. They taught us and made sure we had great manners and that we knew how to respect our elders. They did all of that through the love they poured out onto us. They were amazing mothers. The babies and toddlers had their own set of loving mothers that took care of them day and night. We greeted all of our caregivers and all the staff that worked at Layla house with hugs and kisses every day when they came into work.

Friends Who Become Forever Family

"Family isn't always blood. It's the people in your life who want you in theirs; the ones who accept you for who you are. The ones who would do anything to see you smile and who love you no matter what."

Unknown

Each child, boy, or girl that entered the blue Layla House gates that were accepted to be there came as a stranger. Unknown to ourselves, how life was going to be. Wondering if people were going to like us, if we were going to make friends or how we were going to be treated, entering the gate was a very nerve-racking but exciting moment for each one of us. As we entered and met each person that was in the compound, we all felt peace in our hearts, and we knew that everything was going to be okay. We felt the love and joy that the other kids carried and how they shared it with each other, so we knew it was just a matter of time for each one of us to feel at home as they do and have the joy and love they carried for each other as well! We were excited to make friends and get to know each other.

The environment was so friendly and loving that it became easy for us to get to know each other. It didn't take much time before each one of us blended in and became part of the family. It probably took two to three weeks the most for each one of us to feel and know that we belong there and be immersed in the love, friendship, and atmosphere that was there and feel at home! We had a blast with each other playing different games. We had amazing relationships with our teachers. They weren't just teachers to us but people we looked up to and loved. Our teachers always played hide and seek, soccer, tag, and different games with us during our break time or after school. Some of them would sit down and talk to us or advise us on life. Their job description was only to teach us in class, but they did way more than that. For every child, love is spelled *time*!

There is nothing we desired more than time with people that loved us and that we loved, so they gave us just that. We all love them all so dearly, and we can't wait to see them someday. Each group did their homework together with the ones we clicked with the most and helped each other. If we didn't do our homework, we were always disciplined, so we knew to remind each other to do our homework so we could be the smart kids we knew we were destined to be. We all tutored and helped each other understand each subject. We had a lot of bright kids at Layla House. Everyone was great and had the heart to serve and help each other. Each kid was comfortable around each other. We saw each other as brothers and sisters, and we were all one big happy family, literally. I love how God orchestrates everything in our lives. The Bible says He knows all things. He knows what we need and what needs to happen before the next thing that happens. He not only knows what we need in our future, but He also knows what our hearts need.

Looking back now, He knew that each one of the kids that came to Layla House needed each other first and needed to be in each other's lives before He brought us to our families in America. Whether we knew it or not, our hearts needed each other. We all were in the same situation, losing our parents and becoming orphans. God knew that we needed to be surrounded by other kids that had gone through the same thing. I can't imagine how hard life would have been not only for us but for the families that would adopt us here in the U.S. if we were brought to America right out of our house. We would have not felt like we belonged and would have had a very hard time connecting with our families because we would have felt like they didn't understand us or what we went through in our life back home. But since He had a plan to bring us to Layla House to bond with each other and share each other's stories, connect, heal and strengthen our hearts, our transition was a lot better. Another benefit of going to Layla House before coming to the U.S. is, we could all lean on each other in hard times because of what we went through together. God is too Good! Each kid at Layla House had a unique special connection with each other. We all clicked and got along with each other. It was a lot easier for a lot of the children to open up and share how they lost their parents and family members because all of us there faced the same situation. Nobody was the odd one out. We all understood each other. As we let each other into our hearts, we all connected and had a deep special bond with each other. Everyone that came from Layla House, whether they came at the time we did, or they came after we came to the U.S., we all have a special bond and connection just coming from the same place and did the same things we did. It is funny how we immediately connect, even if it were kids that we never met at Layla House. People that came before or after us. We talk like we have known each other for a long time because of that connection. It is amazing.

All we knew, understood, and felt was Layla House was our home, and all of the boys and girls there or from there were our brothers and sisters. All of the workers were like our parents. We created bond with each other and a friendship that will never be broken forever. We cared for each other and looked out for each other like I have never seen kids care for each other before. We loved each other and were very affectionate, giving brothers and sisters. While others felt it was easy to open up and share. For some, slowly but surely let each other into our lives. We are not friends but family. We were there for each other at Layla House, and we are in each other's life now after coming to America. It's incredible how we all managed to stay in each other's lives in spite of the different states we live in, the different life schedules we have, and the different careers we are all pursuing. It doesn't matter if we haven't talked for a month, six months, or a year; when we do talk, it's like we just talked yesterday. I love those kinds of friendships that last forever. We created those special bonds while we were at Layla House that will never be taken away. We were there for each other through thick and thin. We had many special moments of sharing about our lives and what our life was like before Layla House. We shared with each other how our parents passed away, what happened after that, and the struggle and trials we faced before entering the gates of Layla House. It was incredible to hear everyone's story. I remember being so amazed by how strong these friends of mine were. They were warriors in their families. Warriors in how they took care of their siblings, their sick mom or dad when they were only five to eight years of age themselves. If I listed out everyone's story, you would be in tears and wouldn't be able to finish reading this book. It will be too much to hear and understand, but God has changed all of our lives forever by bringing us to Layla House to be each other's support as sisters and brothers before we come to the unknown all the way to America.

We also gave lots of love, hugs, and kisses every day to the people that cared for us as well like our social worker Desta, Bruk, everyone that worked at the office, our house mothers, our teachers, and everyone that helped clean Layla House. We were very respectful and affectionate towards them. We had a couple of mothers who cooked delicious food for us. We had a bell that one of the kids would ring to let us know when we are being called for breakfast, lunch, or dinner, or when we need to all gather up in the living room. We were fed great food for each meal and ate until we were full. It's a lot to cook for eighty-ninety children every day for breakfast, lunch, and dinner. But our chefs were great and made us delicious food. They showed us they loved us by the time and effort they put into making each meal; they always made leftovers so we can go for seconds. They had ninety energetic hungry children and employees to cook for. The older kids sometimes would go and help prepare dinner. I loved doing that with my friends and helping in the kitchen. We ate peanut butter toast and tea, pancakes, and some type of bread with tea for breakfast. For lunch, we always ate injera (Ethiopian flat bread) with different types of meat or veggie delicious stew (Ethiopian main dish). Ethiopians usually eat that for breakfast, lunch, and dinner. We loved having it once a day, though, so we wouldn't get tired of it even though it was delicious. For dinner, we had Spaghetti, rice, macaroni, and different types of American food. Merrily and the agency wanted us to get used to eating American food while we were in Ethiopia, so it is an easier transition for the child and the family for when we come to America. We loved that idea because we loved every dish that was made for us! We were spoiled by how much we ate and the different types of food we ate. Not a lot of orphanages have that privilege. There were some kids that got transferred to Layla House after staying at a different orphanage, and they said Layla House was 100 times better than the orphanage they were in, in the way they were treated, the environment, and the way they were fed! At Layla House, each kid, all ninety of us ate till we were full and could go for seconds for each meal, and they were great meals made with love. The other children that transferred would tell us we live in heaven compared to the other kids at the other orphanages.

The way they lived at the other orphanage was completely different. Thank you, God, for heaven on earth! If you asked anyone that was at Layla House during the year that I was there in 2003 and after, they would all tell you that Layla House was heaven on earth. We took turns praying for each meal before we ate. Gratitude is everything; we were taught that at a young age. We were very comfortable with each other and ate off of each other's plates. We all loved each other and borrowed each other's clothes all the time. I remember sharing clothes most of the time with one of my best friends Seble. Even though we all had our own beds, the girls always slept with one of their friends. Seble would describe it as having a sleepover with your best friend every night. No one liked to sleep by themselves. We heard that in America, most of the time, you would get your own room and your own bed. It didn't make sense to us. Why sleep alone when you can sleep together with the ones you love? That is a cultural difference. The Adoption advocate workers tried to have us sleep by ourselves, so we can get used to sleeping by ourselves, so when we came to America, it will be an easier transition. But we always climbed into each other's beds when they left. We couldn't stand it; even when we lived in our own houses, there were at least four people in one bed in one room, not one person in one bed in one room. It sounded luxurious, though; we were excited about the life we would have in America. That was our culture, and that was what we loved doing. It was hard to grasp the American way of living. We always told them we would get used to it when we come to the U.S., but for then, we needed to sleep together as much as we could because we won't have that chance ever again.

In the big girls' room, my roommates (fourteen of us) washed and braided each other's hair while we were listening to mezmur (Ethiopian Christian Gospel songs) by Dagi Tilahun and Yosef Ayle. Our house mothers also helped us. We would sing as we were braiding each other's hair. We braided our hair every two weeks. We also took care of the little girls at Layla House as well and washed and braided their hair. That taught us and got us ready to take care of our hair here in the U.S. to make it easier for our families when we would get here. We learned how to be self-sufficient and independent people.

All these memories and more bonded us together closer. I was grateful to make new memories with my friends who came to Layla house with me. We all became really close with each other and with everyone that lived at Layla House. We were not friends but brothers and sisters for life. To Everyone that came from Layla House, this quote is for you.

> *"Family is like branches on a tree, we grow in different directions, yet our roots remain as one."*
>
> Unknown

I love you all, Layla house family!

Christmas at Layla House

Every Layla House child loved Holidays and always looked forward to each holiday that was coming up. Our favorite was American Gena (Christmas)! In Ethiopian culture, it is not very common to give out gifts for Christmas. The tradition was to get new Habesha Kemis (Ethiopian traditional dress) or get new clothes for the holidays if your family was able to afford them. A lot of my friends and I at Layla House have never received any gifts for Christmas before. The first Christmas we had at Layla House, we had a big, tall Christmas tree with all of our pictures on them instead of ornaments. It was our tradition, and it was very cool to see ninety-six beautiful faces on the tree. The manager of Layla House surprised us when she came with her car full of wrapped-up presents to put under the tree. There was a present under the tree for all of ninety-six children and every Layla House employee! It was incredible. We were so excited we could hardly wait for Christmas. We counted down days and watched American Christmas movies every night to get into the spirit of Christmas, just people in America. We didn't have snow in Ethiopia, so to get into the spirit even more, the manager had asked people to make snowflakes out of paper to dump on the ground on the day of Christmas. It was Magical and amazing! We all cleaned up, got our hair braided very nicely, and wore our nicest outfits on Christmas Day! Each one of us was shining. After breakfast that day, we had over 100 chairs outside, and all the young children and employees took their seats to start celebrating Christmas while all the older boys and girls got ready to perform a Christmas Play to all our audience.

We did a Christmas play showing Christ's birth! We had a drama teacher who was directing us to put on an amazing show. We practiced it for weeks. The year 2003 was the year I was there along with many friends. We had Our youth leaders, the eldest in the group, play Mary and Harold. We had angels and wise men, props for the play and the star. You name it, we had it and played out the whole Christmas story! It turned out incredible. We were using a doll as a baby Jesus, and during the play, one of the house mothers brought one of the baby orphans that was at Layla House for Our Mary to carry as baby Jesus! It was epic and perfect timing. The manager of Layla house had someone record a video of the whole Christmas day so we can have it as a memory of when we came to the U.S. It was given to each one of us when we came to the U.S. All of us that were involved in the play had a blast. Afterward, we got into our regular clothes and sat down for the rest of the show. We each got a gift. The A.A.I. staff fund-raised and found a Christmas sponsor for each one of us in America, so they were able to afford it and give us Christmas presents. Thank you so much to all that sponsored us each year. Thank you to All of the A.A.I. staff in the U.S. for working so hard to find a sponsor for each child, on top of everything you all had to do so we can have presents for Christmas! We are forever grateful for everything you all have done for us. May God bless you abundantly for all those who were involved. We were so excited when we opened our presents and found traditional Ethiopian outfits for each person. The boys got theirs, and the girls got *habesha kemis*. It was the first time we owned our own traditional Ethiopian Outfits. It meant a lot to us to own that and be able to bring that to America for memory. It was a way to have part of our culture with us and keep the memory of our country. Even the babies got theirs. It was amazing, and I have kept mine even though I don't fit in it anymore, as most of you Layla house friends have for memory. We also got watches, dolls, cars, and many toys. That place was full of ecstatic children that couldn't contain their excitement. Everyone was so happy and Joyful. It was one of the happiest days ever that we would never forget! We were all decked out in our traditional Ethiopian outfits and got pictures taken, and sang our hearts out in traditional Ethiopian holiday songs. It is all on a video we each own. We all were so blessed and so lucky to live at Layla House. We were all loved and taken care of and were blessed to experience all of those memories together. It is one of our fondest memories from Layla House. We did that every Christmas. I love that it was a continuous thing, and each Layla House kid experienced it during the thirty years Layla House was open. Shout out to Merrily and all of A.A.I. staff for all the years of hard work. Thank you from our hearts to yours from each one of us for everything. During every American and Ethiopian holiday, we had traditional Ethiopian holiday food as well. Traditional Ethiopian food consists of *injera, doro wat*

(Chicken stew), *Kitfo, tibs,* and many other special dishes. Ethiopians love to feast, and so did we at Layla House. We were very blessed to be treated so well. Not a lot of orphanages treated their kids like that or fed their kids like we were fed. We even celebrated Halloween there with Merrily there. When it was dark, they separated us in different groups, and all the leaders went into different rooms as we went to each room to trick and treat. Some of them were dressed up very freaky and scared us. They had people hiding and poking out of different places before we got to every destination. It was very funny because all of us kids were scared and were screaming! You would hear screams and laughs from different groups. It was very cool and well played out. We all had a blast. So many amazing memories. Thank you, A.A.I. staff in America and in Ethiopia, for all the amazing memories! May God bless you!

The Power of Praying Through
(Seble's Story)

Seble, Edil and Sara at Layla House

Seble is one of my best friends from Layla House that I love so dearly, and that has taught me a very valuable lesson that I have been using throughout the years! She taught me and so many of her friends from there the power of praying through. I know that you will be impacted by her story and learn why you never give up praying for things that matter to you the most. She teaches us the power of prayer and the power of praying through and circling our prayers with the promises of God through her incredible story. There is absolutely nothing that God cannot do! Her story illustrates the power of praying through the biggest desires of your heart that you care about the most until God brings it to you, no matter how long it takes, even if it takes years. There is power in praying through, and if you decide to pray through, the promise you have been waiting for will be fulfilled. Her story is a story of loss, struggle, faith, trust, hope, and love!

One night after a fun-filled day of soccer, fun games, laughter and staying up late with all the big girls, our roommates, and sharing what our life was like before Layla House, we all went to bed very late We were all sound asleep until we were awoken by a frightened scream and cry. We all jumped out of our bed with all of our sleepy, exhausted bodies. We were looking around to see who it was and found my best friend Seble asleep but crying and hitting the pillow, saying no! All of us girls rushed to her bed to see what was wrong. She was having a nightmare. We held her down and hugged her, and tried to wake her up. I remember her waking up, and as tears rolled down her face, she asked us where her brother was. She kept saying, "Where is my brother? Where is Joseph?" That night was when I found out that Seble has two brothers. Some of us were shocked to find out she had another brother because we only knew of her brother Ephrem, that was at Layla House with us. We tried to calm her down and tell her everything's okay. She was having an anxiety attack. She wouldn't take no for an answer. She wanted to see her brother then, not in the morning. She demanded to see him then. But her brother was nowhere close to Layla House. Some of the girls knew something I didn't know yet. We helped her calm down, hugged and loved her, and told her we would talk about everything in the morning. We told her she needed to get some rest. One of the girls snuggled with her that night to comfort her and so she doesn't sleep alone. The next morning I asked Seble about her life before Layla House, and that morning, our friendship changed forever when she opened up and shared with me her story that is so close to my heart and has been since that day in 2004.

Seble is a special woman. I knew it from the day I met her, but I just didn't know what that thing was that made her so special and light up. She is very reliable, very responsible, very strong, very loving, kind, sweet, and had the most amazing personality that made everybody like her. She has a magnetic personality that collects people to her, and everyone wants to be friends with Seble. Everyone at Layla House loved her. She had a contagious joy and laugh every day that made people want to be around her. The way she carried herself and the way she treated everyone with kindness, you will never know or figure out that she was going through any hard things in her life or has gone through so much. When I think of Seble and what she was going through and how she handled it, a scripture that comes to mind is Nehemiah 8:10 (NLT): *"The joy of the Lord is your strength."* God gave her his joy in the midst of heartache. As I think back now, I realize that scripture really did come to life in Seble's life truly but not only in her life but every child's life at Layla House. We literally experienced the joy of the Lord that became our strength. American visitors and the employees at Layla House saw that they truly did come to life in all of our lives. When they heard of all our tragic stories and traumas we have been through, they were mesmerized and would ask themselves how in the world we had so much joy and strength. They realized it wasn't from us but that it was from God Himself. All Layla House children have gone through a lot of trials in their young life, trials no child should ever go through. But joy and strength were what was flowing out of us. Joy and strength were what was flowing out of Seble, so I was shocked to hear her story of her life before Layla House.

Seble was the oldest in the house at the age of eight and had two younger siblings. Her dad was absent. Her mom was the caregiver and the provider in the house. It's very hard and expensive to take care of one child as a single mom in Ethiopia, let alone three young kids. Her mom was a beautiful, loving, hardworking mom and adored her kids, so she did all she could to take care of them. They all loved and adored her and were very close to her. Everything was going great until her mom got very sick suddenly. When her mom knew and realized she didn't have long to live, she told Seble to come to her bedside one day, so she could tell her something important and something that would change Seble's life forever.

As they were holding hands, she asked Seble to promise her one very important promise and something that Seble would take to heart and would have to keep forever. She told her that she didn't have much time to live and promised her that she will always take care of her two younger brothers and never let them out of her sight. She was going to be her brother's caregiver from then on, even though she was only eight years old. She had to grow up very fast and be a responsible person. As tears were rolling down Seble's face, she made the promise to her mom. Soon after that, unfortunately, her mom passed away. While not having both parents was already hard enough and hard for an eight-year-old to understand and experience, she was responsible not only for her life but also for her two brothers. They lived with their uncle, who was a great person. Her uncle was unable to provide for three children on his own. He knew the best thing to do was to take them to an orphanage that would take care of them very well and give them a better life than he could. Love is sacrifice. Love is selfless. Seble didn't mind where she lived as long as her two brothers were with her; she needed them with her to keep the promise that she had made to her mom, and they were all the family she had. After a few weeks of living at that orphanage, she was told that Ephrem and her were going to get transferred to another orphanage but not her other brother.

She didn't understand, nor did she know the reason why her other brother couldn't come with them; they never explained to her. All she remembered was her mother's words and the promise she had made to her mom. She flat-out told them no! She told them if Ephrem and her go, then Joseph has to go with them as well. They could not be separated. That could have not been an option; they had to work it out. The employees told her that they were sorry, but it was only her and Ephrem that were going to go to Layla House. That was the saddest day in Seble's life; all she could do was cry. She was heartbroken and had no control over the situation. The decision was already made. How can she keep the promise that she had made to her mom to always take care of them and keep an eye on them? The siblings said goodbye to each other as they were crying. As uncontrollable tears rolled down her face, she felt helpless, distraught, and felt she was letting her mom down. She felt she was breaking that promise that she had made to her mom before she passed away. She didn't know what to think or do as they arrived at Layla House. After she got to Layla house, she loved the place, the kids, the employees, and the Layla house life way better than the other orphanage she was at. She was so happy to have Ephrem with her but still was heartbroken about Joseph. She wished he could come and live with them at Layla House so they could all be together again as a family. She lost hope in how he would get there. When she realized that it wouldn't be too long before Ephrem and her would find a family in America and move, her thought of not having Joseph with her devastated her and broke her heart. The thought of living on different continents and not seeing her brother ever again really was hard for her. She was hopeless. She later found out her brother had some kind of sickness, and that was the reason he wasn't allowed to go to Layla House. When you lose all hope, where does your hope come from? Who can you lean on and trust to be your hope when facing hard trials in your life? It is God! He is the Hope of glory! She learned about Jesus Christ! She learned that God is our hope! Every night, during our worship and praise time, she developed a tight relationship with

God, who became her hope! She believed, prayed, and hoped that God would someday answer her prayer to have the three of them live together again.

> *For we are saved by hope: but hope that is seen is not hope:*
> *for what a man seeth, why doth he yet hope for? But if we*
> *hope for that we see not, then do we with patience wait for it.*
>
> Romans 8:24-25 (NLT)

She hoped for something that was unseen and only possible through God. Something that man cannot do. She hoped and prayed someday that the family that would adopt her would adopt him as well, so they could live as a family again in America. Then she could carry out the promise that she had made to her mother. This girl amazes me because every night during worship, she would get on her knees, cry out to God about her brother's situation. She worshiped and praised God, even though her heart was broken. When she couldn't take it anymore and had an anxiety attack a few times while she was at Layla house, we were there for her and comforted her. We could only be there to support her and be there for her whenever she needed us. But she knew who to lean on as a nine-year-old. It was God, and she reached out to Him for His strength.

"Each time he said, 'My grace is all you need. My power works best in weakness.' So now I am glad to boast about my weaknesses, so that the power of Christ can work through me" (2 Corinthians 12:9, KJV).

We learned so much from her during our time at Layla House. Our hearts were broken for her; we cried with her, slept with her, talked with her, prayed with her, kept her in our prayers that someday God would make this dream come to reality the whole two years she was at Layla House. My beautiful friend went through a lot during that time, but she kept her faith! The time came when she found an amazing family in America, and the adoption process was done, and it was time to start the journey with one of her brothers to a different continent, leaving her heart, her brother, still in Ethiopia. As hard as it was for her to leave, she was praying harder, trusting God and believing it could still happen. She kept the faith and hope, even while she was living in the U.S. that he would someday join her family. Faith is believing in something that is unseen but hoped for! She is a prayer warrior. This is the reason why we all need to pray until we receive what we are believing God for. If it is part of God's plan for our lives, it will happen. The power of praying through is the key to receiving what you are believing God for. The Bible says, "God wants to give us the desires of our hearts." Seble prayed through and believed God for the desire of her heart and that he would give it to her at his own timing. I am here to share with you in tears that God did the miracle. He made the impossible possible. His Word does not come void. He does what He says He will do. He will give you the desire of your heart no matter how long it takes. He is faithful to fulfill His promises in our lives. Her brother Joseph got adopted to her family and is now in America, living with her and Ephrem. They have reunited and finally a family again! Seble doesn't carry the guilt anymore; she is keeping the promise she had made to her mom to always take care of her two brothers and never let them out of her sight. Her brother is home! This is a story that is hard to write without tears rolling down my face. It is a story that is so close to my heart and was a part of my life for many years. I grew to love her little brother that I have never met yet because of experiencing this story with my best friend. God gave Seble the desire of her heart. Because she prayed through, she received what she prayed for, and her brother's life was changed forever! Your commitment to praying through could change your destiny as well as the destiny of others! It shifted and changed her brother's destiny. Thank you, God, for answering Seble's prayer! Thank you to Seble's family that adopted all the siblings. Thank you for being obedient to God when he called you to adopt all of them and being God's hands and feet in this world. Thank you, Seble, for letting me share your beautiful story! I love you, Seblecho. My life and so many other lives are impacted by this story. I hope it teaches you and shows you to keep praying and to pray through until you receive the desires of your hearts from the One and Only One God that fulfills them! Always be in prayer!

"And this is the confidence that we have in him, that, if we ask anything according to his will, he heareth us" (1 John 5:14, KJV).

Fun at Layla House

One of the fun things that the older boys and girls loved was playing pranks on each other! These pranks were very thought out; I will get you no matter what kind of pranks. They were great pranks that I will never forget. It makes me laugh remembering all of them. None of us girls liked going to the bathroom by ourselves, so we always dragged each other to go together. It is not like we needed the buddy system since we never were allowed to go outside the gate. It was only Layla House kids that lived there. There was always a guard on duty, so we were protected. One of the pranks that the boys loved doing was showering us with a bucket of water when we went to the bathroom! They would fill up a bucket of water and somehow tie it to the door and had it way up on the ceiling. So when someone like Seble and I or the other girls opened the door to go to the bathroom, the whole bucket of water poured down on us! I remember Seble and me screaming at the top of our lungs when we were showered with that cold water unexpectedly a few times. Soaking wet and upset, we would run after them to beat them up and get them back. We used our chama (shoes) to beat them. It never hurt them enough; they would just laugh very hard for getting us. It was funny to them but not to us. The boys got each one of the girls at different times. We never knew what they were up to; they were very sneaky, and we could never tell. The girls plotted the same prank on them and got most of them too a couple of times.

They were furious for a little while but would get over it as we were laughing in their faces. Seble and I were two peas in a pod. We were never separated. I remember one time both of us plotted a prank for two specific boys that were getting on our nerves with all the pranks they were doing on us. We loved our brothers, but we were determined to get them. We did the same prank and filled up the bucket of water to get the boys. There were separate boys' and girls' bathrooms in our rooms. We went to the boys' bathroom and plotted the prank, and waited anxiously for the boys to go to the bathroom. They were taking a long time to go to the bathroom, and we were worried that Bereket, our youth leader, would accidentally go into that bathroom instead of the boys. We started becoming obvious and were playing by the bathroom so we could actually see the boys' faces when that water would pour down on them and would tell the boys to go to the bathroom to trick them. They knew something was up, so they weren't going to take our offer. We were standing on guard just in case Bereket or one of the employees didn't accidentally try to go to that bathroom. Unexpectedly all of us kids got called in to our rooms for room inspection. Before we had time to get it down, we were called by name to go to the room. After we left, guess who walked into that bathroom? After all the long wait and anticipation?

Bereket! Our youth leader! Seble and I got called out of our room and were told that Bereket needed us right away. Bereket was the eldest at Layla House. He was our leader and had the privilege of discipling us because of how grown up and wise he was for his age. As we walked out of our room shivering, scared of what he was going to do to us and how mad he was going to be. We both started praying very hard and very fast that he would forgive us for what we did. We heard he was very mad and soaking wet with the bucket of water that was dumped on him trying to go to the bathroom. The prank served the person we didn't intend it for. We wanted to scream and run away because we were sorry and scared. Seble and I behaved well. It wasn't normal for us to do something outrageous like that. Everybody knew that about us and was surprised that we did it. He was sitting up straight on a chair in the middle of the soccer field. He only sits there when he is correcting someone. It felt like the longest walk ever, with our hearts beating faster than we could breathe. When we reached him, both had our heads down and were very ashamed of what we did. He asked us if we were the ones that made the prank and told us to not lie to him. We were not good liars, and we knew we couldn't lie to him because it would get us into more trouble. He was a great leader, had a lot of wisdom, and taught us a lot of values! But when he needs to teach us something, he will do what he needs to do to get his point across and discipline us. So you could see why we were scarred. We told him that it was us and that we were sorry that we will never do it again. We told him we intended to get the boys, not him. He asked us who it was for; we told him and the reason we did it. We were almost in tears without him saying anything yet. Then he did something that we were shocked to see! He gave each of us a handshake and told us we did a good job! We looked at each other in disbelief. Is this really happening? He hugged us and told us not to be scared, and told us not to do it again. We walked away clean. All of our friends loved what we did and always would talk about it while we were at Layla house.

Another time the whole boys' room except Bereket played a prank on the big girls' room. They brought glue and poured it on our cement floor in our big room. They made it so smooth and glued it there that we didn't really notice it until we stepped into our room and found our surprise! We don't know how they got away with that with no one watching them, but they did! We walked into our room, some of us with flip flops and others with bare feet. Our feet were getting stuck to the floor! Wherever we stepped, there was glue on it! We couldn't move. We were so upset with them. They got us good on that prank. We reported them to our house mothers and Bereket. They all got in big trouble and were told to clean our rooms. Instead of having them clean our room, we decided to clean our room ourselves and told the boys to never step into our room ever again. They had lots of good pranks on us. We laughed about it later and forgave them. It became the stories we shared with each other of remembering those good times. For some reason, I only remember them pranking us more than the pranks we did on them. There was a time when they put grass and dirt in the big girls' beds. We were very mad that time, nobody messed with our beds. Most of the pranks they did I expected from the boys; they were troublemakers and always wanted to have fun. The girls would be upset for a little bit and would get over it right away. We laughed about it. They at least timed it at a time when we were going to get our bedding washed. Our mothers, who did our laundry for us, washed all our beddings. Thankfully, we had clean bedding that night. We never held grudges on them; we always made up with them, though, no matter what. We loved our brothers too much to stay mad at them. Other than playing soccer and different games, nobody was allowed to go outside the gate, so they didn't really have much to amuse themselves with for being boys themselves. I only mentioned some of the pranks we did on each other; there were a lot more. They were prank champions, and so were the girls. What kind of siblings doesn't play pranks on each other? They were great memories. This was all for you, Layla House family, to remember some of the things we did at Layla house. I love you all! Cheers to great memories!

Here I Am to Worship

"Light of the world, you stepped down into darkness, opened my eyes, let me see. Beauty that made this heart adore you. Hope of a life spent with you. Here I am to worship, here I am to bow down. Here I am to say that you are my God. You're altogether lovely, altogether worthy, altogether wonderful to me. King of all days, oh so highly exalted Glorious in heaven and above. Humbly you came to the earth you created all for love's sake became poor. Here I am to worship. Here I am to bow down. Here I am to say that you are my God. You are altogether lovely, altogether worthy, altogether wonderful to me. I'll never know how much it cost to see my sin upon that cross. I'll never know how much it cost to see my sin upon that cross. Here I am to worship. Here I am to bow down. Here I am to say that you are my God. You are altogether lovely, altogether worthy, altogether wonderful to me."

Song by Chris Tomlin "Here I am to Worship."

This song explains why we should all worship and the reason we worship. This song was a perfect fit to share with you the reason and why all of the children at Layla House gathered together, packing the living room to worship and pray together with everyone before bed! There were kids sitting on the couches, chairs, and on the floor. Everyone is so scattered during the day playing, doing homework, or whatever they were doing that we don't see everybody on the same day sometimes, even though we all live in the same big house until our night gathering. Gathering with everyone at night was very special to us and one of our favorite times because it was not only for ourselves, but the reason we were gathering was greater than us. It was to worship and pray to the "Great I am." The one we all loved and worshiped. We loved gathering to pray and worship God! "He is our Father. Jesus is our Savior and Redeemer!"

One of our favorite songs we sang and the first song we learned when we first came to Layla House was "Lord I lift Your Name on High." Lyrics are:

> "Lord, I lift your name on High. Lord, I love to sing your praises. I am so glad you're in my life. I am so glad You came to save us. You came from heaven to earth to show the way. From the earth to the cross my debt to pay. From the cross to the grave. From the grave to the sky. Lord, I lift your name on High. Lord, I lift your name on High! Lord, I love to sing your praises. I'm so glad you're in my life. I am so glad You came to save us."

We absolutely love that song, and the words in it describe why we truly love it. We loved singing English worship songs that we understood and Amharic worship songs (mezmur) as well, like Dagi Tilahun and Yosef Ayele Ethiopian Gospel singers. Every night the room was filled up with kids singing their hearts out to their Redeemer, clapping and dancing to worship our Savior. For ten minutes during our praise and worship time, we each prayed out loud to give thanks to God for what he has done for us and made our requests known to Him in prayer to find us families and everything else we prayed for. We prayed for other kids in our situation who needed a home and a family like us and for them to find homes, and for God to take care of them. We loved singing from our heart whenever we sang that song. I remember clearly everyone getting into the song and worshiping our Lord and Savior through our words, hearts, and actions. It was beautiful to hear every child in the room, all ninety of us singing praises to our King with some standing with their arms in the air, some kneeling down, some kneeling down with arms in the air in surrender to worshiping our King. These are little kids ages 5-13 who were worshiping from their hearts. There would be children crying because they felt God's presence and crying in worshiping him. I loved seeing hearts changed in that room. When new kids came to Layla House, at first, they were hesitant in the way we worship and pray but then because of what they are surrounded by, Jesus lovers, they too come to know who Jesus is, and they accept Him as their Lord and Savior. They felt his presence and experienced him. I loved seeing broken smiles change into real genuine smiles. Genuine joy was flowing out of us because of who was in us, Jesus. Greater is He that lives in us than He that lives in the world (1 John 4:4).

We had some powerful prayer warriors that prayed for everyone as well as for themselves. Age doesn't matter when Jesus is inside of you. When you let him in, He will enter in and change you from inside and out, and we did. God's presence was there, and we definitely felt it and believed Him for everything. Some of the nights our youth leader, the oldest at Layla House at the time, were Meron and Bereket. Bereket played his guitar and led us into worship with English and Amharic songs; it was incredible! He always brought God's presence when he sang, and we all loved it when he led us into worship. He was an amazing leader that we all loved and looked up to. Thank you for your leadership Bereket and your love for us, and how you always led us to Christ and corrected us. We can't repay what you have done for us and the big role you played in our lives. I know I am speaking for a lot of people when I say that we love you, Bereket. We appreciate you, and we are grateful for your life and time at Layla House with us! We also formed a choir and put kids in different groups, and they would perform on their night every week. It was beautiful, and each group brought God's presence with them to the rest of the group. God wants our hearts, and we definitely did give him that. No one wanted to miss prayer/ worship every night. As soon as they heard the 8 p.m. bell ringing, they knew what time it was! It was Jesus' time. Kids would come literally running to the living room. They came because they wanted to, not because they were made to. Usually, the older kids or our house mothers, mostly group four, would be in charge of prayer/worship time. When American volunteers came, some of them stayed late so they could be a part of our worship/prayer time. I would see tears rolling down their faces as soon as we started and couldn't control their emotions the whole time! It was amazing for us to see that as well as for them to experience it with us. They cried for two reasons. The main one being, they felt God's presence and saw that we felt his presence as well! They also couldn't believe that we were in the situation we were in but had a lot to praise him for. What can I say? We all knew that Jesus saves, loves, cures, and cares! Like the song by Matt Redman and Steve Angrisano, "10,000 reasons," we had 10,000 reasons to praise Him!

Layla House Goodbye Parties

Families like branches on a tree, we grow in different directions, yet our roots remain as one." Unknown. One by one, all the children at Layla House found families that would adopt them in the U.S. When Merrily came to visit Ethiopia every few months, almost every time, she came with great news! Every time she came, we waited in excitement to find out which one of our friends found a family that would adopt them in America. Every one of my friends was finding families, which was very exciting. As soon as they find a family, the process to come to America is immediately started, which can take about six months to a year to finish. It is lots of paperwork, lots of interviews with the government in Ethiopia, and lots of meetings the children and the social worker attend. For the children, it was always exciting because that was one of the only times Layla house children were allowed to go outside the gate and see the city. I didn't want to find a family right away because it meant coming to America sooner than I wanted. I loved my life at Layla House. I was very happy; it was a place I called home. I wasn't ready to leave Ethiopia, my sisters, and friends. We were allowed to have visitors at Layla house. My sisters came to visit me every couple of months to see how I was doing. A lot of my friends didn't have families to come to visit them; mine were consistent in visiting when they were allowed. The first time they came to visit me, my family and I were in tears. I couldn't control it, so my visit was cut short because of it. All of our friends who had families that came to visit realized we needed to be strong and not cry when our families came because if we did, they would be told to leave right away. We were given a maximum of 1-2 hours to visit, depending on the nanny that was leading that day. I loved when my sisters, aunts, uncles, and neighbors came to visit me.

All of my friends were finding families left and right, and the process to come to America was started for them. Families that adopt are allowed to come to Ethiopia to visit the children as soon as they match them, and then when the process is done for them, they usually come back again to Ethiopia to take them to America. Some families came just once to take the children to America when the process was done for them. When they came, they usually stayed for 1-2 weeks at a guest house AAI had prepared for them. When our friends' families come to visit, they usually take their child's full classroom in the city to do fun activities. We loved it when families came to visit because it was the only time we got to go outside the gate to do fun activities. We went bowling, swimming at a five-star hotel, horseback riding, and ice cream. We went to really nice American restaurants in Ethiopia, which we have never gone to before. Our friends' families paid for everyone in their school classroom to do these fun activities. We loved it and appreciated them. Thank you to all the families who took us out to do these fun things! May the Lord bless you abundantly!

There was a goodbye party put on for every child that came to America, even for babies. The Layla house compound was very big; we put 100 chairs and tables outside where we usually play soccer inside the compound for the party. We had cake, donuts, and soda for all the children to eat and celebrate. The only time we had that kind of food at Layla was during goodbye parties and Christmas. We loved the party except for the goodbye part. When our friends left Layla house to come to America, all of us would cry when we said goodbye to our friends. There would be no dry eyes, especially when it's our closest friends. Our nannies would cry with us as they say goodbye to each child they have grown to love and counted them as their own children. Each child at Layla house found families in different states in America, so we knew possibly we might never see each other again. Saying goodbye to all our friends who became our forever family was very difficult because we were all so close. Our friends, American parents, even though they came for a short time, connected with us right away and would cry with us when they said goodbye to us. It broke their heart separating their children from their friends to bring them to America, but we all grew to be strong because we knew this would happen someday. We loved having American visitors at Layla house; we loved playing with them and talking to them with the little English we knew. Some people came from America to volunteer at Layla house for six months to a year, to teach us English and to teach us about the American way of living so it wouldn't be too much of a culture shock when it would be our turn to come to the U.S. We loved and appreciated all of our volunteers that came to Layla house throughout the years. Thank you so much to each and every volunteer that came to Layla house to love, care for us and teach us! Watching all volunteers come to live with us taught us and made us dream someday to come back to Ethiopia and do the same thing they did and volunteer at orphanages like them. We wanted to pay back what has been done for us in love. A lot of my friends from Layla house, after coming to America when they grew up, have gone back to volunteer at Layla house and other orphanages in Ethiopia to help the children who were in the same situation as them. They have done tremendous work helping orphans in Ethiopia.

"Pure and genuine religion in the sight of God the Father means caring for orphans and widows in their distress and refusing to let the world corrupt you" (James 1:27, NLT).

May the Lord bless you for everything you have done for us.

After I stayed a year at Layla house, I still didn't find a family yet that would adopt me. I didn't mind because it meant staying longer, but I was also nervous. I asked myself, what if I stayed there for so long that nobody wants to adopt me if I grew older. A lot of the time, it was harder for older children aged eleven to fourteen to find families for them because families wanted children younger than that. I knew of a friend who stayed at Layla House for six years before finding a family that adopted her in America. Layla house was a great home for all of us. The staff at A.A.I. worked hard to fundraise for us in the U.S. to make sure every need of ours was met and that we were living an American lifestyle, so it was an easier transition for us for when it was our turn to come to the U.S.

After a year and two months later, I was told by the staff that they found a family for me. Four of my friends and I got told we found families on the same day to different families. I was relieved to find out I had found family and was happy. I also cried because it meant leaving everything I knew behind very soon. Every child's family from America sends a gift to their children as soon as they get matched up. The gift that was sent to them always included a photo album of the family, the home, a letter from the family, a camera so they could take pictures, and some clothes. I received my gift as well. I found out I had a mom and two sisters and no dad. We wrote letters to our families in English while the process was going on to come to America. When American volunteers and friends would ask me what state I wanted to be adopted, too, I always said Washington. I didn't know why but I always wanted to live in Washington state, and to my surprise, my family that wanted to adopt me was from Washington. I was super happy when I found that out; a lot of my friends also were adopted and live in Washington. Mitikay and her sister, who were my childhood friends that came to Layla house with me, have also found a family to adopt them in Washington state. I was hoping someday that I would be able to meet with them after going to the U.S.

After six months, my process was done to come to America. My family didn't come to Ethiopia to visit, and I was told they weren't going to come to pick me up. I understood because I knew it was an expensive trip. I was told by A.A.I staff that Alison, our American volunteer that I loved so much, was going to take me to America! She was going to come back to the U.S. after volunteering for a year at Layla House. I was very comfortable with Alison, so I was happy it was her and not someone else I didn't know that I was traveling with. Alison came to Layla House a few times and stayed six months to volunteer at Layla house. She taught us English and taught us a lot about America. Every day she walks into the blue gate, all the children ran to her to hug and kiss her. Everyone had a great bond with her and adored her. She was our big sister! We all cried every time she left Ethiopia, but she always came back to visit us and kept her word. We were always in awe that she would leave America to volunteer at an orphanage in Ethiopia and take care of us. She had a heart of gold. Thank you, Alison, for everything! May God bless you for everything you did for Layla House's children for so many years! You have inspired us to give back to Ethiopia and those in the same place that we were by the love, care, time you gave to us.

I called my sisters to let them know that my process was done, and I was getting ready to leave Ethiopia in a week. They were happy and sad at the same time to lose me. A lot of times, when American parents come to visit or take their children, they usually take their children back to their home, the place they grew up, so they can visit it one last time and say goodbye to people they knew. It was also so that the families can see where their children are from and understand their upbringing. But if American families don't come, no one was allowed to go back home to visit one last time. I really wanted to see my home one last time, and my sister asked the social workers if I could go visit. They made an exception for me to go. One of the staff took me back home to visit; they did a welcome home and goodbye party for me one last time. They had lots of food, drinks and lots of people that I knew were there to say goodbye to me. I was heartbroken and crying a lot of the time I was there when I realized this was the last time I would see them for years. Everyone in the neighborhood was excited and chanted, "Sara is going to America, Sara is going to America. "God was going to make the impossible possible by taking me to America. After I said goodbye to everyone at home, my sisters gave me some gifts to take, pictures of our family, CDs of Ethiopian singers, and a little bible. I returned to Layla's house crying and packed my stuff as soon as I got there. I gave all my clothes and some of my belongings away to my friends at Layla house.

My sisters came back to visit me a couple of days later to say goodbye to me again. My aunts and uncles and all of my relatives came to the orphanage to say their goodbyes. It was heartbreaking, but I kept being strong so that I could visit them for a long time. They kept reminding me that God was with me, that I wasn't going alone, which was comforting to hear at the time.

A Lot of my friends from Layla house have all gone to America after they found families, and my friends that went to Layla House with me from my neighborhood have also gone to America. I knew it was my turn, but I still had a hard time leaving everything, my culture, my family, Layla house, and all my friends there. Every time when children came to the U.S., new orphan children came to Layla House because there would be room and bed for newcomers. Finally, it was my goodbye party; I was happy and excited. It was an amazing party; I cried a lot as I said goodbye to all my friends, my nannies who loved and took care of me, my teachers, and everyone I knew at Layla House. We all cried together. I left Layla House with Alison that night to go to her guest house to grab her stuff. Our driver came to the guest house and picked us up to take us to the airport! I was going to get on the airplane and fly for the first time ever as an eleven-year-old all the way to a different continent, to a family I didn't know, and a language I didn't speak.

Coming to America

America! The Land of opportunity. The place almost every African and so many others in different countries dreamed about coming to change their life. America is the place where dreams come true. America is the place where you can be someone in life. America is one of the richest places on earth. America, the continent that I thought I would never reach. I was on my way to America; it seemed unbelievable to me. As much as I was nervous, I was also very excited about my new journey to America. Alison and I started the long twenty-seven-hour flight to a place called Seattle, Washington. I was scared to be on the airplane; I was afraid, thinking the plane might crash. I held on to Alison's hands really tight when we took off. I cried a lot on the plane, already missing my friends and family. Alison comforted me and took care of me very well. In different airports, when the airport security saw me, the little African girl with an American woman, they double-checked all of my paperwork and passport to make sure I wasn't being kidnapped. Alison had all the paperwork ready and had guardianship over me to escort me to America to unite me with my family.

Alison spoke really good Amharic, Ethiopian languages, so we were able to communicate very well. I slept on the plane.

As soon as we were going to arrive in Seattle, Alison woke me up and told me to look out the window. I was mesmerized seeing the city; it was so beautiful! As we were coming out of the security in the airport, I saw someone holding a sign that said, "Welcome, Sara." Alison exclaimed, "That is your family, Sara!" We walked to them and hugged my mom and my sisters, who were there. My mom asked me how the flight was and how I was doing. She was surprised when I answered her back in English; she wasn't expecting it. I knew some English; I understood more than I could speak. I kept holding on to Alison's hand because I was scared. I didn't know my new family. A few moments later, Alison's family came. I knew and loved her mom because she came to Layla house many times to visit while I was there. Her mom had adopted six children from Layla House. She brought her two daughters that she adopted from Layla house. I had heard many great things about the girls from our nannies at Layla house and wished someday to meet them. I was happy to meet them; they were the first friends I made in America. We all went to eat at a restaurant together, which I was happy about because I wasn't ready to leave Alison and her family; they were the only ones I knew.

After we ate, I cried as I said goodbye to Alison and her family. I got in the car with my new family to drive home. My mom taught me how to put on a seat belt which was new to me. As we were driving in Seattle, I was mesmerized to see how beautiful America was. I saw big tall buildings that were so beautiful. I was thinking to myself, *this is the America everyone talked about.* It was beautiful; I loved it. I kept looking out the window, totally stunned by everything. We drove a couple of hours then we finally arrived home. As I walked into my new home, I was very shocked. It was beautiful! There were so many rooms in the house like I have never seen before. There was a living room, kitchen, dining room, three bedrooms, two bathrooms, closets, a deck outside. I was mesmerized because I was used to living in a small room house where we cooked, ate, and slept back home. These were luxuries compared to Ethiopia. This was my new house? I was very excited about my new journey and to get to know my family. I wanted to learn English so I could communicate with them better. We communicated with hand signals for a few months and my broken English. When I saw many pictures that were hanging on the wall, I was very scared. I was thinking to myself, all of these people have died. What kind of family did I come into? There were too many people that died. I didn't want to be next. My sister told me who each person was in the picture. When my grandparents came to visit me, I looked at the pictures on the wall and recognized them, then realized everyone on the pictures on the wall was alive, not dead. It was a relief knowing that. In Ethiopia, at that time, a person's picture is hung on the wall when they pass away; I thought it was the same in America. I loved my family. I asked my mom if I could call my sisters in Ethiopia to let them know I arrived in America safe. But she kept telling me you'll call tomorrow and refused to let me call back home. I was worried; I knew my family would be really worried if they didn't hear from me. My sister Hiwet made me promise to call her as soon as I got to America. Weeks went by, and my mom refused to let me call home. I had to live with the new rules. My mom told me that I now have a new family, and that was her and her two daughters, and that was it. She told me I needed to forget my family back home. That was my life in Ethiopia, and now I was told I needed to accept my new family and become American. I couldn't believe my ears, how can she tell me to forget my family back home. How can I forget my life in Ethiopia? I was who I was because of my past and my family. All I asked was if I could call my sisters to let them know I got here safely; that was it. I was heartbroken and very upset but wasn't able to express how I felt because I didn't know much English.

I cried for weeks missing my family and not being able to talk to them; she wouldn't change her mind. She wanted me to forget my whole life in Ethiopia and wanted me to become fully American. What kind of family did I enter into? How can I forget my culture, my language, and especially my family? She refused to understand. I was hoping she would slowly let me transition to my new life as it is hard to leave everything I knew for twelve years behind, all at once. She told me it was her house and her rules. I had no say in it. I was lonely and didn't know what to do. I asked if I could call my friends from Layla House that were living in America. Surprisingly, she agreed and let me call my best friend Seble. It was great hearing Seble's voice; we laughed and talked in Amharic. I was excited to talk in my language because I didn't have anyone else to talk to. Siblings that were adopted together had each other to be there for each other and also to talk in Amharic. But I was adopted by myself, so I had no one. America is very different from Ethiopia. In Ethiopia, children play outside all day. I kept looking out the window to see children but nobody played outside like back home. I never saw children outside; they are used to watching TV and playing video games inside. It was a very quiet neighborhood. Even though I wanted to make friends, I didn't meet anyone for months other than one neighbor who was my sister's friend.

We had family meals together for breakfast, lunch, and dinner. I started getting used to American food. They taught me how to roller skate and do some fun activities. I went to doctor's appointments to make sure I was healthy. I went to a dentist for the first time in my life to get my teeth cleaned and had no cavities, which surprised the dentist. My mom read bedtime stories at night to my sister and me before we went to bed. She hugged and kissed me goodnight and told me she loved me. She was nice as long as I didn't bring up Ethiopia or my family back home. They taught me everything I needed to know about American living. I was home-schooled. My mom's goal was to teach me English and to make me fluent. She worked hard to make sure I learned. I worked hard as well, speaking in broken English. I wanted to go to public school so I can make friends, but it was a good idea to homeschool me until at least I learned English, so I know how to communicate at school. I like surprising people by helping clean the house; I did that at my new home to make my mom happy. She taught me how to cook some food. I was excited about my new future in America with my family. She realized I was a hard worker, which was not a good idea. I was loving life and was excited for my new future in America with my family until my mom completely changed me after three months of living with them.

The Unexpected

There are expectations a person has when starting a new journey. My expectation when I came to America was simple. It was to love and be loved with my new family, to learn English and enjoy my new journey with my family, become someone in life, then return back to Ethiopia to visit and to help my family and make an impact helping orphans and pay it forward. I accepted my family as my own and believed there wouldn't be mistreatment in how they would treat me just because I was adopted. I thought they would treat me like their own family. I thought my mom would treat me like her own daughter, and my sisters would treat me like their own sisters, as I have already experienced a lot of traumatic things in my life at a young age. I didn't expect what was coming!

After about three months, my mom Megan stopped being the nice, loving, caring mom she was to me. She completely changed the way she treated me. Megan was my teacher. I had a hard time learning English as fast as she expected me to learn. English is one of the hardest languages to learn, and it's nothing like Amharic, my Ethiopian language. She made me repeat sentences in complete full sentences every time I was answering and talking to anyone. She did this so I can fully understand

and learn English faster. She started punishing me for not saying sentences correctly or if I said incomplete sentences. I was
learning, and people make mistakes until they become fluent. I
wasn't allowed to speak in broken English anymore; she wanted
me to be fluent asap. She made me write the same sentence
I said wrong over two hundred times on a piece of paper and
pen. Every time I said sentences wrong throughout the day
when speaking to her or my sister, she made me write each
sentence 200-300 times on paper as a punishment. I would
write the same sentence all day, every day, until I was finished.
When I was finished, she would check to see that I didn't cheat
and count how many times I wrote each sentence. My hands
would get tired; when I asked if I could take a break, she told
me no. Sometimes she would time me to write these kinds of
sentences and tell me that I needed to be done at a certain time;
if I wasn't done by that time, she would add more sentences.
Another one of my punishments for not saying sentences correctly was to stand in a corner and repeat the sentences I said
wrong many times out loud. She would make me repeat the
sentences over 2,000 times sometimes. I would stand in a corner downstairs and repeat the sentences all day, every day, and
only got a break when I needed water or when I needed to go to
the restroom. She gave me five minutes to go to the restroom,
and if I took too long, she would add more sentences I needed
to say out loud. I hated doing that but had to do it.

After three months, she stopped treating me like I was part
of the family. Whenever they went to the store, she took me with
them but made me stay in the warm car for a couple of hours.
Sometimes they would stay for three to four hours at the mall

shopping while I waited in the car. She never left the car on for me either. When they visited friends or family, she would leave me in the car as a punishment. I wasn't allowed to spend time with people. While they visit my grandparents and my aunts, uncles, and cousins, I would stay in the car alone. Sometimes they stayed for three hours visiting while I waited for them. My grandparents, aunts, and uncles wouldn't know I was in the car. This happened for a year and a half while I lived with Megan.

I wasn't allowed to eat regular American food with my family. She made me eat peanut butter and jelly sandwiches for breakfast, lunch, and dinner every day while they ate some delicious food as a family. They would eat salmon, rice, spaghetti, chicken, lasagna, burgers, etc. She knew I hated peanut butter, and that was the reason why she made me eat it. She took away the jam and made me eat peanut butter sandwiches for every meal for over six months. I usually ate by myself when they got done eating; I wasn't allowed to eat with them. She told me it was a privilege to eat with them and to eat what they ate. That privilege was taken away from me. Some of the times I ate peanut butter, it didn't settle with my stomach. It made me throw up. I didn't do it on purpose, but when she saw me doing that, she told me I wasn't allowed to go to the bathroom for two hours after I ate so I wouldn't throw up. She locked the bathroom and wouldn't allow me to go inside.

She had no reason to treat me this way other than speaking broken English. I was a good child. I wasn't disobedient. I did everything she told me to do. Small things that I did would make her upset, like not washing the dishes fast enough or not doing chores fast enough, or not speaking loudly, or not speaking English fluently. She continued to treat me like this, and when I think life is going to get better, it kept getting worse. I had no one to talk to about this. I was afraid if I spoke up and shared it with anyone, they would tell her. If they did, I would be in more trouble.

I remember a social worker came to visit from A.A.I, my adoption agency, to see how I was doing and visit my family and me. A day before she would come, she would treat me really nice and let me eat with the family, and would excuse my chores or sentences I would have to say that day so that I wouldn't tell the social worker how she was treating me. She warned me not to say anything that she would do to me to anyone. She would tell me to smile and be happy when the social worker came to check, and if I didn't, I would be in trouble when she left. I kept a happy face and told the social worker everything was great and that I liked my family when she would ask me questions because I was afraid to speak up in front of my mom. Whenever she asked me questions, my mom would answer the question right away so I wouldn't say anything wrong. She was afraid I would tell the social worker everything that she was doing. She acted like she loved me and would kiss me in front of her so she wouldn't notice anything. I was hoping that the social worker would notice something was wrong every time she came, but she never noticed. Every time she came, I wanted her to ask me the questions alone by myself, but she never did. I wanted to speak up and tell her everything my mom was doing to me, but I was afraid of what was going to happen to me when she left our house. She acted completely the opposite of how she would treat me when I was by myself in front of the social worker.

I had a six-month court meeting to finalize the adoption. She continued to treat me horribly. When we went to the meeting in front of the judge, she warned me not to say anything to the judge. She told me if I told the judge of anything she was doing to me, they wouldn't find me another family in the U.S. but that they would send me back to Ethiopia to make me live in the streets with no one to care for me. I told her it would be better than living with her that I would find my family in Ethiopia and I would live with them. She had taken away the notebook with all the phone numbers my Ethiopian sister gave me before I left, so I wouldn't have any way of contacting them if they did send me to Ethiopia. I didn't know Ethiopia much, so I knew I would be lost and living in the streets. Little did I know she was playing with my mind so I wouldn't tell the truth. She promised me that she would change the way she treated me and that she has excused all of my punishments. She told me I would have more freedom in the house when we go back home after the meeting and that I was a good child. She told me sorry for the wrong way she treated me all this time and told me she loved me. I was only twelve years old, I believed her. I told her I wouldn't tell the judge anything. We walked into the room; the judge made her swear on the Bible. She knew that everything she was going to say after the swearing was the truth and nothing else but the truth following the court rules, but she lied her way through the whole meeting. She was good at acting fake and acted super nice. The judge believed everything she was saying. The judge asked me how I liked America and my family. At that moment, I so badly wanted to tell him everything she was doing, I almost did, but I ended up lying to him and telling him everything was great. I told him my family was good, and they treated me nicely. I was afraid of the unknown; what was going to happen to me if I told him the truth, where I was going to live? What if they sent me back to Ethiopia? I came to America to have a new life and a better future. The judge had her sign some paperwork then I was officially adopted. I was her daughter.

In Misery

After our meeting with the judge, I thought my mom would keep her word and change the ways she treated me but got worse instead. She only said those nice things to me because she knew that was an important meeting. After that meeting, I was officially her daughter. The social worker stopped coming to visit; she could treat me however she wanted, and no one was going to come to check on her anymore. I had no clue what to do but tried to stay sane in the difficult days that were coming ahead of me.

She continued punishing me, doing those things I mentioned in my last chapter and got worse when I thought it wouldn't get worse. I was good at cleaning. She wrote down a two pages long list of chores I needed to do as a punishment. Some of the chores on the list were cleaning the bathrooms and scrubbing the toilet, vacuuming the whole house upstairs and downstairs, sweeping and mopping the floor, cleaning the kitchen, doing their dishes after every meal, dusting, cleaning walls, doing laundry, folding their clothes and putting them away, cleaning the car and vacuuming it, cleaning and organizing closets in the house, deep cleaning the kitchen taking everything out, cleaning all windows in the house, pulling weeds in the front and back yard outside, pulling the pine weeds out of red rocks under big arborvitae trees, etc. . The list goes on. I had to wake up every morning at 7 a.m. and take a five-minute timed shower, get ready fast, eat breakfast and start on the chores that were listed. I had to clean everything spotlessly, or she would come to check on it and make me do it again and add more chores for the day if I didn't do it right the first time. I was exhausted every day by nighttime. I only took a break for a meal and to go to the restroom; this went on for months. When I told her I was tired and needed a break, she never listened to me and instead would yell at me to go back to work, so I did.

On Saturday nights and Sunday mornings, we went to a Catholic church. I have nothing against Catholics or church but the way my mom treated me when she was going to a catholic church was wrong. I wasn't catholic, but I was made to go every week with them. In the Catholic church, there are some sentences and sayings that the congregation repeats to the priest throughout the mass. She wanted me to repeat the sayings with a loud voice so everyone can hear me. My voice naturally is very soft and very quiet. It is very hard to make myself speak loudly; I really have to try every time. I didn't want the congregation to hear my voice; I was embarrassed. I didn't believe in it either. She wanted me to speak loudly so everyone could hear my voice so everyone at church would think she was a great mom that made her daughters love God and church. She was very religious but not in the right way. She wanted to be a saint to everyone around her. I knew how she was at home with me, but when she was with people, she was a completely different person. She would be fake and smile a lot with everyone and even treat me nicely around people. So no one had a clue of who she really was. If she didn't hear my voice echoing out of all the people at church, I was in trouble. She would give me hand signals and mouth out, "louder, louder," which I hated when she did that. She bought the book Catholics use for mass at home. She made me repeat the whole mass at home, standing in the corner all day on Sundays after church until I went to bed around 11 at night. I would repeat the same thing over and over again with a loud voice standing in a corner facing the wall downstairs so she could hear me upstairs. If she didn't hear my voice all the way upstairs, she would make me repeat it over and over again. She made me memorize all the sentences that Catholics repeat to the priest so I can do it by memory without looking at a book. She wanted to look good in front of people and to be told that she was a great mom, especially because she adopted me from Ethiopia. This continued for a year and a half every Saturday and Sunday. In Catholic churches, they have confessions every Saturday. They tell the priest their sins and ask for forgiveness. She went every Saturday and took me with her to confess my sins to the priest. My sister went when she felt like it, but I was made to go no matter what.

She wrote down my sins for me and would tell me these are the sins you committed; you need to ask the priest to forgive you. The sins she wrote down for me are like; I disobeyed my mother, I talked back at my mother, I didn't do chores when my mom told me to (which I did), etc., all about her. Every week she wrote me the same sin. The priest told me that I needed to be obedient to my mom, but he had no clue what was going on at home and how she was treating me. I hated going to church and to confession because of all her rules. I loved God, but she made me hate being at church. I was going and speaking loudly only because I was made to go, not because I wanted to go. What kind of mom writes down their sins for you? I was very reserved and a quiet person. After over a year of being patient with her when she treated me like this, I realized I needed to speak up for myself. There was no one to defend me; I had to defend myself. I started talking back at her and telling her no when she was extreme about me doing chores or saying sentences for hours in a corner. I had enough. I wasn't going to be treated like that anymore. But she still made me do those things; she won every time. When I asked her questions and asked where I was disobedient when I was not being disobedient. She would tell me I was being disobedient by asking her the question, or she would make up stuff I didn't say or do. Talking back at her backfired on me and added more chores and sentences to my day, so I knew it was not helping, so I would be quiet. I told her I wasn't her slave. I didn't come to America to be her slave but her daughter. She only made me do chores all day, every day while her daughter watched TV, hung out with friends, went shopping, and did some fun things. I told her it wasn't fair and that she was treating me wrong for nothing I did, which was true. She was evil in her heart and was taking it out on me.

Six months after I came to America, she stopped allowing me to call my Ethiopian friends on the phone. I couldn't meet with them or talk to them anymore. I had no one to talk to about what I was going through. I kept begging her to let me call them because I missed them; she refused every time because she said that was a privilege I had. She was scared I would tell them about how she was treating me. I lost all connection to my family in Ethiopia and all my friends because of her. The only thing I had that reminded me of Ethiopia was a few CDs I brought with me of my favorite singers. I would listen to music when she allowed me. When I would tell her to stop treating me wrong, sometimes when it became really hard on me, she thought I was talking back to her and started taking my CDs away one by one and threw them in the garbage. She knew that was important to me and something that I treasured, so she took them away from me.

She took away all my belongings I brought from Ethiopia and threw them in the garbage as I watched her. I cried, cried, and cried, laying on the floor. I couldn't take it anymore. She was so mean to me, making me work and say sentences all day, she cut off all my connections with the people I love, and now she took away what was left of my childhood and memory. I didn't know what to do; I was heartbroken. I wasn't being a bad kid or disobedient. There were so many children worse than me. I knew I was a good kid and was quiet. I was respectful and was obedient to her except when she was hurting me too much by how she punished me. I was one of the quiet, respectful kids out of all hundred children at Layla House. Everyone knew me for being a great kid in Ethiopia; I was the same person I was in Ethiopia with her. I realized it wasn't because I was a bad child or anything; it was because she hated me and didn't know how to raise me.

She also took away my Ethiopian/English dictionary that I used at night before I went to bed to read. I read it every day because I didn't want to forget my language. Since I couldn't speak it with anyone, I knew I was forgetting Amharic. I kept writing in Amharic on a piece of paper, so I didn't forget. She took that away from me too. If I ever get to see my sisters and family again, I want to be able to communicate with them since they don't know English. She took away all my culture and everything I owned. I was losing hope. I didn't want to live anymore in misery every day; I wanted to die. I was asking God to take me away and to kill me. I was tired of being treated the way she treated me. I felt like this every day, but I knew I needed to live for my sisters. If I died, my sisters would be heartbroken, and Hiwet would never forgive herself for giving me away. I knew I needed to keep being strong and keep going for my sisters. They were my reason for living.

After she took everything away from me and took away all the privileges normal people enjoy in their everyday life, she started scaring me, saying if I talked back at her or said anything, she would make me sleep outside. I was scared to sleep outside by myself. What if I get too cold out there and die? I knew there was a robber that came and checked our door at night to see if it was unlocked to steal stuff. I would hear him every day because I would go to bed late, saying sentences at night or doing chores. I made sure I locked all the doors at night every night. I didn't tell my mom because I was scared to tell her. If she knew I was scared to sleep outside, I didn't want her to have it be one of my punishments. When I would pull weeds outside during the day, I heard my neighbors talking and said someone stole their bike last night. They kept talking about things that had been stolen from them. I knew it was the robber that came and checked our house too. One day I told her again she was treating me badly, and if people heard, she would go to jail for life. When I told her, she got mad, and my worst fear came. She told me to sleep outside. She locked me outside. I knew the robber came at night; I told her about it. She wouldn't listen to me. She thought I was making it up because I was scared, but it was a real story. I knocked on the door constantly, but she refused to open it and closed all the blinds. I sat outside for hours in the cold. I knew he was coming that night, so I hid under the big trees in the backyard so he wouldn't see me. I was scared. What if he kills me when he sees me or what if he stole me or did something to me? I heard big footsteps; I knew it was him, he came and checked the door. I was scared and held my breath the whole time he was in our backyard. He checked the doors; it was locked. He looked around and left the backyard, and went to my neighbors. I was praying that God would protect me and for him not to see him; thank God he didn't. After he left, my mom opened the door to check on me. I told her what happened. She refused to believe me and told me I was still sleeping outside. I told her if I died, she was going to go to jail and to think about that. She let me in the house afterward. She later found out from the neighbors about the robbery.

Another time we had an argument; by this time, I had lived with her for a year and a half. I was tired of living in misery, so sometimes, I would speak up. She told me to do something; I stood up to her and refused to do it. It wasn't because I was disobedient or anything. Even on the days I tried to be so good and speak loudly, say sentences correctly, and was obedient to her, she still punished me. She enjoyed punishing me, and I realized it, so I stood up to her. She was very mad; she told me to pack up my clothes that she was going to drop me off where the homeless people live to live in the streets. I told her I was not going anywhere and that I wasn't going to pack up my clothes. She went to my room mad and packed all my clothes and put them in garbage bags and put them in the car. I kept laughing at her and told her she was going crazy. I refused to cry because she liked to see me cry and hurt. I asked her when AAI, my adoption agency, found out that after you adopted me, you threw me out to live in the street when they found out what you think will happen? What if something happens to me? What if I died? I told her she is the one that is going to be questioned and that she would be in big trouble. I told her she would probably go to jail. She refused to listen to me. She dragged me into the car when I refused to move and drove around the city to take me to the place where the homeless live. Finally, after driving for some time, she came to her senses and thought about what would happen to her if something happened to me. She drove us home; I took my belongings and put them in my room.

My hair was very hard to take care of, even in Ethiopia. It was my sisters that took care of it for me, and at Layla House, our nannies were the ones that braided my hair for me. I didn't do it myself often. I braided other people's hair but not mine. It was very hard to comb and took me some time to wash and braid it. Sometimes I would braid it, and sometimes, I would just comb it and put it in a ponytail. My mom thought it took too long; she didn't understand black hair. It wasn't soft like American people's hair. Theirs is easy to take care of but not mine. She thought I was looking at myself in the mirror and taking a long time which was not true. She covered the whole bathroom mirror with paper so I wouldn't look at myself. My sister would use my mom's bathroom when she wanted to get ready. I wasn't allowed to look at myself in the mirror anymore because she said it was a privilege. The mirror was covered for a whole year. It wasn't because of the mirror that my hair took thirty minutes to one hour to wash and braid. I had thick hair. It was also tiring to braid your own hair. My arms would hurt, so it took me some time. I was only thirteen years old at the time; I really didn't know much about hair. Even after a couple of months of covering the mirror. She told me I took too long still with my hair, and without my consent, she shaved all of my hair. She made me bald. I didn't want to be bald and was embarrassed. I didn't feel beautiful at all after that. I was embarrassed to have a bald head.

While she was doing all these things to me, I can tell you I didn't feel like talking to her or saying anything nice to her. She was making my life miserable every day, to the point I wished I died. Every morning when I woke up, she made me say, "Good morning, mom, thank you for feeding me, thank you for adopting me, thank you for being my mom, thank you for bringing me to America, I love you, etc." and made me hug her and kiss her." I never wanted to say it, but she made me do it every day for two years. If she wasn't so mean to me, I wouldn't mind saying those things.

I always prayed to God to take me out of this family and to give me a new family. I was mad at God. I was mad that she treated me so badly and asked God to find me a new family. I prayed all the time, but I felt like my prayer wasn't answered. I cried out to God every night to make a way where there is no way to free me of this misery. After a while, two years later, I overheard my mom talk to someone on the phone, telling them she is giving me away to a new family. She told them she didn't want me anymore. She told them A.A.I. found a family for me in some other state. What? I was surprised, excited, scared at the same time. Who was going to adopt me? Where? I couldn't contain my excitement. I was excited to leave this miserable life. She never told me yet, and I acted like I didn't hear anything. God heard my prayer! That night I knelt down and thanked God for what was next and prayed it would be a good family this time that would treat me good and love me; that was all I wanted.

One of the chores from spring to fall was to pull weeds, pick up pines and leaves from red rocks under the trees in the front yard and backyard. We had a big yard and lots of trees all around the yard. I worked in the hot sun every day, all day for months. I only took breaks when she allowed me after asking her for bathroom breaks and meal breaks. I hated doing it but had to do it. I was embarrassed when the neighbors would see me working every day. I wondered what they would think of me. They saw my sister ride her bike, play outside, and go on walks with my mom while I was working all day long. They saw my mom and my sister leaving to go somewhere in the car without me while I was working outside every day. One day, my neighbor came and asked my mom if I could babysit her daughter for an hour while she went to the store fast. Surprisingly my mom allowed me to go and babysit. I was excited because I was getting a break from work, and I loved their little daughter.

She was a very cute little girl. I said hi to them and talked to them for a few minutes when I saw them outside while I was working. To my surprise, when I went to her house, her house was full of people. All my neighbors were there. They sat me down and told me they have been watching how my mom was mistreating me. How she made me work outside all day while my sister played outside. They told me it was wrong of her to make me work morning till night every day, especially at my age. They told me they were worried about me, and they were keeping an eye on me but had no way to come and check on me to see how I felt about everything. I told them some other stuff she did to me, not everything; they were furious about it. They told me she wasn't allowed to treat a childlike she treated me in this country. They wanted to call CPS on her. I told them not to do anything; I was scared of what she would do to me. I told them she would get worse if she found out I came and talked to them or if cps showed up and if she acted fake like she usually does in front of people if they see nothing wrong. I was going to be in more trouble.

My mom was getting ready to sell her house to move to another city; they were worried if I moved with her, they wouldn't be able to check on me, and if she got worse, no one would know. I told them I was okay and that I was being a bad child and not listening to her. They told me, "Sara, we know you; you are a good kid; she is using that as an excuse to treat you badly." I went home that day and didn't say anything to her. Two days later, there was a knock on the door. It was CPS! My neighbors called CPS on her. They questioned my mom and questioned me. They told us they would be back tomorrow and left. I was confused; I didn't know what was happening. That night, my mom came to my room and told me to pack all my belongings because I was going to go somewhere else to live with another family. I cried and cried. I wanted to leave so badly, but I feared the unknown. To my surprise, she brought all of my belongings I brought from Ethiopia. I guess she took it out of the garbage after throwing it and kept it someplace where I couldn't find it. I was happy to see that she saved it for me. She told me she was sorry for how she treated me and that she hoped my new family would treat and love me better than she did. The next morning, I was taken to a CPS office to transition to a new family.

Transitioning to a New Family

I walked into the Child Protective Service office confused about what was going to happen to me. I was scared to ask my mom Megan what was going on and where I was going next. I just kept quiet and went with the flow. CPS contacted my adoption agency AAI. and told them what happened. AAI found a foster family that I could stay with for a short time. The family accepted me to be my foster parents. They had adopted two Ethiopian babies from Layla House as well. A CPS worker took me to my foster family home. Heather and Mike welcomed me in with a smile and a hug. They gave me my own room and made sure I felt comfortable and had everything I needed. They were a really nice family. I had breakfast, lunch, dinner with them and ate the delicious food they prepared. I haven't eaten as a family or a regular nice meal for a long time, so it was refreshing to me. I wasn't allowed to watch TV with my previous family for a year because it was a privilege that was taken away from me. I watched as much TV as I wanted with my foster family.

Living like normal people and doing what people do every day was going to be my new norm. Their children enjoyed going to the Zoo and Aquarium. They took them often to Seattle to have fun as a family. I enjoyed going to different fun places with them as they shared their life with me. They went to specific places, so they could take me to do fun things and enjoy life while I was with them. They treated me like their daughter and loved me. They hugged me many times throughout the day and showed me they loved me. They were very loving towards their children and treated them like their own. I was thinking to myself, *this is what a family should be like?* Their home was a place of love. When they asked me, I opened up to them and told them some of the things that my previous mom did to me. They were very upset; they told me I was a good kid and that I should have not been treated like that. They advised me. They told me I was at a safe place with them and that I was loved. They showed it in action in many different ways, as well as in words. Megan came over to drop off some stuff I had left. When we talked, she told me she was sorry again for everything. She told me she didn't know how to raise me; it was better for her and me to be separated and that I am in a better place. She cried as she hugged me; I started crying as well; this was our last goodbye. She hugged, kissed me, and left. Deep down, I knew she cared about me and loved me, but her actions were inexcusable. I cared about her too and loved her, but there was no way we could live together. I was grateful for everything she did for me, bringing me to America; I knew it cost her a lot of money to adopt me. My foster mom came and hugged me as I continued to cry. I had a lot of emotional breakdowns while I stayed with the foster family; Heather was there for me and comforted me every time. We became like family right away, and we clicked.

They wanted to adopt me too. My foster parents told me that my adopted mom was already in the process of giving me away to a new family in Ohio before CPS got called. The family that was going to adopt me had nineteen children. They adopted fourteen children and had five of their own. I was surprised to hear there are nineteen children that live in one house. She told me when my adoption paperwork gets done, I would be going to Ohio.

My neighbors who called CPS came to visit me to say goodbye to me before I headed down to Ohio. They, too, wanted to adopt me and told me they would love to have me as their daughter. We told them that my adoption process was almost done with my second family. My aunts and uncles that I loved so much, also found out that I was with a foster parent. They asked my foster parents for permission if I could go to dinner at their house and spend time with my cousins too for one last time before I headed to Ohio. We have been family for two years and loved each other. I went there and had a great time. They were all heartbroken when they found out I was leaving the state to be adopted to another family. They had no clue this was all happening. They loved me and wanted me to stay in the family. They all shared their concerns with me; they told me they loved me. I said goodbye to them then went to my foster parents. That night when I returned to my foster parents, I was crying and saddened to leave my cousins and aunt and uncle. My foster parents asked me if I wanted my aunt and uncle to adopt me if I wanted to live with them. I told them, yes! It would be a dream come true for me to be adopted by their family. Little did I know that the same night after I left, my cousins cried and told my aunt and uncle that they wanted me to be their sister;

they told them to adopt me! My aunt and uncle were thinking the same thing, so when their children came to ask them, it was like a confirmation to them. Another confirmation was when my foster Dad called my uncle the next morning and told him that he was talking to me and that I told him I wanted to be adopted to my aunt and uncle's family. That same day was when my uncle came and talked to me and asked me a question that I was praying and hoping he would ask. He told me they loved me and wanted me to stay in the family; they wanted to adopt me and wanted me to be their daughter if I wanted to. He told me it was my choice. I could choose whatever I wanted to, and his feelings would not be hurt.

They wanted what was best for me, even if it was going to Ohio. He told me to choose whatever was best for me as he cried and told me he loved me. I was in tears too. This was a question I didn't need to think twice about. I told him, "Yes, I want you to adopt me; I want to be your daughter. I want to stay in the family." I was heartbroken to leave my cousins and aunt. They were all amazing. It was just the circumstances that made us separate. This was an answer to a prayer. A prayer that I didn't think would come true. Thank you, Jesus! I remember when I was with Megan praying and wishing for a different family to adopt me, and one of the main ones was for my aunts and uncles to adopt me. But right away, I would say, it would never happen because they were sisters; it was impossible. I see the Lord making impossible things possible in my life to teach me nothing is impossible for him. As soon as he got my answer, with excitement, my uncle started the adoption process and contacted AAI. When the family in Ohio found out there was another family that wanted to adopt me, they worked really hard to finish the process to take me to Ohio asap. The dad from Ohio was going to come Friday to pick me up. Thursday, the day before, my adoption process was stopped. My uncle and aunt got a lawyer and went to court Thursday to stop the adoption and to make a restriction for me not to travel so they could have time to work on my case if it was possible to adopt me. They fought for me and worked hard to make things possible for me to be adopted by my aunt and uncle. I told the judge I wanted my aunt and uncle to adopt me and that I wanted to stay with them because I loved them. A lot of people worked really hard to finish the long adoption process in a short time. To my surprise, the Lord worked behind the scenes to make everything work out; my dream and wish came true! I was going to be adopted by the family of my choice! My aunts and uncles and cousins were all overjoyed to have me as their daughter and sister! I stopped calling them aunt and uncle and started calling them mom and dad! My cousins became my sisters and brothers! Thank you to everyone involved who helped in my adoption process. Praise God for working everything out to make this happen! I am grateful for the family in Ohio who wanted to adopt me and did everything they could. I can't thank this family enough. Thank you so much. May the Lord bless you for everything.

I have stayed in touch with my foster family throughout the years and have a great bond with them. We visit each other, and we are like family. They still call me their daughter! Thank you to the Haas family, who have impacted my life so much in so many ways! You each are my blessing from God.

My Forever Family

"Adoption—because family isn't made from blood, it's made from love."

Unknown

Adoption is love in one word. Love is what made my new adoptive parents adopt me and have me as their daughter. Adoption is costly in two ways financially and physically. Adoption is a sacrifice. Adoption is giving hope to an orphan child. Adoption is receiving and accepting of something that you didn't think you would ever do. Adoption is accepting an orphan child who needed a family and a home no matter the cost. Adoption is redemption. Adoption is rescuing a child from a life of misery. Adoption is changing the future of a child's life forever. Adoption is receiving and accepting a child just the way they are. Adoption is changing the world, one child at a time. Adoption is messy. Adoption is hard. Adoption is not easy, but it is worth it for both the child and the parents. Adoption is fulfilling. Adoption is giving a new world and a new future to an orphan child. Adoption is giving an orphan child a family again. Adoption is showing an orphan child they matter and that they are loved. That is exactly what my new family did for me. They brought me into their family as their new daughter and brought me into their home to love me and raise me like their own daughter. They had never imagined that they would ever adopt until that phone call from my foster parent was made. It was a phone call that changed both of our worlds, especially mine, forever. They accepted the plan that God had in their life to take me as their daughter. I am forever grateful for them.

Our house was a beautiful three-story castle-like house. There were six bedrooms and five bathrooms. I had two sisters and three brothers. I thought I was in heaven, living in a mansion-like house like this one. Deep down, while I was in Ethiopia, I had wished and dreamed of living in a beautiful, big house someday. It took a few years, but the Lord was fulfilling a desire I had forgotten. Three of my siblings and I were around the same age. We all got along really great. We played together and had lots of fun. They cared for me and treated me like their daughter; my siblings treated me like their own sister. They bought me clothes and shoes whenever they went shopping for my siblings. They treated us all equally. I was part of the family. This was a new change for me to be accepted to be part of the family and be included in all family activities, as it wasn't like that in my previous adoption family. My family made me feel at home and comfortable. I was always told it is your house, eat whatever you want whenever you want. We ate meals together as a family. I ate whatever was prepared for our family, which wasn't the case with my previous family. We had a family devotional every night and prayed together. Sundays were family days to spend time together as a family; I loved spending time with them. We went on vacations together, shopping, to restaurants and movies together as a family and did lots of fun activities. My family put me in public school with my siblings. By that time, my English was great, and I was able to communicate. They made sure I was a great student and made sure I did my homework and checked on my grades often, just like they did to their other kids. There was no difference in the way they treated their biological kids and me. They treated us and loved us all the same. I was able to do normal things that I wasn't able to do when I was with my previous family. I enjoyed and loved life with my new family. They are incredible people and God-sent.

It's normal for adoptees to have their new adoptive family's last name as their own when they come to the U.S. My previous family changed my last name four times. I never knew what my last name was because it was changed often without me knowing. Parents usually don't ask the children they adopt if they want to keep their old last name; they give them their last name, which is normal. My dad knew I went through a lot of traumatic things in my life already, so he let me choose what I wanted my last name to be. He asked me if I wanted to keep my Ethiopian last name and be called Sara Negash or if I wanted it to be changed to their last name. I was really happy when he gave me the choice. I wanted to be called by their last name because I loved them so much, but I chose to be called Sara Negash and kept my Ethiopian last name. Negash was my biological Dad's name. I loved my biological dad, too; it was the only thing I had left of him and something to keep him in my memory. That was the reason I chose to keep my last name.

My mom and dad would proudly introduce me to their friends and people they knew as their daughter. I loved the way they would introduce me. My dad would always tell me I was his Ethiopian Princess; he even bought me a shirt that said, "This is what an Ethiopian Princess Looks Like."

They embraced my Ethiopian culture and who I was, which was completely the opposite of my previous family. My new family didn't want me to forget where I came from or my story. They embraced me and accepted me for who I am. They wanted me to remember my Ethiopian language and did everything they could to help me remember. They bought me Amharic/English dictionary so I can study and remember Amharic. I was allowed to talk to my Ethiopian friends on the phone again anytime I wanted. My Ethiopian friends and I would talk for hours, laughing and talking in my language. I had forgotten a lot, but as I talked to some of my friends who remembered Amharic, it started to come back to me. My Ethiopian friends who lived in Seattle whom I knew from Layla House, the orphanage, drove three hours to visit me at my house often. One of them was Mitikay, the one that was my neighbor in Ethiopia and the one that went to Layla House with me. Meeting her and her sister again and spending quality time together and be in each other's lives was a Miracle that I didn't see coming. They would come and visit me for a week; my family treated them like their own daughters and made them feel at home whenever they visited us. My mom and dad made special food and snacks for us whenever they came. They took us all to do fun things together and paid for them for all of our activities. I was allowed to go to their town as well to visit them after my parents met their parents. I was enjoying life, thanking God for my new life. Adoption Advocate International had gatherings for all Adoptees every year for all of us to visit and have a reunion. The gathering happens in my town every year! It was a full weekend. Children of all ages would come with their families to camp for a full weekend. Our reunions were always amazing and a lot of fun! My dad owned a restaurant in town. My friends my age at the reunion would gather together every year to go to my dad's restaurant to eat. My dad fed thirty of my friends whatever they chose on the menu. They all ate for free every time. My dad is a very generous person. He even fed the parents as well for free every year. I absolutely loved the way my parents were so receptive and accepting of my culture and my Ethiopian friends.

One of my Ethiopian friends that I had experienced a lot of my life with in Ethiopia, and I reconnected when I joined my new family. She was also my neighbor when we lived in Ethiopia. We were both sponsored through World Vision when we lived with our siblings, and then we also went to Layla House to the orphanage on the same day along with Mitikay and her sister. I loved her very much and missed her. Her family asked my parents if I could go visit her in New York because she missed me and talked about me often. After my parents and her parents became good friends, her parents paid for me to go visit her in New York. It was amazing seeing my friend after not seeing her for so many years. We were best friends and sisters. After a while, my parents and her parents had agreements, and she came to live with us for a few years too. I was so grateful and overjoyed to have her live with me. My parents were loving and treated her as their own daughter as well. My parents are truly God-sent. After everything I had gone through with my previous adoption and not being connected to my culture for two years, to have my best friend come live with me was a miracle.

I asked my parents if I could call my sisters in Ethiopia; I told them I had lost communication with them because I wasn't allowed to contact them before. They bought me a calling card to call Ethiopia as soon as I asked. I was finally able to talk to my sisters after two and half years of not talking to them. We were all in tears as we talked over the phone. We talked on the phone often. My family told me to write letters to my Ethiopian sisters and send them pictures so they can see how much I have grown. Whenever I missed them, I called them. We stayed in touch with my family in Ethiopia for years, which healed my hurt heart.

My family bought all the Ethiopian spices and ingredients and learned how to make Ethiopian food for me. They even drove three hours to Seattle to take me to an Ethiopian restaurant because I missed eating Ethiopian food. They did everything they could to connect me to my culture. What was important to me was also important to them. We have a great bond between all my siblings and my parents. Blood is not the only thing that defines a family but love. Love was what made my parents decide to adopt me. Adoption has changed my life forever to have a better future. In my previous family, my hope was taken away by circumstances. I wasn't dreaming about my future, and what and who I will become but taking it day by day on living. My new family was incredible! They made me feel at home and comfortable. I knew I was at a safe place. All I wanted was to be loved and taken care of, and that is exactly what they gave me. I was able to dream about my future, who I wanted to become, and what I wanted to be because my life at home was a place of peace and love.

Love is what heals a broken heart. When I first came to live with my family, my parents wanted to know my story back home in Ethiopia. They didn't know anything about my background other than they knew I had lost my parents and that I was first adopted from an orphanage. They asked me if I was okay with opening up to talk about my past and what I had gone through. They told me they would love to get to know me more so that they know how to care for me. In order to love an adoptee the way they needed to be loved knowing their background is very important. I was surprised to hear them say that, for so long, I wanted to talk to someone that cared enough to know me to share with them what I was struggling with from my past. Someone that was caring and someone I trusted. As I shared stories of my past, both my parents and I cried. Every night, my parents took the time to spend quality time getting to know me by myself, so I could feel comfortable sharing with them about my past. As I cried, they hugged and loved me and cried with me and let me know everything was going to be okay and that they loved me. There was so much reassurance of their love and care. It was easy to bond with my family because they truly wanted what was best for me. They knew I needed extra love because of what I went through. Every morning, night, and during the day, they would come and hug me randomly to share their love with me and tell me they love me. My siblings would come and hug me all the time and share their love for me always! This went on for years! I never had to question if they loved me because they showed it to me in action.

Adoption has healed my broken heart. Adoption has made me who I am today. Adoption is what changed my life forever and gave me a forever family. Thank you, mom and dad, for adopting me and truly loving me the way you do. Thank you for filling up the wounds of losing my parents and feeling like an orphan. Thank you for being my family. I love knowing that I have a mom and dad that I truly love and see as my biological parents. God answered my prayer of having a mom, dad, and brothers and sisters that I prayed many years ago. He is faithful to answer our prayers according to the plan that He has for our lives. I thank God for always taking care of me and loving me through my parents and siblings. God is a restorer. He restored everything I lost through my new family. Each one of my family is an amazing person that I love dearly. They are my treasure and gift from God. My parents are extraordinary! They have supported me in every aspect of my life, even after growing up and after I moved out. We spend holidays together as a family. Love is what ties us all together to become family; I am grateful for love. God gave me a forever family that I love and cherish.

Adoption is Redemption

God adopted us through his son Jesus Christ. We are his spiritual sons and daughters. In the Lord's prayer, it says, *"May your Kingdom come soon. May your will be done on earth, as it is in heave"* (Matthew 6:10, NLT).

Adoption is the heart of God. What God did spiritually adopting us as his sons and daughters is a resemblance in our world today of physical adoption. What has been done in heaven is being done on earth. Just as physical adoption has changed the family I belong to, the continent I would live on, and changed my destiny and future forever, spiritual adoption has also changed the family we belonged to, the place we would go to live after death and changed our life after death forever. There is life after death, as we have seen in the chapter I wrote about why Jesus became our Advocate. Spiritual adoption changed our destination of where we will go after death, hell, or heaven.

"And the LORD God formed man of the dust of the ground, and breathed into his nostrils the breath of life; and man became a living soul" (Genesis 2:7, KJV).

Then when we die in Ecclesiastes 12:7 (KJV), it tells us, *"Then shall the dust return to the earth as it was: and the spirit shall return unto God who gave it."*

Sin disconnected us from living with our Heavenly Father forever. Jesus came in the gap and became the peacemaker between God and His creations which is us. Jesus reconciled man to God. Jesus is the way to the Father and the only way we are able to enter into heaven. Our scriptures tell us in John 14:6-7 (NLT):

> *Jesus told him, "I am the way, the truth, and the life. No one can come to the Father except through me. If you had really known me, you would know who my Father is. From now on, you do know him and have seen him!*

Jesus is the door to heaven, and we can only enter into heaven and be saved by accepting Him into our hearts and believing in him. Jesus, who was sinless, took on the whole world sin's on Himself to die on the cross for us to reunite us back to our Father in heaven.

> *He was despised and rejected a man of sorrows, acquainted with deepest grief. We turned our backs on him and looked the other way. He was despised, and we did not care. Yet*

it was our weaknesses he carried; it was our sorrows that weighed him down. And we thought his troubles were a punishment from God, a punishment for his own sins! But he was pierced for our rebellion, crushed for our sins. He was beaten so we could be whole. He was whipped so we could be healed. All of us, like sheep, have strayed away. We have left God's paths to follow our own. Yet the LORD laid on him the sins of us all.

Isaiah 53:3-6 (NLT)

Jesus was crucified by Roman soldiers on the cross and died in Golgotha over 2,000 years ago. But our Savior didn't stay dead. On the third day, the miraculous happened, He arose from the dead! Mary Magdalene and the other Mary who were close to Jesus went to see His body where His body was lying when an angel appeared to them and gave them the greatest news that would change the lives of the entire world. In Matthew 28:5-6 (NLT), it says:

The angel said to the women, "Then the angel spoke to the women. "Don't be afraid!" he said. "I know you are looking for Jesus, who was crucified. He isn't here! He is risen from the dead, just as he said would happen. Come, see where his body was lying."

Jesus appeared to Mary Magdalene and the other Mary and to His disciples after he rose from the dead and stayed forty days with them before He ascended into heaven.

If a person does not accept Jesus into their heart or believe in Him, before they die, they will go to hell since there is life after death. Hell will be their destination after death. In Revelations 21:8 (NLT), it tells us:

> But cowards, unbelievers, the corrupt, murderers, the immoral, those who practice witchcraft, idol worshipers, and all liars—their fate is in the fiery lake of burning sulfur. This is the second death.

Not believing in Christ is a sin and brings eternal death to a person.

But if you ask God to forgive you of all of your sins and accept Jesus into your heart as your Lord and Savior and believe in Him, you will be saved.

> If you openly declare that Jesus is Lord and believe in your heart that God raised him from the dead, you will be saved. For it is by believing in your heart that you are made right with God, and it is by openly declaring your faith that you are saved.
>
> Romans 10:9-10 (NLT)

After accepting Christ into your heart, you need to learn about Salvation in a deeper way so you can understand deeply about your spiritual adoption to God before you get baptized, which is a commandment. Spiritual adoption is also through water baptism. We need to be baptized in order to be in God's adopted family to enter into heaven. In John 3:3-8, Jesus was explaining how to enter heaven to Nicodemus, who was a religious leader.

> *Jesus replied, "I tell you the truth, unless you are born again, you cannot see the Kingdom of God." "What do you mean?" exclaimed Nicodemus. "How can an old man go back into his mother's womb and be born again?" Jesus replied, "I assure you, no one can enter the Kingdom of God without being born of water and the Spirit. Humans can reproduce only human life, but the Holy Spirit gives birth to spiritual life. So don't be surprised when I say, "You must be born again." The wind blows wherever it wants. Just as you can hear the wind but can't tell where it comes from or where it is going, so you can't explain how people are born of the Spirit.*
> John 3:3-8 (NLT)

Baptism is very important, and it symbolizes the covenant a person makes with God. A person gets baptized by a believer, pastor, or a leader from church, baptizing them in the name of the Father and of the Son and Holy Spirit. When a person's full body is dunk into the water and comes out, it symbolizes spiritual birth! Our sins are all washed away in the water, and we become a new creation in Christ. That is when we receive the Holy Spirit.

> *For you were buried with Christ when you were baptized. And with him you were raised to new life because you trusted the mighty power of God, who raised Christ from the dead. You were dead because of your sins and because your sinful*

nature was not yet cut away. Then God made you alive with Christ, for he forgave all our sins.

Colossians 2:12-13 (NLT)

After baptism, you are no longer a slave to sin, but you have become a new creation in Christ. In the spiritual realm, you are no longer known as a person who is dead in the spirit, but you are known as a person who is alive in Christ. Your name is recorded and written in the book of life. Those who have their names written in the book of life are the ones who enter into the Kingdom of God. That is something to rejoice about!

In 2 Corinthians 5:17 (NLT), it says, *"This means that anyone who belongs to Christ has become a new person. The old life is gone; a new life has begun."*

You are now God's adopted son and daughter! You are now a child of God and have entered God's family. Before, when you were an orphan in spirit, life after death was hell. But now, after becoming a new creation, you will no longer fear death because you know exactly where you're going after death, which is to live with Christ in heaven. You no longer live, but Christ lives in you.

But when the fullness of the time came, God sent forth his Son, made of a woman, made under the law, To redeem them that were under the law, that we might receive the adoption of sons. And because ye are sons, God hath sent forth the Spirit of his Son into your hearts, crying, Abba, Father. Wherefore thou art no more a servant, but a son; and if a son, then an heir of God through Christ.

Galatians 4:4-7 (KJV)

Adoption is redemption! Adoption has made us inherit everything that Jesus owns and inherits. Because we are sons and daughters of God, we have inherited everything that is in Christ. Because we belong to Christ, we share with him his glorious inheritance as well.

In physical adoption, when adoption is finalized, the new adoptive parents and the child that's getting adopted sign the paperwork for legal agreement for the adoption to be processed. What finalizes the adoption is when the judge puts his stamp of his signature on the adoption papers making it legal for the parent to adopt the child. It is the judge's signature on the adoption papers that signifies that the adoption is finished. It signifies that the child is no longer an orphan but belongs to the family that adopted the child. That child now has a legal right to have his last name be the parent's last name and be called their son or daughter. An adoptee is also given the right to be a citizen of the country the family adopts the child in. Being adopted has also given us adoptees new citizenship in a new continent. Just like physical adoption, in spiritual adoption, God is our Heavenly Father, and His children, us human beings who were orphans in spirit, didn't belong to the family of God anymore. In our spiritual adoption, what we sign is not paperwork for our agreement to be adopted sons and daughters of God, but our agreement was accepting the adoption agreement that God our Father sent, who is Jesus Christ our Lord. We agreed by the words that come out of our mouth, confessing and declaring with our mouth in faith, believing in our hearts that Jesus is Lord. We sign off our agreement asking for forgiveness of our sins and believing in the one he sent to save us from eternal death. We also sign off our adoption agreement to God by getting baptized as Jesus commanded us to do. That was our signature to our spiritual adoption to God. Jesus is the Advocate and Judge that God sent to finalize our Spiritual adoption to himself. In Isaiah 33:22 (KJV), it said this.

"For the LORD is our judge, the LORD is our lawgiver, the LORD is our king; he will save us."

Jesus's blood on the cross is the signature of our spiritual adoption. Before, our names were not found in the book of life. The blood of Jesus is the signature that stamped and finalized our spiritual adoption. The blood of Jesus saved us from being thrown into hell, where our names are written, now the blood of Jesus is a sign that says "saved" by our name. Therefore now our name is written in the Book of Life. Our spiritual adoption was finished on the cross when Jesus, our judge, uttered the last words before he died when he said, "It is finished" (John 19:30, NLT).

"When Jesus had tasted it, he said, "It is finished!" Then he bowed his head and gave up his spirit" (John 19:30 (NLT).

An adopted child now inherits the family that adopted them their last name, and everyone that knows them knows they are sons and daughters of the family that adopted them. Just like that, when we get adopted to God spiritually, we become his adopted sons and daughters. In the spiritual realm, we are known as God's adopted sons and daughters. Even the devil knows that we belong to God. On earth, people can tell that we belong to the family of God through our actions, deeds and who we are as a person. Since now we belong to the light, our light who is Christ in us will shine through us.

> You are the light of the world—like a city on a hilltop that cannot be hidden. No one lights a lamp and then puts it under a basket. Instead, a lamp is placed on a stand, where it gives light to everyone in the house. In the same way, let your good deeds shine out for all to see, so that everyone will praise your heavenly Father.
>
> Matthew 5:14-16

After we get adopted spiritually to God, we become citizens of heaven! We are citizens of heaven living on this earth until God calls us home to heaven. In physical adoptions, after a child is adopted to a family if the family member passes away, the child is legally entitled to inherit everything the parents owned. All of the inheritance now will belong to the child because the child belongs to the family. Just like that, in our spiritual adoption, because we are God's children, we have also received God's blessings through Christ.

"And since we are his children, we are his heirs. In fact, together with Christ we are heirs of God's glory. But if we are to share his glory, we must also share his suffering" (Romans 8:17, NLT).

We now have a relationship with Christ and have become God's adopted sons and daughters. If you have not yet received Jesus as your Lord and Savior, it is as simple as saying this prayer in faith, say this prayer so you can receive eternal life.

Prayer:

Lord Jesus, I believe that you have come down from heaven because of your love for me to die on the cross. I believe that you died on the cross to take away my sins. Forgive me for all my sins, for all the wrongs I have done. I believe you are my Lord and Savior. I accept you into my heart right now. Lord Jesus, come into my heart. Change me from inside and out. I believe in you. Wash me by your blood, and I say this in the name of Jesus. Amen.

Finding Christ

Finding Christ is like finding a hidden treasure that you need to live life in this world, but you never knew it existed. Have you found Christ? What was it like when Christ revealed himself to you for the first time? When was the day that you knew in your heart that God is real and he exists? Throughout my life in Ethiopia and America, I relied on God and prayed usually when I was going through a trial or needed help with something. Even though I love God and relied on him for provision and safety, I didn't have a close relationship with him. He was my God that I prayed to but was far away. After coming to the U.S., I stopped praying as I used to when I was in Ethiopia. I was closer to God when I was at the orphanage because we always prayed and worshiped every night before bed and had a devotional with all of my friends. We always felt God's presence in an amazing way whenever we worshiped; I knew I was close to God, and God was close to me. I always felt his presence.

But when I came to America, the atmosphere in my family was different from Layla house; the religion and church were different. I would go to church every Sunday with my family but still never felt God's presence. I always wondered why it didn't feel the same way; worshiping as a Christian in Ethiopia and going to church in America was completely different, as some of you adoptees would agree with me. One of the problems was that religion was different. I lost my relationship with God. Even though I went to church with my family, I didn't pray often. God wasn't far away, but I was far away from God. I prayed sometimes to God, but when I prayed, I always said I am talking to the God I know and that I worshiped when I was at Layla House. I was living life like other people getting up in the morning, eating breakfast, getting ready then going to school or work. That was my norm.

I had gone to Ethiopian orthodox churches when I was in Ethiopia, Catholic church, Mormon church, and was a Christian at Layla House. I have experienced a lot of religions, but none of it satisfied my spirit. It is because religion does not satisfy you. Belonging to a religion doesn't save you. It is a relationship with Christ that saves you. It is a relationship with Christ that fills you up and satisfies your heart. Jesus came to build relationships with us, not to build religion. Religion is all about law; Christ is all about relationships. God wanted a relationship with His children; that is why He sent His one and only on to earth to die on the cross for us because He wanted a relationship with us. I remember one time sitting on my bed, thinking if God is who He says He is. The Bible says He is the same yesterday, today, and forever. If He says that, then He is still a God that does miracles, that heals the sick, raises the dead, and delivers people from the tactics of the enemy, just like in the Bible. I wondered why I wasn't seeing churches that believe in that, why isn't God healing in this day and age like before. If He is God and He is, He is able to. I wanted to go to a church that believes in God that does miracles in this day and age. I wanted to see the impossible become possible through Christ. I often thought about that throughout the years. I was empty and lost and just living life. I was grateful to live in America and was making something of myself. I was going to college and working hard at work and school. But yet I still felt lost. When I was twenty-one years old, I went for a business meeting with some of my American friends to Dallas, Texas. All of my friends were Christians. They have talked to me and shared with me about Christ before and have invited me to their church, but I never took on their offer. They were all Christians. After our meeting, they all decided to go to our friend's Christian church and invited me to go with them. I didn't want to stay by myself, so I decided to go with them. One of the best decisions I have ever made! Bethel Dallas church is a non-denominational Church. I went as a skeptic. I had never gone to a Christian non-denominational church in America before. I was really amazed to see people worshiping from their heart; they were raising their hands in surrender to God, they were kneeling and crying. They were so submitted to God as they worshiped. I could tell this was not fake from the way they were worshiping. They were worshiping in Spirit and in truth, just like it says in the Bible. After worship, the pastor got up and introduced a prophet that came from London who came to serve them for the weekend. After the prophet preached, he started praying for people. A prophet is someone that God uses to speak through them.

A lot of people were getting healed left and right. The presence of God was very strong in the room. God was using this prophet to heal people. There were people that had back pains that got healed instantly; there was a person that was in a wheelchair for years that got completely healed at that moment and got out of their wheelchairs and started walking on their own. God was healing people. There were some prophecies that were given to people. People kept saying it's true when the prophet that didn't know them spoke about their life, hidden things that no one knew about them. I got mad at first and asked, "Why are they using the name of God and doing this?" I was skeptical. After seeing so many miracles, I finally prayed. God, if you are here, the real God that I know and believe in if you are here, please speak to me. I am not going to ask for prayer or anything, but have someone come and pray for me and speak to me through them. I asked God to tell me secrets about my past life in Ethiopia, things that no one would know about me. The only thing my friends knew about my Ethiopian life was that I was adopted, but they didn't know anything else. If God was really there, then He could tell me about my childhood that no one knew. If He did speak through them to me, I told myself I would accept Jesus that day and become a Christian.

When all of my friends went for prayer, I sat down on my chair and told them I didn't want prayer. I was waiting to see if someone would come and ask if they could pray for me because that was my deal with God. To my surprise, a lady that went to that church came and asked if she could pray for me. Shocked, I told her she could. As she prayed, God started speaking to her about my life, and she told me stories about myself that I never told anyone. The Lord used her to show me that he knew me. She told me that I got burned when I was five years old and that I almost died and that it was God that saved me when no one knew I was going to make it. She told me that I was an orphan and lost my mom when I was four years old and that I have also lost my dad too. She prayed for healing for my heart. Then she told me something that was super specific that I was struggling with. When my dad took care of me when I was at the hospital when I got burnt, he slept on the hard cement floor for two months with a little sheet over him. He sacrificed a lot, and I always felt like he died because of me. I felt like he got sick because all of those months of sleeping on the cement floor took care of me, and that was not good for his health. I blamed myself for fourteen years since he passed away.

She started telling me you have been blaming yourself for your dad's death for years; God is telling you that it is not your fault. She told me that I needed to forgive myself and that it wasn't my fault that he was sick or that he died. She told me not to blame myself anymore. I lost it; I cried and cried. I knew it was the real God that was speaking to me about specific things about my life. She told me about my future and about the plans that God had for my life. Things that were on my heart that I planned on doing caring for orphans in the future. She told me the Lord has a plan to use you in that. It was the most incredible experience ever! The Lord revealed Himself to me in a way that I never knew Him before. That day so many miracles happened in my life that I will never forget! I accepted Jesus into my heart that day and promised myself that I will always follow Christ and live for Him! That day I finally met my Savior, I was lost, and now I am found. I wanted to tell everyone about Christ! I was surprised to see that God knew me deeply like that. God knows you and knows what you have gone through. He knows you by name and has been with you in every aspect of your life, taking care of you, guiding you and protecting you, and providing for you. I am reminded of the Samaritan woman who met Jesus at the well when He asked her to give Him some water to drink. She asked Him why He would ask a Samaritan woman for a drink of water.

"Jesus replied, 'If you only knew the gift God has for you and who you are speaking to, you would ask me, and I would give you living water'" (John 4:10, NLT).

"Jesus replied, 'Anyone who drinks this water will soon become thirsty again. But those who drink the water I give will never be thirsty again. It becomes a fresh, bubbling spring within them, giving them eternal life'"(John 4:13-14, NLT).

Jesus is the living water; drink from His well, you will never get thirsty again when you drink from His well. He fills your spirit. Jesus then told her to go get her husband. She told Him she didn't have one. That is when he told her a story about herself that no stranger knew about her. He told her she had had five husbands, and the one she was with now was not her husband either. Surprised that he knew things about her that no one knew, she said you must be a prophet. That was when he revealed who He was to her.

"Then Jesus told her, "I am the Messiah! " (John 4:26, NLT)

She found her Savior, the Messiah. Out of all places to meet Jesus, she met Him where she least expected to meet Him. She wasn't looking for Him, but He came looking for her to set her free and reveal Himself to her. I didn't know I was going to meet Christ, that day, I went to church, but Christ came to meet me. Maybe you are not looking for Christ right now, but He is looking for you and revealing Himself to you. Open your heart to Him, and maybe you will meet Him for the first time through this book. You will meet Him in the least unexpected place you would think you would never find Him in. Accept Him into your heart. He is calling for you. After Jesus told the Samaritan woman about herself, she went to town and testified about the Messiah. She said in John 4;29 (NLT): *"Come, see a man, which told me all things that ever I did: is not this the Christ?"*

She brought the whole town out to see Jesus and to hear Him teach. The Bible tells us many Samaritans from the village believed in Jesus because of this woman's testimony! Share your testimony about Christ and let it change the world, one person at a time.

When I came home from my meeting, I immediately started going to a non-denominational Christian church with my friends. Awaken Church is a Holy Spirit-filled church. Three were testimonies of people coming to Christ being set free from drug and alcohol addiction. There were testimonies of people getting healed from many diseases and cancer! The people there worshiped him in Spirit and in truth. The church had a motto that said, "God would rather have you messy than not at all." I pursued my relationship with Christ. I was hungry and thirsty to know Him in a deeper way and have an intimate relationship with Him. The Lord always feeds those who are hungry and thirsty for Him. He always reveals Himself to those who seek Him just like His Word says, and that is exactly what He did for me. He revealed Himself to me in ways I cannot imagine. He started using me, and I became His mouth and His hands and feet to those he wanted to encounter. That is what we need to do as Christians, we need to make ourselves available for him and ask him to use us, and he will use us in ways that we never imagined. I encourage you to let God use you every day; your life will never be the same.

When we become Christ follower, we need to give up everything and follow Him. I gave up my family's religion when I found Christ. I gave up living for the world and stopped doing things that wouldn't glorify God. After Jesus revealed Himself to me, there was no turning back from what I knew and saw. Those who have found Him know and understand. I decided I wanted to live the rest of my life for Him and fulfill the purpose that God had for my life. I got baptized and became a new creation in Him. After accepting Jesus into our hearts, we need to build a relationship with Him. We need to do daily devotionals to get closer to Christ. We do that by praying and talking to Him every day and night, by reading the Bible His love letter to us every day, by worshiping Him in spirit and in truth and listening to worship music, and by going to church every week to learn about Him and worship Him with other believers. We build our relationship with Him by sitting in his presence to hear His voice and to ask Him for the plans that He has for our lives.

"*My sheep listen to my voice; I know them, and they follow me. I give them eternal life, and they will never perish. No one can snatch them away from me*"(John 10:27-28, NLT).

Not one person will go to heaven by becoming a good person or by doing good works in the world. We go to heaven by believing and accepting Christ into our hearts!

> *God saved you by his grace when you believed. And you can't take credit for this; it is a gift from God. Salvation is not a reward for the good things we have done, so none of us can boast about it. For we are God's masterpiece. He has created us anew in Christ Jesus, so we can do the good things he planned for us long ago.*
>
> Ephesians 2:8-10 (NLT)

After I became a Christian for a year and half, I was going to church regularly and had a close relationship with God. One day, I was at church, and during worship, there was a song we were singing by Kristian Stanfill called "Who you are." The presence of God was there as we worshiped. Everyone at Church was worshiping God and raising their hands in surrender as they worshiped. They lifted their hands up until these verses came up, then everyone's hands went down, and mine went up.

"*You hold the orphans in your loving arms. This is who you are. I know this is who you are. I believe this is who you are.*"

"*Who you are.*"

—Kristian Stanfill

I always raise my hands in surrender and gratitude for what God did for my life anytime a song came up about God caring for orphans. I was an orphan before, and He has changed my life and gave me a family, and brought me to America. I am grateful. Because of that, I always raised my hand. But when that verse comes in the song, it was always just me in my church that raised my hands. I was shy to raise my hand, but it was true he cares for orphans. I have seen it firsthand, so I always raised my hand. Then the Holy Spirit whispered something to me that was going to change my life forever. He told me that I wasn't the only one. He told me I wasn't the only orphan in the room. Everyone there was once an orphan. I knew everyone in the room and their story, and I knew none of them were adopted except me. So I knew I was the only one; what the Holy Spirit was whispering to me didn't make sense to me. Then he explained to me that we were all orphans in spirit. We were all dead in spirit, and that he sent Jesus Christ to be our advocate to adopt us back to God. He revealed to me that we were all God's adopted sons and daughters! That revelation sent me crying down to my knees because I knew it was the Lord speaking to me. I was amazed by this revelation when He explained to me deeply, as I have explained in this book. The Holy Spirit told me He wanted me to write a book about my adoption story and God's adoption story and share the Gospel with people. Earth was doing what heaven already did through adoption! He confirmed to me through many ways to write this book. He confirmed it to me through His prophets and Christian believers when we would pray together. The Holy Spirit would tell them to tell me that there is a book that God told me to write and that I needed to write it and that many people would be blessed by it. After many confirmations, I decided to be obedient to the Holy Spirit and write this book to fulfill the plan that God had for my life. I pray and hope that through this book, the Lord will reveal Himself to you and that you will have an intimate relationship with Christ!

My God Parents

There are some people that are sent by divine appointment by God in our lives. God sends people in our lives to help us to become who we are meant to be and help encourage us to fulfill the purpose that He has for your life. It is not by accident that you meet these people but through divine appointment. God knows exactly how to connect you and the exact place you need to be to meet the people he wants in your life.

When I became a Christ follower as a young adult, I wanted to grow spiritually and live for Christ. God was teaching me new things; I wanted to live an uncharted life for God. I wanted to go wherever he called me to go and do what he called me to do. I wanted to fulfill the purpose he had in my life, but I didn't know how. I prayed that the Lord would send me a spiritual family who are strong in their faith to help guide, teach and encourage me to fulfill his purpose in my life. I had my amazing adopted family, whom I loved and adored with all my heart, but we didn't have the same religion. One day at a business meeting, I met a man named Sandy Stephens talking on stage and sharing stories of how the business had helped him and his amazing wife Deanne financially to sponsor many children in Africa. He had become a father figure to many children in Africa. I heard stories of how his family had helped build a school in Burundi along with some other people from the U.S. so the children could have a place to learn. They also have helped build homes for families who were less fortunate in Burundi and Rwanda, along with some other people. I was touched by that story and their heart to serve children in Africa and were grateful for them. Coming from Ethiopia, I knew the hardships many children and families face because of poverty in Africa because I have experienced it myself. I went to meet him and to thank him for all they have done in Africa, helping the less fortunate. After I met him and his family, we became great friends and stayed in touch. I was in church one day, and the Holy Spirit told me that the Stephens were the spiritual family that I was praying for. As God confirmed it to me many times, I told the Lord, if it was from him, I wasn't going to say anything to them, but that he would reveal that to them and have them tell me that God put it in their heart to be my spiritual parents to teach me about God. To my surprise, a few weeks later, a miracle happened. Sandy contacted me and told me that the Holy Spirit has been putting me in his heart for a while and that he understands and respects that I have my adoptive family already but that the Lord has put it in his heart that I am his God daughter to help encourage me spiritually to fulfill the purpose that God had for me. He told me it wasn't to take the place of my family, that he is so grateful that they adopted me and changed my life. He wanted to share what the Holy Spirit put on his heart. I agreed the Lord had put the same thing in my heart and that I was waiting for him to say something. When something is from God, God will speak and confirm it to both people. Sandy and Deanne have three children.

I was ready to live an uncharted life for God. If you have a close relationship with God, he can tell you about your future and what is to come in your life ahead of time. He will reveal to you the plans and purpose he has for you. In prayer one day, the Lord told me that I was going to move in three months. He kept confirming it many times in many ways. I was supposed to go when he brought the opportunity. The Stephens and I lived in different states. They contacted me and told me they were moving to Arizona to help start a church with their Pastors and friends because God called them to go and invited me to go with them and to pray about it if it is the Lord's will for my life as well. I prayed about it and felt it was this move that God was speaking to me three months prior. I was serving at a Christian church at the time. I had a hard time telling my pastors that my assignment in that church was done and that the Lord wants me to move somewhere else. I prayed the Lord would speak to my pastors and let them know, and that was the last confirmation I needed before I left. I wanted them to know I wasn't just moving; I was trying to be obedient to the Lord's voice. My Pastor Folake Kellogg surprised me one Sunday when she came to tell me, "You're moving, you're leaving us, the Lord told me. God wants to use you somewhere else." I was shocked to hear it and asked how she knew because I didn't tell anyone yet. She told me that the Holy Spirit told her in her prayer time. I knew God speaks to her but was mesmerized by God by what happened. The Awaken church motto was to equip people to be great disciples and send them wherever God calls them to spread the Gospel like wildfire all over the world. The church leaders prayed for me and sent me off to the next chapter in my life. Awaken church and all my friends and leaders in the church truly impacted my spiritual life in so many ways! They believed in the calling God had in my life and always encouraged me. Thank you so much to all of you; you each know who you are who has impacted my life! May the Lord bless you!

The Stephens family and I moved together and started a church in Good Year, Arizona, along with our pastors and friends, called River City Church. We shared the gospel, and many souls were won for the kingdom of God through River City Church. It was the most fulfilling and satisfying service I have ever been a part of.

The Stephens treated me like their own daughter. They showed me Christ's love through the way they loved and cared for me. They helped me grow spiritually and always advised me on life. They believed in me and believed in the purpose that God had for me. They believed in me before I believed in myself; they helped me believe in myself by speaking life into me and supporting me in every way. They helped me financially so that I could focus on the purpose that God had for me. The Lord had put it on my heart for a long time to write this book, but I never had the time to write because of work and college. I wanted to take time off work and be focused solely on the book but wasn't able to financially. My family supported me financially so that I could stay home and write this book! I was able to sit down and write for a few months and write half of my book while serving the church because of them. You are reading this book because of their constant encouragement and support in my life. There were many times I wanted to quit writing this book, but they spoke life into me and encouraged me to do so. God always sent people in my life to speak life into me every time I needed encouragement to keep going to finish this book. Their daughter and my sis Emma was also writing a book the Lord had put on her heart to write. We would both sit down and write our books together and encourage each other.

The Stephens also supported a choir from Uganda, Rwanda, and Burundi that came to the U.S. to tour and worship God in different churches all over the U.S. to raise awareness and find sponsorship for children back home who were less fortunate. Emma had gone on tours with the children's choir since she was fourteen years old as their auntie to care for the children as they toured the U.S. She has had a heart of gold since she was young to serve the Lord and children in Africa. She has given a full year and half of her life touring, serving these children, and finding sponsorship for lots of children in Africa. Emma and the Stephens have gone to Africa many times to visit the children and have impacted many lives there too. Their hearts were sold out to serving the Lord and the plans and purpose he had in their lives. While I was living with them, the children's choir came to Arizona touring. The Holy Spirit told me in advance before they came to go and tour with these children and take care of them as their auntie. When they came, and when I was asked to join. I didn't hesitate; I immediately packed my bag. My family supported me financially and took care of everything for me so that I was able to go serve the Lord loving on his children and taking care of them. It was a three months tour taking care of twenty-one children ages ranging from five to twelve years old.

It was a dream come true for me. I have always wanted to give back with my time to helping orphans and children in Africa, just like some volunteers came to the orphanage like Alison. I loved how they cared for me and my friends when I was at the orphanage. We traveled all over the states and found sponsorship for many children in Burundi and Uganda. The children's choir were Holy Spirit-filled Christians who were very strong in their faith; they brought the presence of God every time they worshiped in every church. The children were amazing. I not only taught them things, but they also taught me a lot of things. I was blessed to be where I was in life now to serve those who were in the same place I was. This would have not happened without God and Stephen's support. Before I went on the tour, I needed a new car because my car was giving me problems; I was thinking about getting a job and working so I could buy one. I was praying and believing that God will provide. When the opportunity came to go on tour, I knew I needed to go because the Lord had told me in advance, but this thought came into my mind, if I stayed, I could get a job and save up in three months' time, I would have had enough money to buy a car. That would have made things go faster, I thought. But then I decided I wasn't going to go with my plan but the Lord's. I believed the Lord would provide a job for me when I came back so I could buy a car. Serving the Lord doing what he called me to do was my main job, so I left. When I came back from tour, to my surprise, as soon as I got out of the car, I was handed a car key by my spiritual family. They surprised me with a new car! The Lord provided for me through the Stephens. There are countless stories of how the Lord showed me his love by using the Stephens to be his hands and feet in my life. Every time I thank them for what they did for me, they always tell me to thank God and give glory to him; it is him that did it. I am truly grateful for them. When you give up something to serve the Lord, the Lord will bless you more than you expected.

The Lord has used the Stephens in my life to encourage me throughout the years to fulfill the purpose he has for my life. I am forever grateful for my spiritual family, whom I love dearly. They are world changers. They have impacted thousands of people's lives in their journey. They are ambassadors for Christ and have won many souls for the kingdom of God!

I encourage you to live an uncharted life, to go wherever God calls you to go, and serve who He calls you to serve! You will have an incredible journey living for the Lord and living a life filled with miracles! I encourage you to ask the Lord to send people in your life who will help encourage and help you to ful-fill the purpose He has for your life. If He has done it for me, He can do it for you! Let us all have a heart like Isaiah, when God said, who should I send a message, Isaiah. He was quick to answer to God and tell Him to send him!

"Also I heard the voice of the Lord, saying, Whom shall I send, and who will go for us? Then said I, Here am I; send me" (Isaiah 6:8, KJV).

Identity

Our identity is not found in culture or through who we spend time with; our true identity as a person is found only in Christ. After coming to America, before accepting Christ, I struggled to find my identity. I didn't know who I was or who to become. Being Ethiopian and living in America was a struggle only because I didn't want to lose my Ethiopian culture and who I was, but I also wanted to fit into the American culture. I wanted to fit in with my American friends as well. Trying to dabble both was hard. People that have been adopted or people that have migrated to a different country usually struggle becoming themselves, trying to fit into the new culture and the new world they live in. Trying to fit into their new culture and friend groups, they usually lose their culture and their character as a person. I have met many people from Ethiopia and other countries that have been adopted or migrated to America and have forgotten their language; some people lose it because they are not able to speak their language or have no one to speak it with, and some lose it on purpose so that they can fully become Americans. Some lose their culture or language because they have been hurt before, and looking back at what they went through would bring out some emotions that they don't want to re-experience.

Some forget completely about their culture because they don't want to remember who they were before, or they don't want to remember the life they used to have because the life they have now is completely different. Some are ashamed of the life they used to live if they have experienced poverty and losing family through death.

Don't forget where you came from; it is what made you, you. Embrace it. Even people that have never migrated to another country or never been adopted do also struggle with identity. Just like some of these examples I have mentioned, I myself went through a phase of trying to find who I am as a person. I lived in a town that had only five Ethiopians. They were all little kids, I was the oldest, so I was never able to talk in my Amharic language often because they didn't know it, just like some adoptees have experienced. I wanted to fit into my friend groups, who were Americans and Mexicans that I loved so much, so I became like them. I acted like them, talked like them, and did things that they wanted to do, trying to fit in. My actions would never say that I was Ethiopian. Unless I told them before, everyone thought I was born in America. I loved being Ethiopian and wanted to share my culture with them but didn't know how, in fear of losing my friends, I didn't. That is something that a lot of Adoptees go through. As adoptees and immigrants, we never share about our life from back home or our struggle unless they are people that are really close to us that we trust. When I told my friends that I was adopted. They would say, "Oh, I am so sorry." I didn't know, nor did I understand, why they would say that. So I would stop them and tell them that I was grateful to be adopted. I am grateful for my family that adopted me. I wasn't ashamed to say that I was adopted; it is what changed my life completely. When I was with my Ethiopian friends, I acted Ethiopian. When I was with my American friends, I acted American. I had two personalities. It was exhausting having two personalities and constantly changing to please people. I wasn't trying to be fake, but I wanted to be accepted by my friends in both of my friends' groups. Some people would even joke around and say, "Who are you? You are not Ethiopian, and you're not American; you're in the middle." As some of you can relate. Being raised by my American family, who were incredible parents, they raised me like an American, which was great! I needed to fit into and learn the American system, but I was also losing my Ethiopian culture because they didn't know my culture. They tried to keep my culture in my life as much as they could. There are some families like mine whom I have met who work really hard to keep their adopted child's culture in their life. They take them to places where they can learn their native language, they let them keep in contact with their friends from back home, or they take them to have cultural food or they make it at home for them, which helps the adoptees stay in touch with their heritage which is great for their development as a person knowing where they come from. They appreciate life more and work hard to become who they are meant to be so they can make an impact in their country when they are reminded of where they come from.

I decided I can become both Ethiopian and American, so I started sharing more of my story and who I am as a person with my American friends. I choose friends wisely. I chose friends who cared about me and loved me for who I was. When they heard my adoption story, they loved me more, and we became close friends. They told me I was a strong person to have gone through what I have gone through and to still have a positive outlook on life; it inspired them. People started telling me I inspired them to push through in life and in school to become who they are meant to be. Be true to who you are because you never know who you will inspire. I was still struggling with my identity though being black in America, especially in my town where there were only five black people. I felt like people wouldn't like me or accept me as their friend because I was black. I struggled with that for a little while; then, I realized if they didn't like me, it was their fault. One of my favorite quotes is:

"Be the change you want to see in the world."

—Gandhi

I decided I am going to accept myself for who I am as an Ethiopian with my scars; if people liked me, that was great, and if they didn't, they didn't. It was their choice. But I decided I am going to love and accept myself first. I decided I am going to be friends with all nationalities and become the change I wanted to see in my town. I became a social butterfly, as my mom would say it, and became friends with everyone. Everyone in town knew me and loved me, but I was still struggling with finding who I really am until I found Christ.

After Accepting Christ into my heart and becoming a new creation, I became a whole new person! In Genesis 1:26 (KJV), the Bible tells us that God said, "Let us make man in our own image, after our likeness." You can be of any race, black or white or etc., but you are created in the image of God and after His likeness. Because of that, women, you are beautiful; men, you are handsome. After you accept Christ into your heart, you become a new creation which means you have a new identity. Your identity is known in the spiritual realm as a son or daughter of God. Your race or culture doesn't define your identity any longer in this world either; you are a new creation in Christ. Jesus came to save every race in the entire world. He doesn't see color. The only color that should matter to us born-again Christians and the only color that matters to God is red; red represents the Blood of Jesus. Jesus paid the price for all our sins on the cross. We are bought by a price that we can never pay by ourselves to become His sons and daughters. Our new identity is defined by who we are in Christ.

> For I through the law am dead to the law, that I might live unto God. I am crucified with Christ: nevertheless I live; yet not I, but Christ liveth in me: and the life which I now live in the flesh I live by the faith of the Son of God, who loved me, and gave himself for me.
>
> Galatians 2:19-20 (KJV)

We no longer live, but Christ lives in us. When we build our relationship with Christ, Christ builds our new character that represents Him in us. We no longer live for ourselves or to please people, but we start living for God. Romans 12:2 (KJV) says, *"Don't copy the behavior and customs of this world, but let God transform you into a new person by changing the way you think. Then you will learn to know God's will for you, which is good and pleasing and perfect."*

Christ becomes the foundation for your identity. He becomes the anchor that holds you up. When you become a born-again Christian, you no longer go with the flow and be tossed to and fro like the wind with your relationships in your life, or trying to become what society or the culture you live in wants you to become, Christ becomes the anchor that holds you. The exhaustion of playing different personalities to please people will stop. You will find rest in becoming who you are as a person because of Christ. When you find Christ, what you find is rest for your soul and rest in knowing and becoming who you really created to be. If you need rest, go to the one who will give you rest and peace for your life. Christ is the one who gave me rest for my life. I no longer needed to please people or needed to change when I was spending time with my American friends or Ethiopian friends; I became my true self. I found my identity in Christ and stayed constant, becoming who He created me to be. I found rest and peace in becoming myself when I found Christ. Instead of doing things to please people, I started doing things to please God. Finding my identity in Christ set me free from so many things. My faith in God disciplined my speech and actions in how I held myself and in how I presented myself as an ambassador for Christ. I no longer spend time at places where God wouldn't be glorified. Through His grace, He took away my old habits and built my character to become more like Him every day. Christ is the example for us to follow in how to live our lives. Don't follow celebrities or even people that you look up to build who you are as a person. If they fall, there is a possible chance you might fall with them. But follow Christ and do everything as he did. Love people like Christ, teach people like Christ, serve people like Christ, forgive people like Christ, bless people as Christ would, and live a life that Christ would be glorified by. As Christians, we are called to become more like Christ every day and be His imitators. Ask yourself this question in everything you do, what would Jesus do? Enjoy your new identity in Christ, living for the one who has called you home to Himself.

"Being confident of this very thing, that he which hath begun a good work in you will perform it until the day of Jesus Christ" (Philippians 1:6, KJV).

Forgiveness

"Forgiveness is defined as a conscious, deliberate decision to release feelings of resentment or vengeance towards a person or group who has harmed you, regardless of whether they actually deserve your forgiveness."

Unknown.

Forgiveness is for you, not for the other person. Forgiveness sets you free. Forgiveness releases anger and resentment that a person carries for years. Forgiveness is relief. Forgiving someone that has hurt you is hard, but it sets you free. One person I had a hard time forgiving in my life was the first mom that adopted me, Megan, that made my life miserable for the two and half years that I lived with her. As you have read in my story, she did lots of horrible things to me and made me feel worthless. I had a lot of anger in me and wasn't willing to forgive her for what she has done to me for many years. Even after I got adopted to my second family, I was still hurt and angry at what she did. I wanted to say lots of mean things to her and was waiting for the day; I would see her again to confront her. If you know me as a person, this is unlike my personality. I am a very forgiving person, but I didn't think I would ever forgive her for everything she has done to me. As I talked to my family that adopted me, I told them about the anger that was boiling inside of me, and I couldn't wait to confront her about it. My excitement about confronting her was shattered right away. My family told me that the best thing to do is not holding a grudge but forgiving her and letting it go. They told me it was my past, but I needed to move on and not let what she did stop me from living my life but rather to live life to the fullest now that I have found freedom. They told me that as long as I lived with them, I was not allowed to say mean things to her or cause any problems with her. As long as I lived under their care, I represented them and their parenting, and what they wanted to teach me was forgiveness, not anger and resentment. They told me when I was eighteen, and out of the house after that, I can do whatever I want as I would as a young adult, but until, then I have to live under their rules. They constantly told me to forgive her and let it go.

I couldn't wait until I was eighteen years old so I could write her the meanest letter. I waited for years, and all of the anger never left me. Everything she did to me always played in my mind. It affected every aspect of my life for years. I had a hard time trusting people and letting people in my life. I always felt like people rejected me, even without them doing anything. The thought of being rejected stopped me from doing a lot of things. I felt like I didn't belong in my family or friends group because of what she did to me. I didn't have self-esteem or confidence for a long time. I suffered for many years physiologically for everything she did to me. It wasn't just about doing chores; it was what it did to my mind, my mindset, and how I viewed myself and viewed life. It was completely wrong. The mean words that she has spoken over me have always been ringing in my ears and playing in my mind for years. When a person goes to jail, and when they are let out after serving many years since what they remember was prison. After getting out of prison, their mindset could still be in imprisonment if they don't realize that they are free. Even though they are free and out in the world, their brain could make them think that they are still in prison. I was out of the cage, I was out of her life, but it was still living like a person that has been imprisoned. My mind was still in prison. I didn't know how to get my mind out of her prison. She didn't know, and she didn't realize that what she has done to me hurt me for years, even after I left her house. She didn't know it would have a long-term effect on me and left a scar. People that have hurt you probably don't know that it affects you. I didn't tell her, and by not forgiving her and holding a grudge, I didn't know this, but I was letting her control me without her knowing. We think by not forgiving people, we are winning, but we are the ones that are losing, and they are the ones that are winning. I was letting her win, and I didn't know it. Holding a grudge puts you in prison and keeps you in imprisonment to that person. Forgiveness sets you free and gets you out of prison. Unforgiveness is staying in prison that you have gotten out of. Forgiveness is for you and not for the other person. I struggled for years with unforgiveness until I found Christ. After accepting Christ, I realized and learned what forgiveness was. An example of forgiveness is Christ hung on the cross. God forgave us of all our sins to give us eternal life.

"For I will be merciful to their unrighteousness, and their sins and their iniquities will I remember no more" (Hebrews 8:12, KJV).

If God forgives all of my sins, who am I not to forgive the people that have hurt me in my life, including my first mom that adopted me. I knew I needed to forgive her from my heart, and that is not possible without the grace of God. I prayed that God would help me to forgive her completely. The Bible tells us to forgive one another as Christ forgave us. If God didn't forgive us, we would not be going to heaven and have eternal life with him. Love is forgiveness, and forgiveness is Jesus dying on the cross for us. We don't deserve forgiveness, but God still chose to forgive us. God commanded us to forgive one another and gave us our own will to choose to forgive. If we forgive those who have hurt us is the only way we will be forgiven by God. The choice is in our hands. Adoption has to be all about forgiveness for both the adoptee and the parent because adoption is messy and hard for both. They are both learning new things about each other. In most cases for both the adoptee and the parent, they are from different cultures, speak different languages, and the way they view life for both are different because they are from different continents. There will be misunderstanding and not having a good relationship from the start because they are both getting to know each other and understanding their way of thinking and how each of them see life. That is why it has to be all about forgiveness from both parties. Adoption is hard on both. Spiritual adoption is all about forgiveness.

The Gospel, which is the good news, is all about God's forgiveness to His children shown by Christ. Without forgiveness, there is no spiritual adoption. You can choose to forgive those who have hurt you and choose to be set free. Those people who have hurt you, you might feel, don't deserve forgiveness, but you and I didn't deserve God to forgive us either for all our sins. As I prayed for the Lord to completely help me to forgive her, God changed my heart, and I forgave her completely. I let it all go. I kept telling the Lord, as you have forgiven me, I have forgiven Megan completely. I asked the Lord if there was a part of me that didn't forgive her to reveal it to me, but I fully surrendered and let it go. I felt a huge burden lifted off of me. There was something that was lifted from my heart and mind. I was set free finally. After baptism, when you become a new creation in Christ, God starts working in your heart. He changes you from inside and out. He takes the heart of stone and gives you a heart of flesh.

"And I will give you a new heart, and I will put a new spirit in you. I will take out your stony, stubborn heart and give you a tender, responsive heart" (Ezekiel 36:26, NLT).

So you no longer want to live in the unforgiveness imprisonment of your past. Since Christ set you free of all bondage, you are no longer a slave to unforgiveness. Unforgiveness comes from the devil, and forgiveness comes from God. The enemy doesn't want you to forgive the person because he doesn't want you to be set free. He doesn't want you to fully live in the freedom Christ paid for you on the cross. One of his tactics is by lying to you and making you think to be upset with the person and having your mind constantly think about all the wrong things they have done to you. Whatever wrong thing has happened to you, it doesn't take away the truth that it was wrong to do what they did. It doesn't take away from the truth, but forgiveness sets you free. Forgiveness unblocks your destiny. It unlocks the blessings that are held up by you not forgiving someone. Forgiving those who have hurt you benefits you because you are able to receive all the blessings that God has prepared for you. God accepted and received you through forgiveness, and everything that he has prepared for you is through you forgiving those who have hurt you as well.

As I prayed for the Lord to completely help me to forgive her, I realized the reason why we don't forgive is because of the hurt and pain we have experienced before. After we forgive that person, we need to get healed by the Lord. God is a healer of diseases and also a healer of a wounded, broken heart. As there is a season for everything, there is a season for healing. I got into my season of healing and got into the presence of God and prayed for the Lord to heal my broken heart and to heal my mind from so much trauma. I got into God's presence as I listened to worship music and asked the Lord to heal me from all wounds I have experienced in my whole life, both in Ethiopia and America. People are afraid to get themselves in the season of healing and be vulnerable before the Lord, but it is the best decision that you will ever make for yourself. It seems hard to open up chapters that you have closed both in your heart and mind. No one wants to go back and relive hurts and pains of the past; people put a band-aid on their aches and pains and live with the bandage on for years. That is what I did, but what set me free is letting the Lord heal me. Every day my prayer was,

"Lord heal my heart and mind to the point that when I remember my past, it doesn't hurt me anymore. I wanted to talk about it without hurting and with a completely forgiven heart. It was a process of healing, a lot of tears shed, but the Lord was gentle and comforted me as he healed me. Psalm 147:4 (NLT) says, "He heals the brokenhearted and bandages their wounds."

I was in the season of healing for a while, but when I was done with my season of healing, I was completely healed. He healed me from my heart being broken from losing my parents at a young age; He healed me from the trauma I experienced when I got burned, He healed me from the spirit of rejection and healed me from all the wounds that I had experienced from my adopted mom and so much more. He can heal you from every wound that you have experienced. Go before your Heavenly Father and ask and let Him heal you in faith. He is a healer and ready to heal your heart. My heart and mind were completely healed. The Lord is a great heart surgeon, and He leaves no mark behind when He heals your heart. I know I had gone through a lot of trauma, as you have read in my story, but He healed me from everything to the point that I got surprised that I went through all that, but when I think of those wounds, they no longer stab and hurt me. It is to the point that it feels like it was almost erased from my memory. I had a new heart and mind. I became a new person, a new Sara. In every aspect of my life, I started blooming and growing, becoming who the Lord created me to be. Forgiveness and healing will set you free and help you become a new person that you will be proud of made by your Creator.

As Jesus has commanded us to forgive those who have hurt us, I wanted to let Megan know that I forgave her so I could act on what the Lord instructs us to do in action, not just in words. Action was harder than words. I didn't want to call her and let her know that I forgive her; I thought that was too easy. I wanted to do it in person, so I prayed that the Lord would make a divine appointment for us to meet somehow so I can tell her I forgave her. God was putting it on my heart to write this book about adoption both physically and spiritually. I told the Lord that adoption is all about forgiveness, and if I didn't get a chance to talk to Megan and tell her that I forgave her completely from my heart, I couldn't write this book. I made a decision that I have to live it out in action in what I am teaching in this book. After a while, the Lord made a way where there is no way for me to meet her. My American brother was going to get married, and I knew she would be coming; I told myself I would tell her then. When I saw her at my brother's wedding, we both hugged each other and greeted each other. I told her I needed to talk to her about something. I told her and her daughter that I forgave them both for everything that happened and everything they did. I told them that there is nothing in my heart, no grudge or unforgiveness. I told her that God healed my heart, and because of Christ, I was able to forgive her for everything. I told her we are family and to continue that without any awkwardness but love. I used to hate her before, but God changed my heart to love her. They told me they were sorry too for everything and we had a great conversation. Now, whenever we see each other at family gatherings, we both greet each other with a hug. She is always surprised by how much I have grown as a person and tells me she is proud of me for what I have accomplished. She is my aunt, and we have continued to be family with love and compassion. This story truly shows the power of God and what God can do in your friendships and relationships when you let him in. I was then free to write this book about adoption and forgiveness.

I encourage you to forgive anyone that has hurt you before. When Peter asked Jesus how many times he should forgive his brother who sins against him. Peter thought seven times was enough. But Jesus's reply was, "No, not seven times, but seventy times seven" (Matthew 18:22, NLT). Jesus is teaching us to forgive people all the time, every time they do us wrong, just like our Father in heaven forgives us every time for all the sins we commit every day. Colossians 3:12-15 shows us how to live our lives.

Since God chose you to be the holy people he loves, you must clothe yourselves with tenderhearted mercy, kindness, humility, gentleness, and patience. Make allowance for each other's faults, and forgive anyone who offends you. Remember, the Lord forgave you, so you must forgive others. Above all, clothe yourselves with love, which binds us all together in perfect harmony. And let the peace that comes from Christ rule in your hearts. For as members of one body you are called to live in peace. And always be thankful.

Colossians 3:12-15 (NLT)

The God That Lives in Us

"God has two dwellings; one in heaven, and the other in a meek and thankful heart."

—Izaak Walton

The Holy Spirit is the God on earth in this day and age. Heaven has come down to earth and dwells in born-again Christians. Jesus's other name is Emmanuel, which translates to God with us. When Jesus came down, it was God dwelling and being with us, his creations. After Jesus was resurrected from the dead, He dwelt with His disciples for forty days before ascending into heaven. After Jesus fulfilled His purpose on earth, which God His Father has sent Him to do, He was going back to the one who sent Him. He finished His assignment. Just like Jesus, when we are done fulfilling our assignment, fulfilling our purpose on earth, which God has sent us to do, we will join Jesus in heaven. Jesus is our advocate when He was on the earth when He left another advocate who is the Holy Spirit was sent to live in born-again Christians until we go to heaven. Jesus told His disciples, it is better that He leaves so that the advocate, who is the Holy Spirit, can come and dwell inside every born-again Christian. If Jesus didn't leave, the Holy Spirit couldn't come. In John 16:8-11 (NLT), Jesus tells His disciples about the Holy Spirit:

> *And when he comes, he will convict the world of its sin, and of God's righteousness, and of the coming judgment. The world's sin is that it refuses to believe in me. Righteousness is available because I go to the Father, and you will see me no more. Judgment will come because the ruler of this world has already been judged.*

Satan is the ruler of the world who has already been judged. In John 16:13-15 (NLT), Jesus tells His disciples about the Holy Spirit:

> *When the Spirit of truth comes, he will guide you into all truth. He will not speak on his own but will tell you what he has heard. He will tell you about the future. He will bring me glory by telling you whatever he receives from me. All that belongs to the Father is mine; this is why I said, 'The Spirit will tell you whatever he receives from me."*

Before Jesus ascended into heaven, He told His disciples to wait to receive the Holy Spirit before they go out to share the Gospel, which is the good news. Just as Jesus instructed the disciples and the believers, they waited for the Holy Spirit to come upon them for fifty days. "

But you will receive power when the Holy Spirit comes upon you. And you will be my witnesses, telling people about me everywhere—in Jerusalem, throughout Judea, in Samaria, and to the ends of the earth.

Acts 1:8 (NLT)

Acts 2:2-4 (NLT) says:

Suddenly, there was a sound from heaven like the roaring of a mighty windstorm, and it filled the house where they were sitting. Then, what looked like flames or tongues of fire appeared and settled on each of them. And everyone present was filled with the Holy Spirit and began speaking in other languages, as the Holy Spirit gave them this ability.

After receiving power from the Holy Spirit, the disciples and the believers went all over the world to share the good news. The church grew rapidly like wildfire; it spread all over the world and now has come down to us. Just as the disciples and the believers shared the Gospel all over the world, it is our turn now to share the gospel to this generation and to the next so that people receive salvation in every generation.

Romans 10:14-15 (NLT) says:

But how can they call on him to save them unless they believe in him? And how can they believe in him if they have never heard about him? And how can they hear about him unless someone tells them? And how will anyone go and tell them without being sent? That is why the Scriptures say, "How beautiful are the feet of messengers who bring good news!

Romans 10:17 (KJV) says, *"So then faith cometh by hearing, and hearing by the word of God."*

The Holy Spirit teaches us and guides us. He reminds us of things we have learned. If you need guidance on decisions you need to make in your life, the Holy Spirit is your companion. Ask him to help guide you to make the right decisions and to help guide you to go and do the will of God in your life. The Holy Spirit is our comforter; when you need comfort, ask the Holy Spirit to comfort you. The Holy Spirit is also our counselor; when you need counsel, ask the Holy Spirit to counsel you. Ask the Holy Spirit to counsel you in your prayer time or quiet time; if you need more counseling, ask the Holy Spirit to counsel you through people he chooses to use in your life. He is full of wisdom. When you feel weak, ask the Holy Spirit to give you strength.

> *Each time he said, "My grace is all you need. My power works best in weakness." So now I am glad to boast about my weaknesses, so that the power of Christ can work through me. That's why I take pleasure in my weaknesses, and in the insults, hardships, persecutions, and troubles that I suffer for Christ. For when I am weak, then I am strong.*
>
> 2 Corinthians 12:9 (NLT)

The Holy Spirit makes his home in our hearts.

Don't you realize that your body is the temple of the Holy
Spirit, who lives in you and was given to you by God? You do
not belong to yourself, for God bought you with a high price.
So you must honor God with your body.

1 Corinthians 6:19-20 (NLT)

We need to keep our bodies pure and clean for the dwelling of the Holy Spirit. If we sin, we need to ask Jesus for forgiveness and ask him to wash and cleanse us by his blood so that the place where the Holy Spirit dwells is always clean.

We feel the presence of God through the Holy Spirit. That is why we need to invite the Holy Spirit when we pray and when we worship alone and when we do this with others. The Holy spirit's presence changes the atmosphere and situations. It is the Holy Spirit that heals our hearts, heals us from sickness and disease. Whenever the Holy Spirit is present, there is freedom!

The Holy Spirit teaches us what and how to pray. Romans 8:26-27 (NLT) says:

And the Holy Spirit helps us in our weakness. For example,
we don't know what God wants us to pray for. But the Holy
Spirit prays for us with groanings that cannot be expressed
in words. And the Father who knows all hearts knows what
the Spirit is saying, for the Spirit pleads for us believer in
harmony with God's own will.

When the Holy Spirit prays through us, we are praying prayers that align with the will of God in our lives. When we are hungry and thirsty for more of God's spirit to work in and through us, he will pour out his Spirit on us. He promises that to us in Acts 2:17-18 (NLT):

> *"In the last days," God says, "I will pour out my Spirit upon all people. Your sons and daughters will prophesy. Your young men will see visions, and your old men will dream dreams. In those days I will pour out my Spirit even on my servants men and women alike and they will prophesy."*
>
> Acts 2:17-18 (NLT)

These are not just words; the Holy Spirit is working in born-again Christians in this day and age who are sold out to serve God. They are seeing visions, dreams, and prophesying. They are bringing the kingdom of God down to earth through the power and presence of the Holy Spirit. If you are searching for more of God, and want to see more of His glory, pray for the outpouring of the Holy Spirit to come upon you! He will show you His wonders and glory. While we are waiting to go to heaven, God has brought heaven to us through the Holy Spirit. God's sons and daughters need to rise up and stand for the truth and boldly share the Gospel with those who don't know Christ. What has been revealed to you has not yet been revealed to other people.

Romans 8:19-23 (NLT) says:

> *For all creation is waiting eagerly for that future day when God will reveal who his children really are. Against its will, all creation was subjected to God's curse. But with eager hope, the creation looks forward to the day when it will join*

God's children in glorious freedom from death and decay. For we know that all creation has been groaning as in the pains of childbirth right up to the present time. And we believers also groan, even though we have the Holy Spirit within us as a foretaste of future glory, for we long for our bodies to be released from sin and suffering. We, too, wait with eager hope for the day when God will give us our full rights as his adopted children, including the new bodies he has promised us.

Returning Back to Ethiopia

Every immigrant or adoptee always looks forward to returning back home to visit their country as soon as they leave their country. Most people start missing home as soon as their foot has stepped out of the country. The wait, the desire, and the anticipation of when you are able to go back home to visit your birth country and family are very hard. I, too, longed for the day I would return back to Ethiopia to visit my family, friends, and country I grew up in for many years. I always dreamed that when I went back to visit, my goal was to go for five months. So I can have quality time to get to know my aunts, uncles, cousins since I have missed many years of their life. Due to finishing High school and starting college, and doing ministry for the Lord, I wasn't able to go for twelve years. I didn't have a gap where I could take five months for vacation because I was busy with life and wanted to accomplish some things before I went back home. America and Ethiopia are my home. I stayed in contact with my sisters in Ethiopia by calling them on the phone and on Facebook throughout the years. I missed them a lot and couldn't wait for the day to see them again face to face.

My spiritual family surprised me by buying my plane ticket to Ethiopia. My adopted family surprised me by blessing me financially for me to be able to go and do the things I wanted to do. God was still writing my story and surprised me with someone special to go with me on this journey back home.

Mitikay is one of my closest friends that I love whom I have known since childhood. She was my neighbor while I was living with my sisters in Ethiopia. We got sponsored together through World Vision, and she is also the one that took the journey with me going to Layla house on the same day, and now, we were going back to Ethiopia to visit our families, and back to the neighborhood, we grew up in twelve years later. It was a trip of a lifetime! I am grateful that God gave me Mitikay to take this special trip that I have been looking forward to for so many years. As we were on the plane, we were thinking back to our childhood in amazement and in awe of God, how the Lord has been there every step of the way, guiding us and caring for us through people he brought into our lives.

After we got off the plane, we were anxious, nervous, and excited to meet our families for the first time after twelve years! There they were, standing in a row holding balloons and flowers, crying as we walked out of the airport. We ran and embraced them with hugs and kisses on their cheeks. We couldn't let go of everyone hugging and holding us tight as we cried with them. It was very emotional for all of us. It was a reunion that I will never forget. I cried when I got in the car; it seemed like a dream. I have dreamed of this day to come for so many years, and now I am living in it. They, too, joined me crying in the car, holding my hand and comforting me. God did it! I was finally home visiting my family. I always prayed for the Lord to make a way where there seems to be no way for me to be reunited with my family again. It was a promise he gave me that he will fulfill. Just as the Bible said in Hebrews 10:23 (KJV), *"Let us hold fast the profession of our faith without wavering; for he is faithful that promised."*

I was mesmerized by how much the city has grown as I looked out the window. It wasn't the Ethiopia I remembered. It has turned out to be more like America. There were so many tall buildings. We finally arrived at the house I grew up in when I was a child. Everyone in the neighborhood came running to hug and kiss me, welcoming me home! There were so many people crying as they hugged me, I couldn't control my tears. It was two hours of people coming in and out of the house to see with their own eyes that Sara has returned back home after twelve years. My house was changed when I returned. There were nice sofas, TV stands with a TV on them, nice coffee table. We never had those things while I lived in Ethiopia; they made the house look absolutely beautiful. They added to the house, so it was bigger than I remembered. It felt great to be home again with my sisters and my aunts. I also came home to be an aunt to two of my nephews. The whole week was a week of people coming to visit friends and family from far away who came to see me. Every person that came brought some delicious Ethiopian food with them. I was in awe of God for bringing me to this moment to spend quality time with my family.

I remembered and understood Amharic well but speaking it was hard for me. I was speaking in broken Amharic, but we understood each other. I went to the rural part of the country, to the country Laman that my parents were from. I met my parents' neighbors, and they shared with us special stories I didn't know about my biological Mom and Dad. It was special meeting them and hearing stories of how they all lived together. I met so many aunts, uncles, and cousins that I have never met before when I was in Ethiopia. I didn't know I had lots of family like that. I was grateful and happy to meet them. There were cousins my age that I loved and spent lots of time with. I went back and forth from the capital city Addis Ababa and to Laman so I could spend quality time with everyone during the five months I stayed there. Quality time was everything to me and something I looked forward to for many years; I had a great time with everyone. I took gifts with me to give to all my family members.

One of my dreams and hopes were to see one of my sisters get married. I missed one of my sister's wedding, and I didn't want to miss the other one. My sister, Lydia, bless her heart, had waited for me for years to get married so I could be present at her wedding! I was able to witness her wedding and be there to see her get married. That was a dream of mine that the Lord fulfilled. It was a beautiful wedding! All of my family members were there and lots of people we knew and loved. It was a wedding that I will never forget!

I wanted to go to a church in Ethiopia that was Holy Spirit-filled. I was so happy to find an incredible church called Presence TV Worldwide church. The prophet there is a man of God that God uses in a mighty way. In that church, just like the church's name, the presence of God is very strong. I saw miracles happen every single week! There were people that were walking out of their wheelchairs that have not been able to walk for twenty years and be set free in the name of Jesus! There were people that used to walk with canes for years, and the Lord healed their legs completely right in the spot. They walked into the building with their canes and wheelchairs and left without it! Praise God! They come to that church believing and receiving their healing. There were people getting healed of HIV and cancer! Many diseases were healed in the powerful name of Jesus in that church! Every week there was healing and testimonies of God's goodness. There were people delivered from the enemy. In that church, I saw miracles, signs, and wonders! God healed my aunt's eyes. She wasn't able to read or see that much before because her eyes were weak. The Lord healed her as she was worshiping Him.

We both were praying for healing for her eyes, and the Lord heard us. I was with her when she got healed. I had back pain for a long time that I was going to physical therapy for while I was in the U.S., it never got better through physical therapy. Even when I went to Ethiopia, it was hurting so bad that I was going to massage places often to feel better. But when I was worshiping one day, the prophet told us to put our hands on our bodies at a place that hurts us. I put my hand on my back, and instantly, the Holy Spirit touched me and healed me. I didn't have any back pains after that. Glory to God! Every week was astonishing to witness so many miracles! I never missed a week. Even if I went on vacation to another town in Ethiopia out of the city, I always came back for the two days of service they had during the five months I stayed. How can I miss heaven coming down to earth? Being in God's presence is the best place on earth; there is nothing that can compare to it. God is a healer, if you need healing, believe and pray for it, and the Lord will heal you.

For those who believe, In Mark 16:17 (NLT), the Bible tells us:

> These miraculous signs will accompany those who believe: They will cast out demons in my name, and they will speak in new languages. They will be able to handle snakes with safety, and if they drink anything poisonous, it won't hurt them. They will be able to place their hands on the sick, and they will be healed.

Mitikay and I had an amazing time visiting with our families and visiting different places in Ethiopia. God made a way for this special person in my life to go back to our roots together. For that, I am truly grateful. I love you Mitikay; you hold a special place in my heart.

During my five months stay, Mitikay and I visited the Sele Enat Charitable organization. It was the house that we were at before we came to the U.S. We went to see the children and serve the kids there just like we hoped and dreamed we would someday come back to Ethiopia to serve orphans like us. It was an amazing experience we both had. Seleenat means in place of a mother in English. They take care of children who have lost their parents and have no one to care for them. It was a place of love; the children were loved by their nannies and everyone that served at Seleenat. I was amazed by their work. A few of our friends that were adopted from the same orphanage were also in Ethiopia at the same time; we went to volunteer together at the orphanage and took the children swimming, ice cream, to restaurants and took them shopping. We had lots of fun with them. It was an amazingly humbling experience to be a volunteer and not an orphan. God truly takes people from the bottom and puts them on top. I have seen it in my life and so many other people's lives.

Seleenat children

Sara (me) with Seleenat children

Mitikay holding a baby at Selenat orphanage

During the holidays, I would spend the day with the children and celebrate with them as they don't have anyone, just the management, nannies, and volunteers that come to celebrate with them as they don't have a family of their own. I would come home in the evening and spend the holiday with my sisters. It was the most fulfilling experience that I have never had helping orphans. On Sundays, one of the volunteers from the orphanage and I would take some of the older children to church. They are not allowed to leave the gate by themselves, but they are able to go to church if they want to, with volunteers. They always begged me to take them to church and made sure I showed up every Sunday. It was the most fulfilling experience that I have ever had helping orphans. God fulfilled the desire of my heart to give back to orphans just like I have dreamed about for so many years.

James 1:7 (NLT) says, *"Pure and genuine religion in the sight of God the Father means caring for orphans and widows in their distress and refusing to let the world corrupt you."*

The management at Seleenat Charitable Organization are incredible people who love the children they support. They have made the place a home for all the children there. I am grateful for non-profits like Seleenat and many more organizations in Ethiopia and all over the world that care for orphans. If you would like to sponsor a child from Seleenat Charitable Organization, contact them! I encourage you to sponsor a child and help a child get an education, medical expenses paid, and necessities that the child will need to have a brighter future. You can be the person that changes a child's life forever! Their Facebook page is called Sele Enat Mahiber.

I had the best time of my life in the five months I stayed with my family and my friend Mitikay in Ethiopia. Going back to my country answered so many questions I had in my heart about my family, my family history, and my country. Every question that I had was answered. If you haven't yet gone back to your roots, to where you came from, to visit your country or family as an adoptee, I highly encourage you to go back and visit and find out more about yourself and find answers to the questions in your heart. You are going to be so grateful and happy that you did that. That emptiness will be filled. If you don't know how to find your families or don't have connections with them, contact agencies and people that would know how to find families.

There are so many families who didn't have contact with their families back home but have been reunited through research. Even if you are not looking for your families, know that your families could possibly be looking for you. Look for them and find your roots. It is hard for a lot of adoptees to go back to their roots as there are many traumatic things that have happened in their past that they don't want to remember, but know it will be the best decision you have ever made looking for your family. If you don't have your parents, you might have aunts, uncles, and cousins wondering where you are and how to find you. Always know they love you and want to be reunited with you. It is the greatest feeling in the world to find the missing piece you have been looking for all along. I was loved and taken care of by my family. They treated me like a queen. Every piece of the puzzle in my heart was filled. My trip made me whole as a person. It was a reunion that I will never forget. Praise be to God, who made everything beautiful in my life at the right time. I am grateful to the Lord for everything He has done in my life. He has been the rock that never left my side and has been by my side every step of the way. He is the anchor of my heart. Through finding myself through adoption, I have found the true lover of my heart, that is Jesus Christ, my Savior, the advocate and judge for our spiritual adoption to God.

Returning Home to Heaven

Heaven is the place where the Creator of the Universe, the one who is the Alpha and the Omega, the beginning and the end dwells with his adopted children. It is the place where our Spirit and God's Spirit dwell. Heaven is what our hearts and souls long for. Heaven is the place of eternity, the place of rest, the place that is already ready for God's adopted sons and daughters to live after we pass from this life. Before Jesus ascended into heaven, He promised His disciples and other believers He would come back for them.

> *There is more than enough room in my Father's home. If this were not so, would I have told you that I am going to prepare a place for you? When everything is ready, I will come and get you, so that you will always be with me where I am. And you know the way to where I am going.*
>
> John 14:2-4 (NLT)

John 14:18 (NLT) says, "No, I will not abandon you as orphans, I will come to you." Jesus went to prepare a place for us and will come back again to take us home to where he is. Jesus is also the judge to let us into heaven because he is our advocate for our spiritual adoption to God. When we confess and acknowledge Him publicly on earth, He will also acknowledge us before His Father in heaven. But if we deny Him on earth, He will deny us in heaven. That is why it is important for us to speak boldly and confidently about our faith in the Lord while we live on this earth. Our eternity is tied to it. The Bible tells us people look in the outward appearance, but God Lord looks in our hearts. (See 1 Samuel 16:7.) When we speak boldly about our faith in Jesus Christ, we need to do it from our hearts, not just to look holy in front of people. Because the Bible also tells us that there are people that honor God with their mouths, but their hearts are far from him. If your heart is far from God, and if you don't have a relationship with him, you might not get into heaven (see Matthew 15:8).

Matthew 7:21-23 (NLT) says:

> Not everyone who calls out to me, Lord! Lord! Will enter the Kingdom of Heaven. Only those who actually do the will of my Father in heaven will enter. On Judgement day many will say to me, "Lord, Lord! We prophesied in your name, and cast out demons in your name and performed many miracles in your name. But I will reply, I never knew you. Get away from me, you who break God's laws.

We need to have a true relationship with Christ. It is not by our works, we go to heaven but by the grace of God and doing the will of God in our lives while on earth. When we do the will of God in our lives, we need to do it for the Lord and not to be seen by men. There is a reward waiting for us in heaven for doing the will of God in our lives with a pure heart. Let us fight the good fight just like Paul in the Bible and finish strong. Paul tells us in 2 Timothy 4:7-8 (NLT):

> *I have fought the good fight, I have finished the race, and I have remained faithful. And now the prize awaits me the crown of righteousness, which the Lord, the righteous Judge, will give me on the day of his return. And the prize is not just for me but for all who eagerly look forward to his appearing.*

Let this be our prayer for our lives to finish the race faithfully to receive our crown of righteousness. Rick Warren said, "The way you store up treasure in Heaven is by investing in getting people there."

Jesus is coming soon! Mark 13:32-33 (NLT) says, *"But of that day or hour no one knows, not even the angels in heaven, nor the Son, but the Father alone. Watch out! Stay alert! For you do not know when the time will come."* The Bible describes Jesus as the Bridegroom, and we the church, born again Christians, are His bride. He is coming for us to take us home. We have to be prepared and ready to go when our Bridegroom shows up. Just as His words say, no one knows of his return, but we have to be ready as if He is coming today! If Jesus was coming today, would you be ready? If not, get ready now and be ready. He can come any moment. The Bible tells us signs of Jesus's return is that there will be wars and rumors of wars, there will be earthquakes and famines.

We are citizens of heaven living on this earth! We are going to the place of everlasting joy and happiness. It is a beautiful place no person can imagine with physical eyes. It is a place of absolute love and peace. Heaven is a place where we will live with our loving Father and our Savior, Jesus Christ, forever. It is a place where we will reunite with our loved ones who also are born-again Christians. Philippians 3:20-21 (NLT) states:

> *But we are citizens of heaven, where the Lord Jesus Christ lives. And we are eagerly waiting for him to return as our Saviour. He will take our weak mortal bodies and change them into glorious bodies like his own, using the same power with which he will bring everything under his control.*

Solutions for Adoptions and Foster Care

Are you adopted? Are you adopting a child for the first time? Do you already have an adopted child? Are you in the Foster care system? Are you a foster parent? Adoption and Foster care are very important in this world and generation. Children need homes and families to care for them, and families desire and want to share their love and home to those afflicted children who are in need. Adoption and foster care is the answer and solution for the children and for families, but first, before you adopt a child or decide to be a foster parent, you need to understand what it means to adopt or be a foster parent for an orphan child or for a person in the foster care system. Being a parent to a child in need is the most selfless thing a person can do; it could also be the hardest thing a parent can experience. Love and the desire to help impact a child's life and future is the main cause that leads a parent to adopt or be a foster parent. This main reason can never be forgotten after a parent adopts or becomes a foster parent. When it gets difficult, which it can, the parent always needs to have the reason they made the decision to bring the child in their life in the first place. I encourage parents to write down the reason you decided to adopt or be a foster parent and put it where you can see it every day, put it on your wall in your house or room. Remembering the purpose will always help you to be able to love and care for the child in a deeper way and will also help you go through it in challenging times.

Being a parent to a child in need is very rewarding and the most fulfilling thing a person can ever experience to change a child's future. But when a parent decides to adopt a child or chooses to be a foster parent, they need to first research about adoption or the foster care system and learn from people who have gone through it. Read books and articles that have been written by people that have experienced it before that can advise you on how to raise a child who is vulnerable. Learning from their mistakes and also learning from the positive method they used to raise their child can help you tremendously on what to expect and how to raise your new child. Every child is different, and what worked for them may not work for your child, but having information beforehand will help get your mind ready for the job ahead of you. You will find information from the parent's perspective and the child's perspective as you join into this new world of adoption and foster care system. You will learn a lot about how your new child thinks and what to expect from an orphan child, what their wants and desires are, and the hurt and heartache they have gone through that has been a scar in their life. You'll learn what the child expects from you as a parent to them. Wisdom is wealth.

Unmet expectations from the child and from the parent can lead to division and chaos in the home. When entering the world of adoption and foster care, there are expectations parents have, and there are also expectations that the child being adopted has. Some of the expectations a child being adopted has are to be loved and taken care of well by the person that adopts them. The child expects the parent to love them and treat them just like they would treat their own biological children, which is true. Parents, if you are not treating and raising your adopted or foster child just as you would your biological child, it is wrong. You should treat them the same and love them. If the child feels mistreated, the child will feel unwanted, rejected, and unloved by the parent. Even if you don't feel like they wouldn't feel and experience that, they automatically do. The child may have experienced rejection and feeling unwanted by their biological parents, giving them up for adoption and the foster care system. They might not understand that their biological families wanted what is best for them by giving them up. After joining a new family and if they see and feel that their new parents are also treating them differently. That wound that hasn't been healed will rise up, and they would feel hurt and unloved. Help them heal that wound by constantly making sure they feel loved and included in the family. When a child experiences rejection or if they feel unloved by the parents or their new siblings, they would start a new behavior, not being obedient to the parent and not doing what the parents ask them to do. When you see a child being disobedient, don't look at the disobedience first but ask yourself what the cause of their disobedience could be. What is hurting or bothering them to make them feel act that way, is the key. Talk to the child with love and ask them if there is something bothering them and the reason they are not being obedient. Finding the root of the problem will help you find a solution for the problem. Don't add punishments on them for disobeying, and don't take away privileges that could possibly fix the problem temporarily. This would make the child get more upset and add more reasons to disobey the parent, which would cause more chaos in the home for everyone. Have a conversation with them by being understanding and loving and ask them the real reason they are acting the way they are, ask them what is really hurting them, and keep asking questions until you get to the root. When you find out the reason, help them heal and help them understand and fix the problem. The healer of hearts is Jesus! Pray for them so that the Lord would heal their heart and make them whole. Do your part as well, and treat them with love and care and raise your children, both adopted and biological, equally to cover up their wounds of their past.

There is an expectation that parents have that their children they adopt or foster will be perfect children who follow and obey all their rules. Parents expect as long as the adopted or foster child lives in their home and under their roof, they expect the child to follow their rules in the home. Adoptees or foster children, it is true, you need to accept and follow the rules set by your parents because they are the adults who took guardianship over you to care for you and love you. Parents expect the children to be grateful, which is true; the children should be grateful for everything the parent does for them and always live in gratitude. Adoptees or foster children come into their new family thinking and expecting that the parents will give them everything they wanted. Some children come in thinking that they would even help their families back home in their country as well.

Parents, you are not expected of that; you are expected to care for the child that you adopt. But if you choose to help their families back home out of the kindness of your hearts, by sending a little bit of money to support their families, your adopted child and their family would truly be grateful for you forever as life is truly hard for those that live in third world country. Adoptees don't expect your parents to help your families; they can if they choose too and don't be upset if they don't. Let it be something to inspire you when you grow up and when you're on your own; you'll be able to help your families back home as much as you want. Adoptees hear of some of their friends' families helping their family back home for them, so when they join their new family, they think and expect all families to do what they have heard from their friends and expect their parents to help their families. If this is causing problems in the home, talk about it with your child and help them understand that you are not able to financially. It is something that is fixable.

Some parents feel if they allow their adopted child to be in contact with their biological families, that their child would not love them as much. Some fear that their new adopted child wouldn't accept and be close to their new families if they let them be in connection to their past families. That is a lie. Some parents don't allow their child to be in contact with their families back home in fear that the child would ask their parents to help their families back home financially. That is all a lie. Parents do allow your adopted child to be in contact with their families; they were there in their life before you. Your child, no matter what you do, can never forget their past or their families back home. It is their root, and you should encourage them to stay in touch with their families. If you allow them to stay in touch with their birth families, they would love you more and appreciate you for letting them. You're a child, and you will probably become closer in your relationship because you allowed them to not forget their families and where they come from. Your child would someday ask themselves who they are, where they came from, who their families are back home. They would want to know answers to these questions, and you allowing them to stay in touch with their families will help them get their answers. Don't let your child live with questions all their life on who they are by not allowing them to build relationships with their biological family. These are the questions every adoptee will someday ask themselves and have the answers ready for them. If they are too young to know and understand, get their families information from the adoption agency and stay in touch with their families, letting them know how they're doing as they are growing up. It wasn't easy for their biological family, as in siblings or aunts and uncles, to give them up for adoption, but they loved them enough to want what's best for them. They thought what is best for them is to give them up to be your son or daughter. Help the biological families heal by allowing your child to stay in connection with them. Some biological families regret ever giving up their child to adoption because adoptive parents don't allow their children to contact their birth family. Some promise that their child would stay in touch, but after adopting them, they don't allow the child or the family to talk. Be true to your word and keep the promise you make to the biological family and to the agency that you adopted your child from. Some biological families don't know where the child they gave up for adoption lives, how to find the children, and they live all their life with a question of if they are still alive or dead. A lot of adoptive parents change their child's name after they adopt them, so it is easier for people to remember the child's name, so it is not foreign to the country they adopted the child into.

While that is normal and okay to do. Birth families are not able to find the children because of the name change and the adoptive families not updating the birth family. Allow your child and their birth families to stay in touch through phone calls, skype, or writing letters to each other; you will be blessed by it too. This is a big question for your child as your child grows up; it would create a big hole in their heart not knowing. Help your child heal and help their heart to be whole by allowing them to be families with their birth families as well. By allowing your children, they will grow in a stronger relationship with you, and they will be able to open up about their past and allow you into their hearts. They will love you more for doing this for them! Some, if not all adoptees, will want to meet their biological families in person someday, as a parent will be willing and open for that if they talk to you about making a trip to go see them. Some adoptive parents bless their hearts and take their children back to their country so they can visit their biological families and their birth country. Some take their children every few years because they know it is important to their child and to their birth families.

Some parents don't allow their adopted child to stay in touch with their culture and friends from back home. They want their adopted child to completely forget where they come from. They shut off all connections to their past and their culture. Some don't allow their adopted children to speak in their native language, even if they have a sibling that speaks the language. Because of the lack of speaking, a lot of adoptees forget their native language. Some don't allow their children to stay in connection with their friends who are also adopted from the same orphanage. They are told to forget about everything and everyone they know and told to adapt and accept to the new culture in the new country they live in, language, families. They are told to make new friends and forget their old friends. This is all wrong. Allow your children to keep their culture from back home while accepting and learning about the new culture they live in. While they are learning the new language, allow and encourage your adopted child to speak in their native language. That is the only way they will be able to talk to their families back home. Learning new languages is a gift and wisdom. In fact, learning about your child's history and culture and understanding where they come from, that will help you as you raise your child. Understand your child by knowing and talking to them about where they came from and asking them about their past. When you try and speak some words in their language or when you allow them to practice their culture and when you appreciate their culture, that is an open the door to your child's heart to have a real connection with them. They would know you accepted them for who they are and where they came from. That will bring joy to them and knowing how understanding you are. I know some adoptive parents who take Amharic classes to learn the Ethiopian language so they can teach their children and also relate to their children. I know some families who take cooking lessons on how to cook Ethiopian food so they can cook it at home for their children. I know some families watch YouTube to learn how to make Ethiopian food so they can teach their children as well.

Doing things together with your adopted child that relates to their culture or where they come from will bring a greater bond between you and your child. Some adopted children miss their culture and their country by cooking together, by allowing them to call their friends on the phone, by meeting up with other adoptee families, and by going to adoption gatherings. It will help your child heal and help them not to miss their country or their families back home. I know some families who make sacrifices to meet up with other adopted parents and children that don't live in the same state every month so that their child can keep in touch with their friends. Adoption is sacrifice. Adoption is looking out for the best interest of the child, not only the parent. Allow them to be immersed in their culture while teaching them the new system and culture in the new country they live in. When you learn new things about your adopted child's culture, also learn the behaviors of their culture, understand and see what is considered rude and what is considered polite in their culture. What is considered rude in their culture might not be considered rude in your country. What is considered rude in your country might not be considered rude in their country. Understanding the behavior and learning about them will help you understand your child and how to raise your child. It will save you from confusion, misunderstanding, and not getting along with your child.

For example, my adoptive mom thought I was being rude when I didn't look her in her eyes when she would talk to me or scold me for something. She would yell at me to look her in the eyes. What she didn't understand was in my culture, it was a sign of respect to not look at adults in the eye when you're being scolded or when you're talking to an adult; you look down as a sign of showing them respect. I was respecting her in my own thoughts, but in America, in this culture, she thought I was being disrespectful to her and not listening to her when she would tell me to look her in the eye, and I wouldn't. That caused misunderstanding and brought some unneeded tension in the house. It is hard for adoptees to break habits they learn from their culture, whether it is good or bad, right away. I came as an eleven-year-old to America; it was hard for me to break all the things I learned all the behaviors I practiced in Ethiopia when I came to America all at once. Not that my behaviors were bad, but they weren't accepted in America as normal since it is a new country and a new way of living. My mom needed to be patient with me as I tried to break off some of the things I learned growing up. It wasn't me being disobedient; it was me being obedient to her in my thoughts. Understand your child and where they came from. Understand they have developed habits good or bad from their culture or what their families taught them in their country, so learning and developing new habits is going to take some time in a new country.

They don't do it on purpose. Don't add punishment while they are breaking their old habits and developing the new habits you are teaching them. If you add punishment, they might be upset and be resistant to change their ways. Teach them new habits with love and patience. Patience is very important for both the adoptee and the parent in adoption. A lot of misunderstandings between adoptees and adoptive parents can be fixed by learning about each other's culture. There wouldn't be second adoptions if adoptive families and adoptees have patience in understanding culture and behavior and learn how to get along with each other. If adoptive parents are too strict, they could lose their children. They are used to living in freedom in their country. Being too strict too fast might cause problems in your relationships with your adopted child because they are not used to the new rules. Teach them and raise them well but do it in a way that shows them whatever you are teaching them will benefit them in life later.

If there are problems between the parent and the adopted child, I encourage you to go to counseling. Don't go to any counseling though, find a counselor who specializes and has worked with adoption cases or foster care systems. Usually, adoptees don't want to share what they are going through with someone that doesn't understand them or to someone that doesn't have a background in adoptions. Because they know they can't relate to them. Both of you can go to counseling to make your relationships better.

Don't be surprised if your adopted child is not opening up to share about their past and the traumatic things they have gone through in their lives. Don't feel hurt or don't feel or think they don't love you if they don't share their past. For a lot of adoptees, it is hard for them to open up about their past and share their stories because they are wounds that they haven't healed from yet. Trust takes time. They will open up and share their life with you when they feel comfortable with you and when they feel comfortable to go back in their memory to see everything they experienced. Some adoptees shut it off from their memory as soon as they start a new life with their adopted family and try not to remember the life they used to live. They do that because they of hurt and pain. A lot of adoptees have experienced watching their parents die in their hands; they have experienced lots of death in their home. They have experienced living in the streets with no one taking care of them and some other traumatic things that happened to them in their past. While talking about it is healing for them, talking about it is also hard for them. Some adoptees want to share their past experiences with their families, but their adoptive families are not open to knowing their past, or they never ask them to share with them. I wanted to share with the first mom that adopted me all of my experiences, but she wasn't open. She never asked m,e and we were always fighting to the point that I never felt comfortable to share with her. I always felt like she didn't care about me because she never wanted to know my past to understand who I was. When my second family adopted me, my parents and I would stay up late talking about my past. They always told me if I felt comfortable to share; they wanted to know about my family back home and all the traumatic things I experienced. Because they were loving and open, I was open to share with them. As I shared with them, I cried; they let me cry and held and comforted me. I felt relief sharing with them about my past because it feels good to let it out and share so they can understand me. It created a closer bond between my family and me. Adoptees, it is okay to open up and share about your past with your parents. They are there to comfort you, to love you, and be there for you. You will also heal by sharing, and they will know how to treat you and raise you if they know your background.

Some families get counselors for their adopted children to get them help; while that is a great idea, make sure you find a counselor who understands adoptions and has a background in helping adopted children. Your children would be willing to open up and share if they know they can relate.

Adoptive parents become friends with your adopted child, so they can come and talk to you whenever they are going through a hard time. Be a parent and a friend at the same time. If they shared something they are struggling with you or if they shared something of their past with you, don't use it against them when you and the child have a disagreement. This will show them they can trust you with anything. Some adoptees might be okay with the traumatic things they went through at some time in their life, but at another time in their life, it might rise up as an issue and something they struggle with. You never know when that trigger would come and what causes it but don't make them feel like they have been good and okay with it all that time, don't question why it became a problem now. It is a question for them too; they can't answer. Be there for them to listen and comfort them. The struggle of an adoptee is huge. Be patient with them and speak life into them.

Adoptive parents, if you are religious, don't shove religion onto the child. Teach them about God and how to live life as a Christ follower and take your children to church. But don't be so religiously strict that they end up hating the religion. Don't be so strict that they don't stop believing in God. Your main job as a parent is to teach them the ways of God. I know of some adoptees that had parents that were very strict, that they didn't want anything to do with God when they turned eighteen years old and were on their own. You want them to keep the behaviors and standards that you teach them even after they move out; teach them in a way that they want to keep everything they learned from you! Proverbs 22:6 says, *"Train up a child in the way he should go; and when he is old, he will not depart from it."* When you train up a child in the way they should go, you do it in love, not anger or scolding them. Jesus brought us to himself with his love. We believe in God because he first loved us first. Love was the way to salvation. Love is the answer for adoptions both physically and spiritually.

You are doing a great job teaching them about God and life but always do it in love. While you do it in love, some children might not see or realize that what you are doing and your expectations for them is because you love them but do it in love with your tone of voice and action as well. Adoptees know and understand everything your parents do for you is because they love you and want what is best for you and your future. Listen to them and obey them.

Adoption agencies should check on the adopted child every six months at least twice a year, every year, until the child turns eighteen years old. Adoptive parents do send in updates on the child to the adoption agency with pictures and a message on how their child is doing. But that is not enough. While some adoptive parents are doing an excellent job raising their adopted child and the updates they send to the agency are true, some adoptive parents do lie on the update of how the child is doing. Agencies don't believe only the families but also check on the adopted child to make sure the updates you are receiving are true and accurate. Adoption agencies need to have a social worker for their agency to check on the adopted child periodically. The social worker needs to interview the child on how they are being treated by the parent separately alone where they feel comfortable. The child will not speak up if they are being treated badly in front of the parent in fear of being in trouble when the social worker leaves, so they will be quiet. The child needs to feel comfortable about sharing what is going on in the home; you can make that happen by creating a safe environment for them. The interview between the social worker and the child needs to be confidential so that the child can freely open up without fearing the family would find out what he or she shared. If the child shares they are being treated badly, the social worker needs to address it to the agency, and the agency needs to investigate as soon as possible to fix the problem. If it means finding a new family for the child, the agency needs to do what is best for the child as their main priority is to serve the child. I suggest for a social worker to check on each child every six months until the child turns eighteen years old because some adoptees have experienced after six months or a year was when some parents started treating them badly. My agency followed up with a social worker to check on the child until the adoption process was fully complete; after that, they never came back. The agency needs to budget and have enough social workers to check on all the children that get adopted periodically, which will fix issues that rise up in adoptions.

After interviewing different adoptees, these are the main problems that were spoken, and solutions for each of the problems are listed. I hope and pray this chapter and my story will encourage parents to adopt and also equip parents to adopt or do foster care to care for orphans in many continents! Adoptive parents are needed and need to always be celebrated. You are one in a million! May the Lord equip and strengthen you as you care for His little children! May God bless you abundantly as you love His children!

Adoption Testimony

Betrese

Chosen

I was born in Ethiopia. My parents got divorced when I was three years old. My dad passed away when I was six years old. When I was twelve years old, my biological mom was diagnosed with HIV. In the hardest time and scariest time, I found Jesus and accepted him into my heart. When my mom got HIV, she couldn't take care of me anymore. It was hard for her to provide for us while she was sick, so she decided to give me away to be adopted because she wanted a better life than the one she could give me.

The following year, God brought someone into my life who was going to adopt me from America. My dad, who was going to adopt me, came to my house in Ethiopia to visit me while he was on a mission trip to Ethiopia. I stayed with my biological mom while the adoption process started. About a year after starting the adoption process, when the adoption process was done, I went to the orphanage. I stayed there three weeks before I came to America. I was grateful to stay with my mom until my adoption process was done, so I can have more time with her. I was adopted with three other girls from the orphanage who became my sisters.

Coming to America was one of the hardest things I had ever experienced in that time of my life, apart from losing my biological dad. I was very scared and was missing my family from Ethiopia. I cried every day for years. My tears were the only way I could let out how I was feeling inside. My parents who adopted me would hug me, hold me and cry with me when I was going through a hard time. They wanted to help. It broke my heart to see them so sad with me and wishing that they could change things. There was no way I could share with them fully what I was feeling because of the language barrier when I first came to the U.S. It was hard to have deep conversations enough for them to understand and help me. So I did my best to only cry at night when they didn't see me because I knew it would break their heart to see me crying.

Adoption is so hard but so worth it! As I became a part of the family, I transitioned from an only daughter in Ethiopia to one of twelve daughters adopted from all over the world. (One from the United States, one from Korea, four from China, seven from Ethiopia.) My parents are my role models, and I will forever admire them for what they have done for me and my siblings.

My parents had one goal, which was that all their children in their house would know God and be saved. They sacrificed so much for us. I was in the "second round" of them raising kids. They had raised two biological daughters already; then, God called them to get eleven more daughters.

So at the age where they should have been retiring, they chose to start over again and introduce 11 children to Jesus. My parents changed our earthly lives! They became a part of all of our stories, choosing to surrender our lives to Jesus for eternity. The verse in 3 John 1:4 describes my parents hearts' desire for all of their children.

"I have no greater joy than to hear that my children walk in truth"
(3 John 1:4, KJV).

So, what does Adoption really mean to me, and why do I associate the word "Chosen" with it? I was chosen and adopted in a time where I wasn't even seeking to be adopted, not just to a physical family but also into a heavenly family. I became their daughter and got a new name. A few years later, God reminded me of some of the stories in the Bible, how people got new names because God changed their life and they were no longer their old selves. Abram to Abraham, Saul to Paul. It's the same for me and many of my sisters. We all either added a new middle and last name or a first and last name. I am now a new creation in Christ! He has given me a new name and identity.

When I was in Ethiopia, I used to cry because I wanted a sister or a brother because I was an only child. After many years of tears, God blessed me with more than a dozen. I may have forgotten about my hopes and wishes, but God didn't. He chose me to be a daughter of the most sacrificial loving, amazing parents, that live each day to serve Him and not waste their time here on earth.

I was "chosen" to be in God's family and my earthly family in the least convenient but also the most special time in my life. I was chosen by my parents, who taught me about Jesus, who is the foundation of my life. I can live every day in praise of Him because He not only saved me from hardship, but He gave me an incredible life through His instruments, my parents. He gave me eternal life by adopting me as his daughter through his one and only son, Jesus Christ.

If you're planning on adopting a child or doing foster care, in the process of adoption or foster care, you must pray and ask God to go before you and behind you. God's heart is all for adoption. It's the core of His heart because it is what He did to save us to be His adopted sons and daughters again. So let Him lead you through it. He knows the way! May the Lord bless you for caring for His children! You will change their lives forever!

"God decided in advance to adopt us into his own family by bringing us to himself through Jesus Christ. This is what he wanted to do, and it gave him great pleasure"(Ephesians 1:5, NLT).

Adoption Testimony
by Zerihun

To my dear brothers and sisters who are here to listen to my testimony, my name is Zerihun. I was born in Addis Ababa, Ethiopia. I had a difficult childhood growing up. I began losing family members at an early age. Before the age of five, I lost my brother, my sister, and my father. Which was heartbreaking. Before I could heal from one death, one by one, those that I love were taken away from me. As a single mother in a third-world country, my mom tried to take care of my two other sisters and me. My mother was doing all sorts of types of jobs to provide for us and doing the best that she could with the opportunities that were presented to her, which wasn't much. Soon afterward, my mom got very ill. When I was nine years old, my mother passed away. That was the moment when I realized that at that young age, I had become an orphan. Deep inside, I realized and knew I had no biological parents anymore. I felt like I had lost everything and didn't know what my future was going to be like.

A few months later, I met a woman from an adoption agency called Adoption Advocate International. I remember her picking us up in a big blue van, telling us that we are going to live in a better place. My extended family, who were taking care of me and my sisters at that moment, were delighted when the opportunity came to go to an orphanage and to get adopted into a family. Without any hesitation, they accepted the offer because they wanted a better life for us! They couldn't give us the life they desired for us. So we ended up going to the orphanage. It was difficult at first because they separated my little sister and me between two different orphanages with the same branch. The orphanage had many children and couldn't house all of them in one place. So they had two big houses in order to take care of more orphans. There was a separate house for babies and younger children to live in, and there was a bigger house for older kids.

We went to visit the children in the younger house every week, but it was still hard to be separated from my little sister, who was the only person I had left. Soon after we went to Layla's house, I was told that a family wanted to adopt us from Chicago. We had no idea really what that meant. Our adoption process went fast, and a few months later, my father and my mother came to pick us up from Addis Abeba, Ethiopia. My little sister and I didn't really understand what was happening.

All we knew was, we were going to end up in a place where we had no idea the language or the culture. When we landed in Chicago, it was a big city with a lot of people. It was extremely loud; we saw people with different hair colors, different eye colors, different skin colors, and most of all, different ways of life. While living in the U.S., I didn't really experience Jesus Christ. My family and I had a falling out when I was about seventeen years old. In the process of rekindling that relationship because of Christ. I remember the day I got saved. A man of God laid his hand on me and prayed for me. I promise you I blocked out, and when I woke up, I was a totally different person. I stopped doing every worldly thing that I used to do and moved two hours away from the city that I'm from to go to an internship to get to know God in a deeper way. I gave up everything in the world to go to the internship and follow the plan that God had for me. I was reckoned by God's love and have experienced him in such a deep way my heart's desire and hunger was to know Christ and make Him known by sharing the Gospel! Jesus set me free from the bondage of sin. God adopted me as his son. Being adopted physically, I have experienced a lot of hardships in my life, but God healed me of all I have gone through and made me whole. He changed my world completely. I began to know about the Word of God and what it means to be a believer and a follower of Jesus Christ every day. Jesus took away all my shame and guilt, all my addiction, and all of my suffering from the past has been lifted. I'm a different man now. I am a man of God, eager and excited to see what God's going to do through me for the kingdom of God! Being adopted has saved me from many trials and tribulations, and for that, I am forever grateful! I don't know where I would be if my family didn't adopt me. My family is amazing, and I am grateful to them for changing my life.

My heart's desire is for people to taste what I have tasted and experience God in a way they have never experienced him before. You can be a young adult and be on fire for Jesus! Just as Jesus was about doing His Father's will, I have surrendered my life to my Heavenly Father's plan for my life. I am grateful to be adopted twice, both physically and spiritually. May God bless you, and may He reveal Himself to you in a new way!

Adoption Testimony
by Leamlake

They said all kinds of things. "You were an unplanned child. You're as good as nothing." "You will never make it." "You are an orphan...." Little did they know, and I never thought I would ever be able to say this. But it's okay to lose a parent; it's okay to feel alone. It's okay to be undervalued. It's okay to be mistreated. That is just the world we live in, broken and full of darkness. The only reason that makes it okay is because of Jesus. For the longest time, I lived my life without knowing him. Well, Jesus knew me all along. It was Him who carried me through the darkest times in my life. He was and is my Good Shepherd while the enemy lurked around to destroy me. Little did they all know, I was created in his image, plan, knowledge, authority. The Lord is not one to mess with. For the first time, as I was searching to find myself and who I was, instead of the world, I found my identity in Him. Jesus showed me what love is. He gave me everything I thought I lacked and beyond. He washed my sins away, made me clean, and granted me forever with Him. He provided for me for everything. He gave me a loving family who adopted me in America. He healed all my wounds, whipped my tears away, and broke my chains. He showed me my worth and my purpose for why He created me. He loved me unconditionally and still loves me! I am forever grateful for Jesus! He is the best thing that ever happened to me!

While adoption is a beautiful thing, I don't believe it's everyone's calling. It's a commitment that ought to be taken seriously. Seeking the Lord's will and counsel is vital before taking on this journey, as it will include making sacrifices of love. Adoption is a simple resemblance to what God did for His people. The love He has poured out on us through His son Jesus Christ enabled us to be His children. High price was paid for this to happen. For whoever this calling may be, the Lord will provide the sacrifice.

For you created my innermost being; you knit me together in my mother's womb. I praise you because I am fearfully and wonderfully made. your works are wonderful, I know that full well. My frame was not hidden from you when I was made in the secret place, when I was woven together in the depths of the earth. Your eyes saw my unformed body; all the days ordained for me were written in your book before one of them came to be.

Psalm 139:13-16 (NIV)

Testimony of Adoptive Mom: Carrie Strawn

"Merrily holding baby Mihret in 2007"

When Mihret was referred to AAI. for adoption, Merrily held Mihret on her lap for the journey from Nazret to Layla House, which was a two-hour drive. She told Mihret's adoptive parents that the two had "bonded" on the trip. A few months later, her adoptive parents asked if Merrily would take a picture with Mihret to include in her baby book. This picture is the result.

As Mihret's mom, it means a lot to me to know that there were people like Merrily and the nurse we met at Adama Hospital and the nannies at Layla House (AAI) who cared for our daughter at a time when she was incredibly vulnerable. This picture speaks to me of how God surrounded Mihret with the love of His people, even in the midst of the loss of her first family. Life can be incredibly hard, but God is always good.

My daughters, Mihret and Zinash, are two of the most beautiful blessings in my life. I was initially devastated when I found out that I wouldn't be able to bring children into the world, but I knew that there were also children in the world who needed parents. God brought our family together in a way that filled the desires of all of our hearts and gave us the deeply sacred gift of loving each other well. We thank God for making us family!

Adoptive Mom Carrie Strawn

Bruk Birhnu Testimony

Bruk Birhnu

As an adoption specialist and a children psychologist, I worked for three consecutive years in one of the International organizations located in Ethiopia. I have seen many heartbreaking cases in my years of helping children get adopted internationally. As I look back, most of the stories fill my eyes with tears; some of the children's stories shocked me, others made me very sad to see children in a vulnerable state like they were. When I saw these children in heartbreaking situations, it became my passion and calling to help them have a better life by standing in the gap and advocating for them through the non-profit organization I was working for to help them have a better life through adoptions. I worked hard along with my fellow coworkers to help as many children as possible have a better life through adoption. After the children got adopted, I still check on the children that got adopted all over the world through the non-profit organization I was working for. I check on them often and have a great friendship with their parents as well. I advise the parents on anything they need help with and have visited many of the children throughout the years in different states and continents. It's important for me to know of their well-being after their adoption as well. That is why it is my passion. It was one of the best times of my life working to help these orphan children who couldn't help themselves. I gained so much wisdom working for three years from 2012 to 2015 as an adoption specialist and psychologist.

Adoption is very important, and it gives extra life for that specific child. Many reasons lead children to be adopted for international adoption, such as death of biological parents or when the children are found left in the streets by themselves and abandoned by their family members. Some need to be adopted due to bad culture's practices in the community's for example, "blood for blood," which means killing of any family member will result in revenge by the victim's family so that they will try to kill anyone from the killer family. In this case, taking the child for international adoption becomes mandatory.

I personally agree with adoption because I feel like it is saving one's soul. As a Christian, the Bible teaches me to help anyone who needs help. As the Bible says in John 13:34 (KJV):*"A new commandment I give unto you, That ye love one another; as I have loved you, that ye also love one another."* Helping children who have lost their parents through tragic circumstances and helping children who don't have anyone to care for them is very important. They wait on people like you and me to stand up and care for them. I understand that not all adoptive parents are very nice. Since we all are human beings, we are not perfect. Physical adoption isn't perfect. Most people make mistakes, knowingly or unknowingly. For those kinds of people, all I can do is pray both for the child and the parents.

In this world, we are sons and daughters of God. As he is our father, we all are his adopted children. He created us, He owns us, He leads our life, he makes our path straight, and more importantly, He loves us like nobody does. That is why He says this in John 14:18 (NLT), *"No, I will not abandon you as orphans, I will come to you."*

He never left us abandoned; he is with us all the time because he sent the Holy Spirit to live in us to be our constant companion. He showed His love for us on the cross, giving up His life to give us eternal life with Him if we choose to believe in the work that has been done for us through Jesus Christ. Earthly adoption is not perfect, but earthly adoption is necessary because the children who are orphans living in the streets of the world need us to care for them because they are the future generation leaders of our world! Earthly adoption is not perfect, but heavenly adoption is. Heavenly adoption is perfect because Heavenly adoption was formed by the one who is perfect Himself that is our Heavenly Father.

—Bruk Birhanu
adoption specialist and children psychologist

Testimony of Adoption by Eskedar Cochrhan

Eskedar

I was the youngest of four daughters in my family, and I had a fairly normal early childhood in Ethiopia. I enjoyed playing with friends in my close-knit community. My dad had left us when I was young, and my mom was the single mom taking care of us. My mom got really sick, and she didn't know how long she had left to live. She wanted to make sure that my older sister and I were in a safe place with good education so we can have a good future. She loved us dearly but knew if anything was going to happen to her, she knew we would be living in the streets with no one to take care of us. She wanted to make sure that we would be ok.

One day my whole world changed when I had to be separated from the family I loved and the only home I had ever known. The only thing I recall in those first few weeks of my time at Layla House orphanage were lots of tears, confusion, and longing to go back home to my family. I remember being afraid and confused, even as I adjusted and tried to make new friends in the orphanage. It wasn't until a few years after coming to the U.S. that I was finally able to catch my breath and really start to take in everything that happened.

When my American adoptive family came to get my older sister and me when I was twelve years old, I felt a mixture of relief, excitement, fear, and sadness. I was leaving my birth family, my country, and the memories and friends I had made in the orphanage. I can remember so vividly how terrifying that flight to Oregon was. It felt more permanent than I was ready for, and I held onto my Ethiopian blanket, realizing how real everything had become.

Teenage years in any culture are difficult, but the hardest parts for me were needing to learn a new language quickly, adjusting to a new family, and to my huge middle school full of many cultures that were new to me. It was through the friends that I met that I was able to pursue a deeper relationship with Christ. As my faith grew, my relationship with my adoptive parents grew as well. I realized through my faith journey that my story wasn't finished. My view of being adopted also changed from feeling all alone and left behind to feeling chosen and loved.

Finding my identity and learning that I am deeply known and loved by Jesus has transformed my life. This is where I got to see my life here on earth, the one I didn't think mattered or made sense, colliding with God's eternal plan. I realize now that He had been with me all along. He was with me as a little girl playing with my friends; He was with me in the hard years in the orphanage when I had to make new ones, and He was with me in America through all the changes I struggled through.

I watched a video of my birth mom that someone had made from when I was that young girl in Ethiopia. In the video, I saw her expressing her heart's deepest desires and prayers for her daughters. She prayed that she would live long enough to see us safe and healthy with opportunities for education. God heard her prayer and gave me a life that was better than she could've hoped for. He also kept her healthy and has allowed us to merge both families into one.

The truth I have discovered from the Bible is that no matter where we've come from or the kind of childhood we had, we are all, in fact, adopted into the family of God. God decided in advance to adopt us into His own family by bringing us to Himself through Jesus Christ. This is what He wanted to do, and it gave Him great pleasure. So we praise God for the glorious grace He has poured out on us who belong to His dear Son.

—Eskedar Cochran

Testimony of Adoptive Mom: Carrie Cochran

I had always known that I was going to adopt, even as a kid. I was drawn to Ethiopia and the experience of other adoption stories, and one orphanage in particular: Layla House. Through internet connections, I heard of a group of women heading to Layla House to take medical supplies and volunteer. I emailed the coordinator and begged for a spot on the team. I didn't understand the relentless compulsion to go to that specific place at that specific time, but in late March 2008, I flew out to meet a team I didn't know to head to a place I knew I needed to be.

On one of the first days, I volunteered to help take a group of elementary kids horseback riding. We all crowded into a van to get there. I took pictures of the kids on top of their horses, most beaming at the experience. I felt compelled to take a picture of one sweet girl in particular, who turned out to be named Eskedar. She was quiet and sad, and I would find out later had only been in the orphanage for about two weeks. She was just beginning to find her smile again, and I noticed a spark in her eyes that felt familiar somehow. As I took her picture, I hoped it might be special to her and to her adoptive family one day.

When it was time to leave, we all piled into the van to head back to the orphanage. I took a middle seat towards the back, and Eskedar ended up needing a seat, so I offered my lap. She was tiny, the size of my six-year-old foster daughter back home. As the van pulled out, Eskedar turned back towards me and placed her hand on my upper chest, saying clearly in English, "my family." This was the first time I had heard her speak, and I felt the breath leave my body in astonishment. I looked at her, maybe shaking my head and trying to explain that I wasn't her adoptive mom since I realized she might have misunderstood something someone had said.

But as she turned back away from me, I felt like I couldn't regain my air. I felt a strong feeling of pressure I couldn't understand, and I heard a voice, not from the van, say clearly, "This is her." I felt myself answer this voice, "Is this her?" And I heard the steady, clear voice say, "This is the one you have been looking for."

I soaked that in for a moment and then began trying to talk to Eskedar with my few Amharic words and her tentative English. I desperately needed to find out more about this child that had just entered my life so profoundly. When I later landed on American soil, my first task was to call my waiting husband and tell him what he wasn't surprised to hear, "So there's this special girl...."

Over the next twenty-nine months, as our love deepened for Eskedar and her older sister, we tried to reconcile the profound grief and loss on their side of the adoption with our own excitement to embrace them into our family. At thirteen and 1sixteen, we wanted them to keep their language, their names, their culture and hoped that somehow we could weave our stories together in a way that felt right to them. Because of my experience with God in that Ethiopian van, I had to believe there was a way to do that. We wanted to help them adjust, feel loved, be fully part of our family while also remaining fully part of their loving Ethiopian family. In our story, it was important for the girls to be 100 percent both.

In September 2010, we brought both girls to their new home in Oregon. It was time to begin figuring out what it meant to be a family together. We have watched them grow into their lives, through many ups and downs, with tears and laughter, as they decided to accept us into their stories. Helping them find their places in the world has been one of the greatest honors of our lives.

—Carrie Cochran Adoptive Mom

About the Author

Sara Negash was born in Addis Ababa, Ethiopia. Adoption has impacted and changed her life forever. Sara's passion is to help orphans and those in the foster care system to become a voice for those who don't have a voice. She enjoys mentoring children who have gone through adoption and the foster care system. Sara has toured with a children's choir from Uganda, who came to the U.S. to raise awareness for poverty-stricken children in Uganda and Rwanda. They worked hard to find sponsors for a sponsorship program that helps children go to school and pay for their medical bills. Sara's desire is for others to take the initiative to help orphans, who will be the next generation leaders in the world! Adoption is the heart of God. He calls us to care for his children in James 1:27.

Sara serves as a young adult leader at her church. Sara's passion is to serve God and share the Gospel with those that are lost who haven't yet received Christ. Her desire is to make Jesus known all over the world and win souls for the kingdom of God!

Contact Information

If you would like to contact the author, Sara Negash, for any inquiries such as speaking engagements, mentorship, etc., you can use any of this contact info. I look forward to hearing from you! Blessings!

Email: adoptionisredemption@gmail.com

Facebook page: Adoption is Redemption

Website: www.adoptionisredemption.com

CPSIA information can be obtained
at www.ICGtesting.com
Printed in the USA
BVHW060508171121
621781BV00007B/300